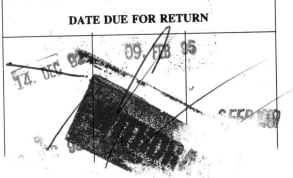

RESHAPING EUROPE IN THE
TWENTY-FIRST CENTURY

Reshaping Europe in the Twenty-First Century

Edited by

Patrick Robertson
Secretary, The Bruges Group

Foreword by

The Rt Hon. Margaret Thatcher, OM, FRS, MP

MACMILLAN in association with The Bruges Group

First published 1992 by
THE MACMILLAN PRESS LTD
Houndmills, Basingstoke, Hampshire RG21 2XS
and London
Companies and representatives
throughout the world

ISBN 0–333–55108–7 c ℓ

A catalogue record for this book is available
from the British Library

Printed and bound in Great Britain by
Billing and Sons Ltd, Worcester

6003673766

Contents

Foreword

In my Bruges speech I said that we should never forget the peoples east of the Iron Curtain, who once enjoyed a full share of European culture, freedom and identity. Now those peoples have torn down the Iron Curtain. They are relishing again the joys of nationhood and are anxious to return to the European fold.

There is today a unique opportunity for Europe to come together as a family of nations. But unity in Europe must be built on willing cooperation between independent sovereign states. For it is with the nation state that people's natural loyalties still lie, and from the nation state that Europe draws its strength and vitality. As we move at last towards the completion of a real Single Market in the European Community, we must take the right decisions about the Community's future. That means creating a Europe that is a model of economic freedom, open to the world.

The essays that Patrick Robertson has compiled in this volume point the way towards a wider and a more generous European Community. I am delighted to commend them to all Europeans.

MARGARET THATCHER

Preface

Most of the essays in the volume were presented to The Bruges Group at a conference held in November 1990. Others were prepared at the request of the editor, and still more, mainly speeches, were included because of their importance to the present debate on the future of the European Community. Together, they form the starting point of a fundamental re-appraisal of the way in which we have viewed the continent of Europe the last forty years.

Reshaping Europe in the Twenty-First Century contains a varied and exciting collection of ideas ranging from strictly economic questions such as European monetary union to schemes for reforming the European institutions which increasingly affect our daily lives. Taken together, the essays illustrate the extent to which Europeans still follow in the tradition of Rousseau, Adam Smith and other classical liberals who played a major part in shaping the societies in which we live today. In short, this volume represents a contribution to the debate about the role of individuals within a modern country, and the extent to which the state should play a part in the functioning of a free society.

The three main sections of this volume deal with the philosophical, economic and political questions that have arisen ever since it has become clear beyond any doubt that many Europeans would transform relations between European nations into a federal European state.

The first Part, 'Building a New Europe', opens with a detailed presentation of Europe's past and present in an essay by Alan Sked originally published by The Bruges Group in May 1990. Drawing extensively – like much of this volume – from historical experience, the author constructs an intricate and balanced scheme for a European confederation that would enshrine liberty and free trade in a modern constitution. The richness of Europe's past and the separate polities which have developed over the last thousand years are brought into relief in a paper presented to the conference by Kenneth Minogue, 'Transcending the European State'. There, Minogue questions whether Europe is about to create something new and better,

or if, instead, we are merely reasserting assumptions from the
past. Wayne Hunt, writing at the time of our Conference, brings
us the perspectives of a Canadian living in Europe, as he draws
parallels with the constitutional entanglements which now en-
velop his own country. Gavin Smith discusses the legal com-
plexities of national sovereignty, demonstrating the importance
of maintaining strict adherence to the agreed positions of international treaties.

The final essay of this Part, by Conrad Black, examines the
British Conservative Party and asks how the Party of the Nation
accepted a series of beliefs that may lead to the end of Britain
as an independent country. This paper was originally delivered
at a fringe meeting of the 1990 Conservative Party Conference.

The second Part, 'Money, Competition and Price Stability',
contains a series of expert contributions from a group of European economists who, writing for The Bruges Group and elsewhere, have been at the forefront of the debate on European
monetary union. Geoffrey Wood introduces their positions in
his own 'Introduction to European Monetary Union'. Tackling
one of the most contentious economic questions of our time,
the authors underline the principles which guide liberals in
their approach to economic matters: what are the minimal
rules which will guarantee the free exchange of goods, and can
they be secured in a European context? The political and
constitutional implications of their thoughts are examined in
the last Part of this volume in a series of speeches recently
delivered to The Bruges Group.

For specialists interested in particular aspects of European
economic integration, Part Three provides a range of essays
touching upon EC competition policy, employment law and
industrial relations. 'Competition, Employment and the World
Economy' opens with an analysis of Europe's position in the
world economy, by Christian Watrin. There, writing less than a
year after the revolutions, he concludes that Western Europe
owes a special debt to those Eastern countries which, until
1989, were subjected to Soviet political and economic domination. He asks whether it is possible or even desirable for the
West to pursue its own plans for integration without taking into
account the need for trade and prosperity in the East. Francis
Maude concludes this Part with a wide-ranging defence of international free trade, embodied in the General Agreement on

Tariffs and Trade, the latest round of which appears perilously close to being derailed as I write. This paper was originally published in 1990 by the London-based Centre for Policy Studies.

Part Four, 'Security and Defence in a New World Order' discusses for the first time in a Bruges Group context the important security and military considerations of a future world order. Is Europe ready to take up its own defence policy? Is the European Community the right organisation to defend the security of Western Europe? In papers specially prepared for our Conference, Peter Schmidt and Miguel Herrero de Miñón question the justification for a European security union and examine the role of NATO in maintaining world peace.

The final Part of *Reshaping Europe* contains some very personal contributions. We publish for the first time a wide-ranging speech to The Bruges Group in January 1991 by Peter Lilley, in which he challenges the supremacy of out-dated ideas and beliefs. Enoch Powell, in a moving conference speech, rejects what he perceives to be the feeble political compromise that has always confused the European issue for the people of Britain. And Norman Tebbit, who closed our London gathering, points to the opportunities and dangers of the phase which Europe is entering. Lastly, Patrick Robertson views Europe through the experiences of his childhood in Italy and France. This volume provided the opportunity to publish these thoughts for the first time.

To conclude. The debate about Europe's future arouses deeply-held emotions and convictions that cut right across the political spectrum. Given their different backgrounds and political beliefs, what factors determine the way in which Europeans think? This volume deals with much more than the technical questions of economic interdependency: it examines the very assumptions of the European ideal, and sets it on a path which may eventually bring it to fruition.

PATRICK ROBERTSON

Notes on the Contributors

Conrad Black is Chairman and Chief Executive of Argus Corporation Ltd and Proprietor of The Telegraph Group. He was educated at Carleton University, Laval University and McGill University.

Tim Congdon was educated at St John's College and Nuffield College, Oxford. He has worked for *The Times* and in the City, where he is Economic Adviser to Gerrard & National and Managing Director of Lombard Street Research Ltd. He is the author of a dictionary of economics, *Monetary Control in Britain* and *The Debt Threat*, as well as *Monetarism: An Essay in Definition* and *Against Import Controls.* He is a frequent contributor to the financial press, particularly *The Spectator* and *The Times,* and is one of the City's leading financial commentators.

Miguel Herrero de Miñón received his PhD in Law in Madrid and for many years was a top legal adviser in the Civil Service before going to work for the Spanish government. In July 1976, he assumed the position of General Secretary at the Ministry of Justice in order to assist in the political transition to democracy. He was elected to Parliament in 1977, being one of the seven drafters of the democratic Constitution. He subsequently served as Parliamentary leader for UCD, the party in government (1980–1). In October 1982 he was re-elected to Parliament on the Alianza Popular ticket. He was executive President of the parliamentary group of the Opposition 1982–7) and is now the Popular Party's spokesman in the Foreign Affairs Committee of the House.

Wayne Hunt was educated at Laurentian University, the London School of Economics and Massey College, the University of Toronto. He is currently Associate Professor of Politics at Mount Allison University in Sackville, New Brunswick, Canada, where he is also a Fellow of the Centre for Canadian Studies. In 1989–90 he was Visiting Fellow at the Centre for International Studies at the London School of Economics.

Tim Johnson leads Coopers & Lybrand Deloitte's employment law practice. He joined the firm in 1989 after practising for several years as a solicitor specialising in employment law. He is Joint Editor of *Employment Law Manual* and is Editor of the Employment Law Bulletin of *Encyclopedia of Labour Relations Law*. He has also contributed articles to numerous publications.

The Rt Hon. Peter Lilley MP was educated at Clare College, Cambridge, and worked as an economic consultant in under-developed countries (1966–72). As an investment adviser on energy industries (1972–84), he was chairman of the London Oil Analysts Group (1979–80) and Director of W. Greenwell & Co. (1986–7). Before becoming the Conservative MP for St Albans in 1983, he was Chairman of the Bow Group (1972–5) and Consultant Director of the Conservative Research Department (1979–83). After serving as Parliamentary Private Secretary to the Chancellor of the Exchequer, he became the Economic Secretary to HM Treasury (1987–9) and the Financial Secretary to HM Treasury (1989–90). He is currently the Secretary of State for Trade and Industry.

Antonio Martino has been Professor of Monetary History and Policy at the University of Rome since 1979, and Professor of Economics at the Free University (LUISS) since its foundation in 1982. He has written many books, including *Appunti di Economia Internazionale*, *Scritti Monetari* and *Constraining Inflationary Government*. He regularly contributes to the Italian and international press on monetary and fiscal issues. He is President of the Mont Pelerin Society.

The Hon. Francis Maude MP was educated at Corpus Christi College, Cambridge. He was called to the Bar in 1977 before becoming the Conservative MP for Warwickshire North in 1983. He held several posts in this capacity, including Assistant Government Whip (1985–7), Parliamentary Undersecretary of State at the Department of Trade and Industry (1987–9) and Minister of State at the Foreign Office (1989–90). He is currently the Financial Secretary to HM Treasury.

Kenneth Minogue is Professor of Political Science at the London School of Economics. Born in New Zealand, he was educated in Australia, earning his degree at the University of Sydney before moving to London where he was awarded a First Class Honours in Economics at the LSE. His activities are too numerous to list, but he is probably best known to the public at large through his presentation of the British Channel Four television series *The New Enlightenment* in 1986. He has lectured throughout the world and is the author of many books.

Manfred J. M. Neumann is Professor of Economics and Director of the Institut für Internationale Wirtschaftspolitik in Bonn. He has published extensively in the field of monetary and international economics and is an authority on German monetary policy. He is a member of the EC-advising CEPS macroeconomic policy group.

Daniel Oliver was Chairman of the US Federal Trade Commission, 1986–9. Prior to becoming Chairman, he served as General Counsel of the US Department of Education and General Counsel of the US Department of Agriculture. He is now a Distinguished Fellow at The Heritage Foundation.

The Rt Hon. Enoch Powell was educated at Trinity College, Cambridge. He became an MBE in 1943. From 1950–74 he was the Conservative MP for Wolverhampton South, also serving during this period as Parliamentary Secretary, Ministry of Housing and Local Government (1955–7), Financial Secretary to HM Treasury (1957–8) and Minister of Health (1960–3). In 1974, he left the Conservative Party due to disagreements over Britain's EC membership and became the Ulster Unionist MP for Down South and South Down (1974–87).

B. C. Roberts graduated from the London School of Economics and New College Oxford before teaching briefly at Ruskin College and then at the LSE since 1949. He was Professor of Industrial Relations, 1962–84, and is now Emeritus Professor. He has written and lectured widely, served on the Council of the Advisory Conciliation and Arbitration Service 1979–86 and has been Editor of the *British Journal of Industrial Relations* since 1963. Professor Roberts was founder and first President of the International Industrial Relations Association.

Patrick Robertson was born in Edinburgh and educated in Rome and Paris. He later read Modern History at Keble College, Oxford, where he began to organise a group of British academics around a campaign to halt the march of European centralism. In February 1989 the newly-named Bruges Group was launched, and he quit his studies to become the full-time Secretary of the group.

Pascal Salin is Professor of Economics at the University of Paris-Dauphine. He is a member of the Board of the Mont Pelerin Society, and has been a consultant at the IMF, the EEC, USAID, the Harvard Institute for International Development, FAO, the Economic Commission for Africa and the French Ministry of Finance. He has published numerous articles and books on monetary policy and taxation, including *L'ordre monetaire mondial, L'arbitraire fiscal, Currency Competition* and *Monetary Union.*

Alan Sked is Senior Lecturer in International History at the London School of Economics. He was educated at the University of Glasgow and Merton College, Oxford. He is a pupil of A. J. P. Taylor and, like Taylor himself, a historian of both Britain and Europe. He has published books in several languages and his works include *The Decline and Fall of the Habsburg Empire, 1815–1918, Post-War Britain, a Political History, Britain's Decline: Problems and Perspectives* and *Europe's Balance of Power, 1815–1848.*

Peter Schmidt is a senior research fellow in the Research Institute for International Affairs at the Stiftung Wissenschaft und Politik (Foundation for Science and Politics), Ebenhausen, Germany. He has published extensively on European security and defence issues in American, French and German journals and has recently co-edited two books on Franco–German relations and on European integration and security policy.

Roger Gavin Abbey Smith graduated from Corpus Christi College, Oxford. After being called to the Bar by the Middle Temple in 1981, he went to Brussels in 1983 as a 'stagiaire' in DG XI and the Commission Legal Service. He worked for a British MEP, and became EC Affairs adviser with Coopers & Lybrand (Brussels). After returning to England he worked for a London-based consultant on EC affairs, and has now returned to Chambers.

The Rt Hon. Norman Tebbit CH MP has been a member of the Conservative Party since 1946. In 1974 he became MP for Chingford, also acting as Minister of State, Department of Industry (1981), Secretary of State for Employment (1981–3), Secretary of State, Trade and Industry (1983–5), and Chairman of the Conservative Party (1985–7). His autobiography, *Upwardly Mobile*, was published in 1988.

Christian Watrin received his Doctorate in Economics at the University of Cologne where he is currently a Full Professor in the Faculty of Economics and Social Sciences, the Chair for Economic Policy and Managing Director of the Institute for Economic Policy. Since 1987 he has also worked as Chairman of the Advisory Council to the Federal Ministry of Economic Affairs.

Geoffrey E. Wood is Professor of Economics at the Centre for Banking and International Finance at the City University, London. He previously taught at the University of Warwick, and has been a member of the Economic Section of the Bank of England and Visiting Scholar at the Federal Reserve Bank of St Louis. His publications include research papers on the demand for money, inflation and the balance of payments; he is co-author of *The Financing Procedures of British Foreign Trade* and co-editor of *Monetary Targets* (with Brian Griffiths), *Exchange Rate Policy* (with Roy A. Batchelor), *Monetarism in the United Kingdom* (with Brian Griffiths), and *Financial Crises and the World Banking System* (with Forrest Capie).

Part One
Building a New Europe

1 A Proposal for European Union

Alan Sked

INTRODUCTION

No less than forty-five million people died during World War Two. The vast majority of them were civilians, often killed under the most appalling circumstances. The vast majority, too, were Europeans, victims of what has been called 'Europe's Second Civil War'. It is little wonder, therefore, that after 1945 European statesmen should have sought to banish war for ever from the European Continent.

To date at least, their efforts appear to have been successful. On the one hand, NATO was established to contain the threat of Soviet Communism; on the other, economic recovery was assisted by the establishment of, first, OEEC, and later, of the ECSC and the EEC. Particular attention was paid to integrating West Germany with the European democracies, militarily through WEU and NATO, thanks largely to Sir Anthony Eden, and economically through the Treaties of Paris and Rome, thanks largely to the work of such men as Jean Monnet, Konrad Adenauer and Robert Schuman. Today there is no longer any possibility of war occurring between Germany and France. Indeed, thanks in no small measure to the political wisdom of Konrad Adenauer, we can once again begin to refer to 'Germany' – a state, we hope, which will soon be united in liberty. And given the record of the Federal Republic since 1949, we have every reason to expect that a united Germany, despite her size and economic strength, will play a positive and constructive role in European affairs.

Today, then, the vision of the 'founding fathers' of the postwar period is becoming a reality. Europe stands on the verge of a new era of peace and prosperity. Even the economic vision they shared of a single-market economy encompassing the whole Continent is in the process of being made real. From 1 January 1993, Europe should have finalised arrangements to guarantee the free movement of goods, services, people and capital within the frontiers of the Community. This process is now almost half-way to completion and is based on the principle of unhindered competition.

If there has been much progress on the economic front, however, problems still remain. Monetary union will prove extremely difficult to achieve. More particularly, the Common Agricultural Policy represents a standing rebuke to the original aims of the founding fathers. Not only does it account for two-thirds of the entire Community budget, but, by its very nature, makes a mockery of free market principles. Its costs the average European family of four approximately £1,000 per year; it transfers resources from poor urban dwellers to rich rural ones; it has grossly inflated the value of land; and it helps obstruct the efforts of poor, Third World countries to develop their economies. It would be wrong therefore to pretend that the record of the Community is perfect, or that the guiding principles of the founding fathers have always been consistently implemented. Yet The Bruges Group have no hesitation in paying tribute to the many positive achievements of the Community to date.

Politically, the founding fathers of the EEC looked forward to an 'ever-closer union' of the peoples of Europe. Exactly what they meant by that remains unclear, but it is certain that they foresaw increasing political cooperation between Europe's individual states leading to some form of political unity. Today, once again, there are calls for a political union emanating from many leading European statesmen. And, very soon, the question will be placed on the agenda of an inter-governmental conference.

What sort of political union should Europeans seek to create?

Times have changed since the 1950s and 1960s. Then European states were growing ever stronger, raising more and more revenue, developing wide-ranging social programmes, and spending ever more money. Among the less beneficial consequences were inflation, higher taxes and bureaucracy. Since the 1980s a political reaction has set in, with the result that today, there is everywhere in Europe a greater awareness of the need for smaller government, less taxation and greater competition. All this, of course, is absolutely in line with the original aims of the founding fathers.

It is difficult to believe, therefore, that were they alive today, they would be in favour of creating a highly centralised political union with a powerful federal government in Brussels dictating economic and social priorities to enfeebled member states. On the contrary, recent demands that the vast majority of policy-decisions should emanate from Brussels would be regarded by them as a nightmare. They would surely agree that the principle of free competition is required to uphold political as well as economic freedom. Hence their vision of a political union would almost certainly be one of a European Confederation, meaning a union of free states cooperating as closely as possible to maintain peace and to enhance the prosperity and freedom of all.

Developments in Eastern Europe today reinforce this conclusion. The democratisation of countries formerly behind the Iron Curtain means that many new democracies will soon have the right to participate in any future European Union. Their adherence should be warmly welcomed. Yet it must be abundantly clear that they will be unwilling to subordinate their newly-won freedom to new forms of central control. They will not wish, surely, to replace masters in Moscow with masters in Brussels. Besides, Europe, East and West, is simply too diverse, too sophisticated and too large to lend itself to central control.

Only a European Confederation, therefore, can, in our opinion, be the model for political union. This alone can sustain the diversity of Europe, which we wish to foster rather than suppress. This alone can give rise to that mutual trust and respect which in the end can arise only from the habit of cooperation. Last, but not least, it is the only way in which Europe can be united. Any other model will threaten to keep Great Britain out, to keep out Eastern Europe, and to revive suspicion between France and Germany. The following proposals, therefore, after a review of the arguments and principles involved, will set out a plan for political unity which will not merely obviate these dangers, but will demonstrate how to end the democratic deficit and increase the powers of parliamentary accountability for Europe as a whole. They are put forward as a constructive attempt to further the cause of European union.

THE DEBATE ON EUROPE: THE WEAKNESSES OF THE FEDERALIST (CENTRALIST) CASE

Until the founding of The Bruges Group a year ago, nearly all the initiatives towards European Union were made by the federalists. In 1984, for example, the European Parliament adopted by 231 votes to 31 (with 43 abstentions), a *Draft Treaty of European Union*, which was to come into force if ratified by two-thirds of the member states. In 1988, the President of the European Commission, M. Jacques Delors, declared: 'We will not be able to take all decisions that need to be taken between now and 1995 without moves towards a European government of one kind or another ... In ten years time 80 per cent of economic, and perhaps even fiscal and social, legislation will originate in the Community.' The Belgian Prime Minister, Mr Martens, went further, calling for a full political union, with 'common sovereignty' covering foreign policy, defence and security, as well as monetary, economic, environmental, and social policy. His views were subsequently endorsed by other Christian Democratic heads of government in the Community (i.e. those of Holland, Luxembourg, West Germany and Italy) who associated themselves with a declaration avowing their commitment to a full European economic, political, and security union. Indeed, Article 38 of the *Foreign Policy Platform of the Christian Democratic Union of the Federal Republic of West Germany* of 14 June 1988 states: 'The CDU wants to gradually build a United States of Europe with an accountable government as a counterpart of the European Parliament.'

The Bruges Group alone has undertaken the task of examining how European Union might be made consistent with individual freedom, national integrity, and parliamentary accountability.

Our work so far has exposed the weak intellectual basis on which the federalist case rests. Take for example the following four claims:

1. that the nation-state is obsolescent;
2. that a United States of Europe would be like the United States of America;
3. that a federally united Europe is needed to defend European interests against America and Japan; and

4. that federalists stand for peace and progress, whereas those who defend national sovereignty are old-fashioned nationalists who live in the past.

On the first claim, the truth is that the most successful states today are nation states – Japan, the USA, West Germany – whereas large multinational states are almost everywhere in difficulties – the USSR, Yugoslavia, India and Nigeria, for example. In Asia, meanwhile, it is the small states which are forging ahead economically – Taiwan, Singapore, Hong Kong and South Korea – without any apparent need to pool their currencies or form a federal union out of ASEAN. In Eastern Europe, likewise, the former satellite states of the Soviet empire appear in no way ready to surrender their new-found national independence. Hence the nation state is hardly obsolete; nor is bigger better. Indeed, recent research into the question of why Europe, rather than India, China or Arabia surged ahead economically and technologically after the fourteenth century, points to the fact that Europe remained divided, whereas the Mogul, Ming and Ottoman Empires, by militarily and bureaucratically uniting these other parts of the world, helped destroy their ability to adapt. Europe's historic success, in other words, has been due to her diversity rather than her political and administrative unity.

The second claim, that there is an analogy between a United States of Europe and the United States of America, is quite clearly misleading. It fails to recognise that the American colonists were a fairly homogeneous group who were starting government from scratch. Europe today is definitely not starting from scratch; rather it contains nations whose histories go back almost a thousand years. They are culturally diverse and speak a large number of different languages. Finally, they have developed different political institutions, many of which would find themselves in direct competition with any European federal government. A true analogy between Europe and America, therefore, would only arise were the USA to form a *United States of the Americas* with Brazil, Ecuador, Mexico, Argentina, Peru and Chile, etc., with a federal capital in, say, Managua, and with a common currency managed by a system of largely Latin American banks. This is not a prospect which appeals to the many supporters of European unity who are to be found today in the United States.

The third claim, that Europe requires a federal government to protect its interests against Japan and the United States is based upon incorrect assumptions, as is another argument that only a European federal government can prevent war breaking out between France and Germany. It must surely be true that Europe today is already sufficiently united to fulfil both these tasks. There is no danger any longer of a Franco-German war, while the European Commission has proved perfectly capable, in all sorts of commercial negotiations, of protecting European trading interests around the world.

With respect to the fourth claim, the persistence of such arguments highlights the way in which it is the European federalists who still think in old-fashioned terms about the international system and the world balance of power. Far from being progressive, anti-nationalists, seeking to put an end to the inherently dangerous competition between nation-states, their real objective is to construct a larger nation-state called 'Europe', which, with its own national sovereignty, will prove able to indulge in that competition more efficiently on a global scale. By talking of a 'European culture' and 'European interests', their aim is simply to create a European nationalism. Their quarrel with those of us who continue to defend *national* sovereignty therefore is not one of principle, but one of scale.

The Bruges Group has been able to demonstrate in these and other ways (without mentioning the economic fallacies pursued by Brussels) that European federalists have, intellectually, a very weak case. It is now time for us to enter the institutional debate and to do that we have to be sure about our arguments. These will be convincing only if they are based on sound principles, so in the rest of this paper, these principles will first be outlined, and then specific reforms will be proposed.

FIRST PRINCIPLES

The principles on which the institutional proposals are based are the following:

1. the need to protect and increase individual freedom;
2. the need to create the fewest possible layers of government;
3. the need to build on achievements to date;

4. the need to preserve flexibility of structure;
5. the need for checks and balances;
6. the need to guarantee human rights;
7. the need to guarantee peace in Europe;
8. the need to reject imperial or superpower status;
9. the need to preserve national sovereignty.

Let us now examine these principles in more detail.

1. At the heart of all the work of The Bruges Group has been the determination to increase the freedom of the individual to compete politically, socially and economically. We must strive to ensure that he does not become the prisoner of a European bureaucracy; that his economic freedom is not limited by harmonisation for the sake of harmonisation; and that integration takes place only for his greater good and not merely for the sake of integration. These proposals, therefore, will concern themselves with limiting government, restraining bureaucracy, guaranteeing human rights and enhancing peace.

2. It is more or less an axiom of government that the more levels of government that are provided for, the more government and bureaucracy we will get. The idea that government can be redistributed so that the same amount can be spread over more layers is proved false by all human history. Hence the assurances of the federalists, namely that the creation of a European government would merely entail a transfer of powers to Brussels, leaving correspondingly less government below, are empty of substance. These proposals, therefore, will not involve the creation of any new layers of government. They will attempt instead to rationalise present structures and to inhibit the growth of bureaucracy by controlling the role of the European Commission.

3. The Community has proved itself quite able in the past to develop institutional procedures which are both efficient and appropriate. Examples include the rotating presidency of the Council of Ministers; the right of the Commission to take member states to the European Court; the convention of always trying to arrive at a unanimous decision even when majority voting is allowed for under the Single European Act. These are precedents upon which we should build.

4. The proposals contained in this paper are based on the situation which obtains in Europe today. They assume that if

there is such a thing as a 'European interest' it is either fairly
obvious – in which case national governments will be able to
deal with it – or it is obscure – in which case the majority votes
of a federal parliament are unlikely to illuminate it, since most
European elections are fought along national lines. The time
may come, however, when European citizens will vote on genuinely European issues, and will expect a genuinely federal
government to take decisions and to be answerable for those to
a genuinely federal parliament. That day, however, has not yet
arrived. Nonetheless, there has to be room for change if that
change is demanded. After all, both Swiss and American history
provide examples of states moving from a loose confederation
a more federalist union. These proposals therefore will allow
room for change – but not by imposing change on member
states which prefer the status quo. Flexibility, in other words,
must not be a one-way street to federalism.

5.   All democratic institutional arrangements require checks
and balances to preserve accountability and to prevent the
emergence of elected dictatorships. The proposals in this paper
include checks and balances not only to enhance the accountability of the Council but to check the growth of government
and bureaucracy.

6.   The need to guarantee human rights complements the
need for democratic institutions. But whereas democratic institutions may take different forms to suit national tastes, human
rights by definition must be uniform in nature. If rights are
rights, then all Europeans have an equal claim to them. It is
therefore proposed that the Community should include within
its purview the supervision of human rights in member states.

7.   The commitment to peace in Europe is surely the *raison
d'être* of the Community. It is therefore proposed to make this
explicit and to proclaim the Community a *Friedensbund.*

8.   There is an assumption among federalists that a united
Europe 'speaking with one voice' would exercise more influence in the world and would be able to take its place among the
superpowers. Apart from the fact that much would depend on
what that voice would have to say, it seems evident that this
premise is illusory. Superpower status has not saved the Soviet
Union from economic collapse; nor has it saved the USA from
unnecessary wars and military commitments merely to safeguard
prestige. Japan, on the other hand, has done much better by

neglecting defence, foreign affairs, and the striving after international status altogether. Europe would do well to follow her example. Otherwise, the pursuit of world power status is likely to involve unnecessary expense in order (most probably) to exert some kind of dominance over Africa. The rejection of federalism would help Europe reject the kind of vainglorious foreign policy which would all too likely accompany it.

9. National sovereignty is not to be confused with nationalism and certainly not with aggressive nationalism. It has nothing to do with illiberalism and is at heart a defensive and libertarian concept. It does not imply the superiority of one nation over another. Quite the reverse. It is the legal defence of small nations against aggressive neighbours. It was Poland's answer to Hitler; Czechoslovakia's to Brezhnev; and is Lithuania's to Gorbachev. It is to nations in international society what civil rights are to individuals in civil society: their legal defence against superior power. To ask a nation to surrender its sovereignty is like asking an individual to surrender his civil rights. In Europe, historically, the enemies of national sovereignty have always been the enemies of freedom.

Nor is national sovereignty to be confused with national irresponsibility, the belief that the nation state has either the right or the capacity to do anything it desires. That is an illusion. At heart national sovereignty is a legal concept. It is the authority vested in the government of each state to take decisions on behalf of the people of that state. As such it cannot be shared. In an interdependent world, of course, states may choose to exercise their sovereignty by associating with other states and to do things in common. However, in so doing they do not relinquish their national sovereignty, but merely agree to act jointly *in a specific sphere* for a specific or unspecific length of time. They always retain the right to put an end to their cooperation with others, even if that right may entail certain political or economic costs. Sovereignty is the right to exercise authority; it is not the ability to avoid consequences.

With regard to the European Community, this means that the United Kingdom, for example, has chosen to exercise its national sovereignty by associating itself with other states in certain institutional arrangements; her decision to do so, however, has not – indeed could not – involve the transfer of sovereignty to others. Constitutionally, sovereignty in the United

Kingdom resides with the Queen in Parliament. Hence the work of the European Parliament, the European Commission, the Council of Ministers and indeed the European Court can only have meaning for the United Kingdom so long as Parliament enforces their decisions and retains the right at any time to end that cooperation. The same is true for all the other sovereign parliaments of all the other member states.

Given this situation, it would seem to be desirable to form institutional arrangements in Europe which reflect this basic principle. At present there is a great deal of loose talk about 'pooling' or 'sharing' sovereignty; there are even voices making the mistaken and illogical claim that the European Parliament has developed a sovereignty of its own. This is untrue, but the very fact that MEPs and others believe it means that the European Parliament, if given more powers, would seek to undermine the status of national parliaments and to subordinate them to its pretended authority. I will therefore propose new institutional and budgetary arrangements which will guarantee the status, and delineate the role, of national parliaments.

PROPOSALS

A European Community has developed because European states have recognised that there are certain areas in which they must work together. Cooperation between states is a common experience in international affairs, as the existence of NATO, OECD, the UNO, the IMF and many other bodies testify. Even so, the existence of a directly elected European Parliament has caused several Europeans to call for the establishment of a federal (i.e. supranational) government as the logical counterpart to that body. This should be rejected as totally unnecessary. European states are highly sophisticated organs which are already used to operating an enormous range of policies. They do not require supranational supervision. At the heart of these proposals therefore is the reform of the European Parliament in order to put an end to the centralising dynamic which it creates. In short, it is proposed that Europe should be run along a parliamentary structure which establishes at the outset that sovereignty derives from the individual member states. This in my opinion is the only way to insert a protective shield between the freedom of the individual and the bureaucratic tendency, already all too apparent in Brussels, which treats Europeans as indentikit beings to be shaped according to institutional needs rather than personal desires.

The European Parliament

Europe needs a parliament. Given the existence of European legislation and a Council of Ministers, it is imperative that a parliament should exist to scrutinise the men and measures involved. Ideally, each national parliament should agree on all legislation first, but in practice this is impossible. Hence the need for a common forum. There are many advantages to be gained by the parliamentarians concerned, quite apart from the obvious one of accountable government: the habit of co-operation; increased knowledge of European politics; an awareness of different cultures and values.

Today, alas, the European Parliament has too few powers to act as an effective brake on the European Commission. It has no formal links with national parliaments, little public profile, and ambitions which are undermined by the general indifference of national electorates.

Given the self-expanding powers of the Commission, the result is a 'democratic deficit' at European and national levels which is exacerbated on the one hand by the incipient competition between the European Parliament and national legislatures, and on the other by the fact that most politicians of the first rank choose to pursue their careers in domestic politics.

It is therefore proposed to strengthen parliamentary accountability in the EC and to eliminate the 'democratic deficit' by integrating the parliamentary process at national and Community levels.

Proposals
1. *Structure.* That, by reaffirming the wisdom of the founders of the Community, the European Parliament will be constituted according to the original Article 138 of the Treaty of Rome (1957) and will therefore become an assembly of representatives from national parliaments.
2. *Procedure:*
   - Delegations from each national parliament will reflect the

political composition of their domestic legislature according to the procedures selected by the national parliaments themselves. They will be responsible for explaining their actions to their domestic parliaments as a whole. National parliaments will retain the right to elect their European representatives from amongst their members, through internal parliamentary elections every two years.

- Individual MEPs from national parliaments will vote according to conscience but will have the right to form 'parties' or blocs with MEPs from other member states.
- If a majority of any national delegation objects to legislation proposed in the European Cabinet on the grounds that it undermines a vital national interest, and find their objections sustained by a majority in their national parliament, the proposed legislation, even if passed, will not be applicable to the country concerned.

3. *Scrutiny of the EC budget:*
   - Members of the European Parliament will have their powers strengthened by gaining the right to scrutinise the EC budget in detail and to amend or reject it by a majority vote. The European Parliament will not have the right to increase the EC budget without the consent of the EC Cabinet and Council.
   - In order to ensure that all member states contribute equitably, funds for the EC budget will derive from national quotas defined as an agreed proportion of national GDP. (There should therefore be no need for individual national rebates.)
   - It is proposed that, within the framework of the Single European Act, and with respect for national procedures, financial accountability be consolidated through the establishment, in each member state, of a visible European Community tax to raise the national contribution to the EC budget.

4. *Legislation:*
   - *All* European legislation must be approved by a majority in the European Parliament.
   - The European Parliament will have the right to censure, by a majority vote, all members of the EC Cabinet.
   - Proposed changes to the Treaty of Union must be approved, in the first instance, by two-thirds of the European Parliament.

The European Cabinet

1. The present Council of Ministers will be given increased status and responsibility by becoming a European Cabinet consisting of one national minister from each member state. The European Cabinet will be permanently resident in Brussels, responsible for proposing and agreeing European legislation, as well as the EC budget.
2. The European Cabinet will be responsible, in true parliamentary tradition, to the European Parliament, and all EC Cabinet members will be ex-officio members of the European Parliament.
3. Each member of the European Cabinet will also have cabinet status in his domestic government (e.g. Secretary of State for Europe, instead of Secretary of State for Scotland, Wales or Northern Ireland, to use the United Kingdom model as an example).
4. Each national Secretary of State for Europe will serve at the behest of his national government and will be responsible for coordinating the work of the European Cabinet with the work of his domestic cabinet.
5. The European Cabinet will distribute European portfolios amongst its members under the direction of a rotating President who will make annual 'state of the Union' reports to the European Parliament.
6. The Presidency of the European Cabinet will rotate annually, from amongst its members.
7. The voting procedure in the European Cabinet will rest upon the principle of unanimity, except for areas specifically designated by the European Council for majority voting.
8. The European Cabinet will sign trade and membership agreements on behalf of the European Union provided these fall within the competence of the Treaty and are approved by the European Parliament.
9. The European Cabinet will have the right to propose amendments to the Treaty of Union.

The European Council (Heads of Government)

1. The European Council will continue to meet every six months as the highest level coordinating body and will take respon-

sibility for defence and foreign policy of the European Union.

2. European political cooperation will be supervised by Heads of Government and Foreign Ministers working with their own existing Secretariat.
3. The voting procedure of the European Council will rest upon the principle of unanimity, save for areas specifically designated for majority voting, which will not include defence, foreign affairs and constitutional amendments.
4. The European Council will have the right, shared with the European Cabinet, to propose European legislation. Council initiatives will be put to the European Parliament for approval via the European Cabinet.
5. Proposed changes to the Treaty of Union, initiated in the first instance by the European Cabinet, and approved by a two-thirds majority in the European Parliament, will be referred to the European Council for acceptance. If adopted, amendments to the Treaty of Union will only come into force if passed with majority approval of two-thirds of all national parliaments.
6. Countries whose national parliaments reject these amendments will not be compelled to enter into new constitutional arrangements.
7. The European Council will suspend member states found to be in breach of the Peace Protocol.

The European Commission

At present, there is no proper European civil service. The nearest equivalent body is the European Commission, whose powers include:

1. the right to review the progress of legislation among member states;
2. the right to negotiate agreements and to administer certain funds;
3. the right to issue directives and regulations and to take member states to the European Court of Justice;
4. the power to initiate and propose legislation.

The first three of these powers are appropriate to the functions of a European civil service. The fourth is not. In a democratically accountable Europe these powers can only be exercised by the European Cabinet.

Proposals
1. The European Cabinet will be assisted in its work by the European Commission formed by amalgamating the present Commission, the Council Secretariat and the Committee of Permanent Representatives.
2. The European Commission, though no longer retaining the right of initiative, will exercise the following responsibilities:
   - to review legislative progress and to take member states to the European Court if they default on their obligations under the Treaty of Union;
   - the right to issue directives, to issue regulations, etc., once these have been approved by the European Cabinet;
   - the right to negotiate treaties and administer funds under the supervision of the European Cabinet.
3. The European Commission will cease to have any political role, (unlike the present Commission), and will not, for example, function as a middleman between the European Parliament and the European Cabinet. Given the increase in powers of the European Parliament, this will no longer be necessary or desirable.

The European Court of Justice

Europe needs a supreme court. Given the number of member states, the diversity of their legal traditions, and the vested interests which have to be confronted in breaking down barriers in Europe, a supreme court is indispensable for furthering economic unity. It must also provide a guarantee of civil rights in Europe and help maintain the peace between European states. Democracy, in short, depends upon the rule of law and which rule is law in Europe can only be decided in a European court.

Today, on the other hand, the European Court of Justice has an institutional self-interest in extending the competence of EC institutions and law by adopting a teleogical interpretation of legislation. The Court has also tended to boost the powers of the present European Commission and to neglect the exercise of judicial restraint. In short, there is insufficient provision within the existing treaties to impose a doctrine of *ultra vires* or to encourage the Court to adhere to a strict interpretation of European law. Finally, as presently constituted, the Court has no responsibility for guaranteeing civil rights.

Proposals
1. The European Court of Justice will ensure the legality of European legislation proposed by the European Cabinet.
2. The Court will ensure that the European Cabinet and European Commission do not act *ultra vires*.
3. The Court will ensure that the Treaty of Union and all European legislation is strictly interpreted.
4. The Court will guarantee the maintenance of human rights in the Community by entrenching the European Convention of Human Rights.
5. Member states failing to uphold human rights will be expelled from the Community on the initiative of the European Court.

Amendments to the Treaty of Union

Procedure
1. Changes in the Treaty must originate in the European Cabinet.
2. Proposed changes must be approved by two-thirds of the European Parliament and be unanimously adopted by the European Council.
3. Changes will only come into force if passed by a two-thirds majority of all national parliaments.
4. Member states wishing to retain the status quo will not be obliged to accept amendments to the Treaty of Union. *The possibility of a multi-tiered Community will therefore be enshrined in the Treaty of Union.*

Membership of the European Union

1. All democratic European states will have the right to apply to join the European Union.
2. No member state may be expelled save in cases of persistent violation of human rights or violation of the Peace Protocol.

3. Any member state may choose to secede from the Union.
4. Membership of the Union must be approved by a two-thirds majority in the European Council and by a two-thirds majority in the European Parliament.
5. Negotiations regarding new membership will be conducted by the European Commission under the supervision of the European Cabinet.

The Head of the European Union

1. The Head of State of the presiding member state of the European Cabinet will act as 'symbolic head' of the European Union for the duration of one year.
2. The Head of the European Union will open sessions of the European Parliament with a speech setting out the objectives of the Union for the forthcoming year.

A European Peace Protocol

All member states will pledge themselves never to declare war, enter into hostilities, or sign alliances against one another. Any member state in breach of this Protocol will be suspended from the Union by a declaration of the European Council.

CONCLUSIONS

The advantages of these proposals are manifold. First of all, they are logically consistent. The proposed Union is based on the national sovereignty of the member states. Their parliaments send delegations to the European Parliament to question ministers and scrutinise the budget. The budget is made up from national quotas, financed in a manner decided upon by national parliaments, albeit in a way consistent with the integrated market. The fact that members of the European Parliament and Cabinet will be functioning on both European and national levels would correct the 'democratic deficit'. There will also be no rivalry between the European Parliament and the national parliaments. Finally, no single state could dominate the others, or find itself contributing disproportionately financially.

Secondly, inherent within these arrangements are both explicit and implicit safeguards against 'big' government. The dynamic towards ever more centralisation is checked by the abolition of direct elections; the removal of the right to initiate legislation from the present European Commission; the empowering of the Court of Justice to rule against acts considered *ultra vires*; and the ending of the role of today's Commission as middleman between the Parliament and the present Council. The dual role of both the Ministers and the Members of the European Parliament should also be a disincentive to unnecessary legislative initiatives.

Thirdly, these proposals contain a number of checks and balances. For example, although the right of initiative is restricted to the European Cabinet and the European Council, MEPs will be able to put pressure on Ministers through their national parliaments and governments if they believe initiatives should be taken. Again, although MEPs might wish to block the application of legislation to their own state in order to preserve a vital national interest, this could only be done if both a majority of their own delegation and of the MPs of the state concerned agree to do so. Finally, applicants for membership would have to be European and commend themselves to two-thirds of the European Council and two-thirds of the European Parliament. This would prevent any single state from vetoing an application for membership.

Fourthly, these proposals contain many positive advances. They allow for greater scrutiny of the budget by MEPs and for greater powers for the European Parliament in general. They thus bring real parliamentary government to Europe without undermining the role of national parliaments. They also make human rights a European concern, provide for explicit undertakings to maintain peace in Europe, and provide Europe with a 'symbolic head'.

Finally, they have the advantage of providing a means of attracting to both the European Parliament and Cabinet politicians of the first rank who would view membership of both these institutions as important stepping stones to a successful domestic political career.

These arrangements represent a positive, parliamentary and practical proposal for European Union. They are designed to appeal to the loyalty of *all* Europeans, and to prevent an unnecessary division between those on the one hand who seek a uniform Europe, and those on the other who nationalism impedes further cooperation and unity.

2 Transcending the European State

Kenneth Minogue

The word 'international' was invented by Jeremy Bentham in 1780, and promoted to an 'ism' a century later, in 1877 according to the *OED*. It breathes the pure air of universal values, and it stands for the grand Western vision of today. It was an important component in the set of ideas which finally brought Communism down. Although Communism itself had purported to be an international movement, bringing liberation to the whole of mankind, it was actually imprisoning, and had the effect of incarcerating whole peoples behind walls, and blocking intercourse with foreigners. The Czechs, Poles, Russians and the rest yearned for the oxygen of unfettered contact with the rest of the world, especially Western Europe and America. They wanted trade, travel, tourism, talk – human, philosophical talk, not ideological cliché or the suffocating intimacies of the narrower kinds of nationalism. No doubt they wanted prosperity as well, but they knew that prosperity came from breaking down barriers between people, not erecting them. Internationalism stands, then, for one of the grand visions of contemporary life. Like all visions, it will have some bad effects. It will vulgarise and homogenise many valuable local forms. But in our generation, most people find it liberating.

In Europe, however, there is another vision riding piggyback on internationalism. It is a doctrine arising from the belief that in a world of superstates, European nations are, separately, too small to be economically prosperous and politically powerful. If, however, they unite to form a single state which can represent the interests of Europe, then we Europeans can get back into the big league. Such a state promises to increase our wealth, and seeks the authority to impose whatever uniformities it thinks necessary on the entire population. Curiously enough, much in this vision of a united Europe resembles the Communism which has recently collapsed in the East: like Communism, it claims to be the vision of the future, while actually it is a return to much earlier types of thought – in the case of the European Community in its present form, a return to the mercantilist and cameralist doctrines of European absolutism in the seventeenth and eighteenth centuries. This is supranationalism, and again like communism, it can hitch a ride on the idealism of internationality by pointing out that it seeks to transcend the limits of the nation-state. But this claim is dishonest. What it does not make clear is that it merely reproduces all the worst characteristics of the nation-state at a higher, and therefore more dangerous, level.

My basic distinction, therefore, is between internationalism and the supranationalism[1] of the European Community, as it has so far developed. I am convinced that nothing less than a confusion between these two quite separate movements is what explains why adherence to the European Community in its present form has become for many educated people in Britain and elsewhere nothing less than a religion. To question any move towards closer union is seen as an act of the old unregenerate humanity which has stained history with wars and tribal conflicts. Yet there is no doubt that the real thinking that lies behind Brussels and Strasbourg includes not only the idealism of the Franco-German pioneers whose attitude to two world wars was 'never again!' but also a very strong dose of *realpolitik.* Ambitious European political architects have been dazzled by the power supposedly exercised by the United States, Japan and (in the old days) the Soviet Union. They wish to join the superpower club. But they believe they can only do so by creating a single sovereign centre of power having the authority to reduce the nations of Europe to an orderly subordination. How such a European sovereign would act remains for the most part in the womb of time, but we already know (as I shall argue) that it involves some pretty rough treatment of the rest of the world.

The confusion between the idea of internationalism and the reality of supranationality is found throughout European public opinion, but it has flowered in Great Britain in an acute and interesting form, which I propose to analyse. The issue revolves around the question of what it is to be a sovereign state. Sovereignty is a basically legal term used to refer to the ultimate authority which can determine the law and government of a

human community. It is thus a basic idea necessary in understanding any modern state. The word is a piece of metonymy in
which the person of king or emperor in late medieval and early
modern times stood for the supreme will of the community.
The absolute monarchs of that period were never despots,
since they ruled over independent subjects with established
property rights, but their absolutism, coming to seem oppressive after an earlier period when it was felt to be liberatory, has
been attacked and destroyed in recent centuries. The world of
absolute monarchs has given way to a new theory of authority
(democracy), and new ways of preventing officials exercising
sovereign powers from using them oppressively (the separation
of powers). We now live in a world of written constitutions, in
which the executive and legislative powers of sovereignty are
sovereignly allocated to different institutions, with judicial bodies having the power to settle disagreements. The history of
Britain has in basic respects followed this pattern; indeed, many
of the aspects of modern constitutions are actually imitations of
the British model. But precisely because Britain took the lead
in this evolution of constitutionalism, and because its constitutionalism was successful enough to avoid any serious breakdown
after the 'revolution' of 1688, it has some interesting eccentricities of its own. Most basic of all, perhaps, is the fact that no
single document is especially privileged as *the* constitution, and
that its sovereign power is the complex unity of the Crown in
Parliament which has, in principle, utterly unlimited powers. It
is this constitutional fact, taken in isolation from the British
political process, which leads Mr Tony Benn and others to try
curdling the blood of the bourgeoisie with the observation that
the British have no rights. Mr William Wallace describes parliamentary sovereignty as 'an outdated constitutional myth which
we should now abandon' – the beneficiary of the abandonment
being the authorities of the European Community.[2] Mr Neal
Ascherson, who echoes Mr Wallace, even down to his little
ironies, thinks that 'The Community is not about sovereignty in
that British sense at all.'[3] And an assortment of European enthusiasts talk about the 'pooling' and 'sharing' of sovereignty
with our European partners.

All of this is a muddle. You cannot share sovereignty. You can
only do three things with it: exercise it, delegate it, or give it
away. Britain might, for example, enter into a federal union

and abandon its sovereignty completely. What it would get in return is no doubt some political influence alongside fellow federalists in how the new sovereign power would act. This is a perfectly possible thing to do, and many people are in favour of it, but the pretence that it constitutes a sharing or pooling of sovereignty is strictly for simple and gullible people. How much difference it would actually make to our lives is another matter, a matter difficult to judge because it depends on how extensively the new sovereign would seek to regulate our lives. The European Commission in Brussels has proved to be an enthusiastic regulator.

So much for abandoning sovereignty. We might also delegate or devolve sovereignty, which is what happens when Britain pledges itself to abide by future international treaties, and it happened when Britain entered the Community in 1972. The government then officially told the people that Britain's sovereignty was in no way threatened. This was somewhat disingenuous, but it was strictly correct. In the European Communities Act of that year, we agreed to abide by Community legislation (in whose framing of course we might take part) so long as it did not involve certain restricted areas: imposing new taxation, for example, legislating retroactively, or creating new criminal offences.[4] These agreements are authoritative in Britain for no other reason than that the British Parliament, in its exercise of sovereignty, has declared them so. But it is one of the powers of sovereignty that, following the principle *salus populi suprema lex*, it may abrogate treaties. The European continent has in the relatively recent past been swept by rather unsavoury enthusiasms which have found their way into the law. One hopes that this will not happen again, but the safety of the people cannot be grounded on hopes. If it did happen again, Britain would no doubt exercise its sovereignty and refuse to implement such laws, even at the cost of a major political crisis in the Community.

The current questions about sovereignty involve monetary union and the possibility of federal institutions. The question thus arises as to how far Britain (or any other member of the Community) could go on delegating bits of its sovereignty and still have anything left. One is reminded of the philosophical question of how many grains of sand are necessary to constitute a heap. It might well be argued that in principle, a sovereign power might devolve every substantive decision, while retaining only the one vestigial power to reassert its sovereignty if it so chose. We might call this the 'cheshire cat' theory of sovereignty. These are difficult legal questions, and they are difficult for a very specific reason: that sovereignty is a highly paradoxical legal conception because it is at the junction between law and politics. The reality behind legal sovereignty is the effective political will of a people, and if that comes into conflict with a legally alienated sovereignty, we move from constitutional doctrine to political reality. Quebec may be subordinate to Canada, the Southern States in 1860 to Washington, Lithuania etc. to the Soviet Union, and so on, but when organised discontent becomes effective, a new political reality beginning to express itself in a demand for sovereignty has come into existence, and legalities fall into the background. This is an important point, with two important implications for our current situation. The first is that it is in everyone's interest that Britain (and other countries) should not be untimely hustled out of their legal rights of sovereignty, because if the matter is miscalculated, there will soon be serious political trouble. The other implication bears upon the dangerous illusion that the economic and political dominance in the Community of 80 million Germans can be blocked by waving the magic wand of constitutionality. A united Germany may perhaps be no problem at all, but if it is, legalities won't solve it.

If I am right about these things, the idea that Britain has a special problem with Communal cooperation because of the doctrine (myth *chez* Wallace) of parliamentary sovereignty is a mistake. The countries of Europe do indeed have written constitutions in which the sovereign power is limited by being parcelled out among various institutions. In fact, they have often had many such constitutions – five since 1789 in the case of the French. Every so often, political reality tears them up, and the politicians have to start all over again – a fitting commentary on constitutionalism as an illusion of permanence. Nor have all those admirable written declarations of rights produced the reign of virtue dreamed of by our current radical republicans. Britain has always been, and remains, a beacon of freedom to those suffering oppression. This evident fact was obscured for some intellectuals because, during the intellectual dominance of Marxist ideas, they picked up the foolish notion that current liberal democratic states were profoundly oppressive in ways concealed by capitalist ideology. For a time, they imagined freedom and true community were to be found in the Soviet Union and elsewhere. With the collapse of Communism, they have lost their utopias, but retained their hatred of contemporary European and especially British life. The European Community has now become, for many of them, a new utopia, and it will remain so for just so long as it remains incomplete; it has all the charm of potentiality.

This, I take it, is why so many people are enthusiastic about abandoning the tried and (for many of us) much-loved institutions of Britain in favour of this paper utopia being built up in Brussels. Thus Wallace:

> Institutional co-operation among different levels of government, sharing powers, is fundamentally different from an allpowerful parliament at Westminster, delegating subordinate powers to lesser authorities as and when it desires.

Wherein, we may ask, lies this fundamental difference? That 'all-powerful parliament at Westminster' sounds pretty despotic until one remembers that it exercises its power through limited officeholders dependent upon representatives who must be regularly elected by the people. Hence it is in the highest degree misleading of Neal Ascherson to headline his version of this argument: 'the spectre of popular sovereignty looms over Greater England'. The people are no less, and no more, sovereign in Britain than in any of the liberal democracies of the continent, and has been so for longer than any of them. Hostile radicals (and even misguided reformers like Lord Hailsham) are fond of talking of British government as an 'elective dictatorship'. When was the last real dictatorship subject to regular election and the continuous competition of political parties?

The main device for discrediting British sovereignty lies in identifying it with policies of narrow national interest. At its crudest, this is actually to identify national sovereignty (a legal concept) with nationalism (a political enthusiasm). In fact, the history of British politics over many centuries (ranging from its unilateral decision to abolish the slave trade in the early nineteenth century to its adherence to international organisations in the twentieth), shows that Britain has been in a high degree

internationalist in its conduct of foreign affairs. It is certainly
wrong to believe that the move from British sovereignty to the
supranationalism of the European Community is a move from
narrow to universal values. Consider an obvious and striking
example. One of the areas in which the British government has
delegated its sovereign right of decision to the Community has
been agriculture. Britain has become part of the Common
Agricultural Policy. That policy is highly protectionist. It has
encouraged the degradation of the soil by overproduction of
food. It has cost the families of the Community some hundreds
of pounds each year in overpriced food. It has impoverished
Third World countries (not to mention members of the Commonwealth) who are excluded by its protectionist barriers. It
has fossilised agriculture in a structural condition long since
made obsolete by changing conditions, and it threatens to
wreck the liberalisation of world trade in the Uruguay Round of
the GATT negotiations. Is this not the most spectacular exhibi-
tion of the narrow interests of a (supra)nationalism that might
be imagined? And is it not also a case where British sovereign
policy is clearly by contrast far more internationalist in its aims?

It thus seems to me that nearly all the things which are widely
believed about the relation between British sovereignty and the
Community are contrary to reason and logic. To confuse a
power with the way it might be used (but in fact usually is not)
is rather like the absurd feminist argument that all men are
rapists. They have the equipment, after all.

Still, once we have cleared our heads of these muddles, there
are two types of argument which may seriously be advanced in
favour of supporting greater integration with Europe *along the
presently established lines*. I emphasise the last phrase because I
shall presently suggest that there are better forms of European
integration. The first argument is that a federal structure will
indeed be a permanent cession of sovereignty but that it will be
limited by constitutional guarantees. This is an argument which
has been influentially advanced by James Buchanan[5] and Peter
Bernholz.[6] It happens that these two writers believe in a state
with strictly limited powers, one that would leave the citizens of
Europe free to trade with each other unhindered. I am in
strong agreement with such aims. My problem, however, is that
it is politically unlikely that any written constitution that might
emerge from the contemporary European process would be of

the kind they hope for. It is much more likely to be awash with declarations of economic and social rights whose whole point would be to license bureaucratic interference with every detail of civil life. But even if a thoroughly liberal constitution were to emerge, its value would depend on the legal institutions of the Community. The history of federal states tends to be a history of power moving from the parts to the centre; I know of no real exceptions, nor of any countervailing tendency giving hope for the future. Indeed, the centralising tendency seems to me to be increasing, because of the popularity of solving problems by regulation. And there is little doubt that the authorised interpreters of Community law, the Court at Luxembourg, with its propensity for teleological interpretation of the Treaty of Rome, would be a weak instrument for the protection of liberal freedoms.

The second type of argument encourages us to have faith in the Commission's own doctrine of subsidiarity. Decisions should not be made, according to this doctrine, at the highest level unless they cannot properly be made at a lower level. I have no quarrel with this principle. It is, indeed, the pure milk of liberal individualism – until an actual problem arises of deciding just what is the appropriate level for decision. That question is one of power. It is a question of who would have the power to coerce whom. And power, we know, is delightful stuff; many people can't get enough of it. The Commission in Brussels is the source of a constant stream of regulations, directives and proposals which express its power to regulate our lives. It seeks, for example, to regulate the age at which sporting guns can be purchased, or magpies shot. It has proposals about protection against sexual harassment, and the employment of part-time workers. Its operations are like a blunderbuss, in that the pellets seem to go all over the place. And what is then left of subsidiarity? As Sir Leon Brittain has admitted, it is impossible to operationalise.[7] No doubt federalism itself would be a partial attempt to implement subsidiarity in general terms. If the Commission's use of this idea were serious, I would expect it to have already been very much more specific about whole areas of European life where it firmly excluded itself from having any competence. I am not aware that it has done so; indeed, it is difficult to see how it *could* do so in any conclusive way. Hence we are left only with the protection of the Council of Ministers, each Minister being appropriately sensitive to the national interests of his country. The only final protection is the unanimity rule. Unanimity is an excellent rule at this high level. If all countries agree, we have some evidence that a rule is in the wider interest. Majorities, on the other hand, are very far from infallible. The minority is sometimes right. Even a minority of one. Even Mrs Thatcher.

Coercion is the central point. Brussels has acquired considerable powers, and no one doubts its appetite for more. Talk of subsidarity, talk of remedying what is significantly called 'the democratic deficit', is beside the point, because what is meant here by democracy is merely a warrant for legitimating the wider exercise of powers. The dream of internationalism, the reaching out of Europeans towards each other, and of Europe towards the world, has awakened to an alarming reality: the creation of a whole new layer of government superimposed upon the layers of government we already have. Supranationalism is, quite predictably, producing exactly the opposite results from those at which internationalism aims. Power being delightful, and profitable, governments and bureaucracies tend to expand. To extend the powers of Brussels would be to put ourselves under a power whose future course we could not predict, and it would not even have the effect of diminishing the powers already exercised over us by national governments. But we do at least have some real influence on *them*.

The power to coerce, I repeat, is the point. What proposals for political and economic union mean is that Brussels will have not only the power to dissolve outmoded restrictions on trade between states, but also the power to impose new restrictions on every aspect of European life. Now it is a central point in the theory of the state that sovereign governments must have the power to ensure that their subjects conform to laws whose purpose is to minimise collisions between individuals each pursuing his or her own projects. This elementary requirement of civil order is already performed by the national governments of the Community. My argument is, then, that all the coercion which human communities need to maintain order is already done by the national states, and therefore that the Community's lust for the power to coerce subserves no other purpose than a pure bureaucratic passion for imposing harmonisation and uniformity upon everyone within range.

In the end, this passion will undoubtedly defeat itself, but it could cause a great deal of trouble first. In the wake of the revolutions of 1989, the central European issue is often posed as the choice between widening and deepening the Community. But this is a false choice. It makes the basic Brussellian assumption that a deep Community is one subject to the entire range of regulations the Commission can get the Council to agree to. But as Richard Body has argued, Europe is a vast and complex group of countries which can associate differently according to the problems involved.[8] He cites the condition of the North Sea, the environment of the Alps, centralisation of patents and many other issues on which different groups of countries will get together, and in doing so, solve common problems without attempting to coerce each other. A process of this kind can grow by creating the conditions of its own success, not needing to live in a condition of perpetual crisis (as the Community does), nor to spend millions on public relations, nor to seek power by exploiting the hysteria of momentum. The European Community is by no means the only transnational organisation dealing with common problems: apart from NATO, the Council of Europe, the Western European Union, the Economic Commission for Europe, and many others, each suitable for its own specific purposes. The Council of Europe, for example, has its own Social Charter, and Britain is a signatory; but it leaves to each state the details and the timing of any implementation of its principles. Seen in terms of the quiet, steady progress made by these bodies, the Community can only look increasingly exigent and hysterical in its passion to govern us more and more.

I cite these considerations in order to open up discussion on the two principles which would guide a real European internationalism. I am assuming that such a European Community would be a free market in people, goods and services. That granted, I would see the European Community based on consultation and marked by the principle of *consensus*. No doubt this would mean that on a variety of issues, some countries would take steps before others did. I see no difficulty about this, because I know of few regulations so unmistakably wise that they would not benefit from being implemented by a few pioneers to test out how they would work. No doubt there are some measures which would only work, or at least only have their full effect, if done by all. Environmental measures often come into this class. But here we should have to weigh up the disadvantages (which I imagine would only be temporary) of some countries holding out against a reform, against the disadvantage of erecting a coercive apparatus over the peoples of Europe, an apparatus which would undoubtedly find increasing numbers of things needing to be regulated. For I see institutional arteriosclerosis as the major danger not just to Europe but to the world at large. It grows when authorities with coercive power respond to a continuing stream of lobbyists, pressure groups, single issue enthusiasts and cranks of many kinds, all of them eager to pull the levers of power. Quite apart from the intrusiveness, there are the transaction costs imposed by regulations. The regulation on trade in caramel is reported to be nearly 27,000 words long, and it cannot possibly be any fun to read. For businessmen above all, to have to operate in such an environment would be an ordeal. The proclaimed aim of the European Community is to allow Europe to compete economically on level terms with Japan and the United States. A Europe left free to produce and to trade has nothing to fear from such competition; a Europe increasingly regulated, inspected, directed, harmonised and levelled would soon suffer the fate so brilliantly analysed by Mancur Olsen in *The Rise and Decline of Nations*.[9]

The two principles on which a new Europe capable of pioneering the shape of the next century must be based are therefore *consensus* and *competition*. To build on consensus is to have faith in the rationality of Europeans, a faith which entails no serious political risks because all the elements of order which are essential to a civil community have been democratically achieved in the established practices of the national states. The defect of many politicians is that they fail to recognise that in modern states, the very conditions of association change every generation or so. The very complexity of modern societies has rendered obsolete the old understanding of a society as a collection of manifest interests in conflict with each other, except in a few areas such as agriculture. It has created what I have elsewhere described as a 'loquocentric society' – a society, that is, in which political decisions emerge from the deliberations of an articulate population relatively remote from any direct interest in particular outcomes.[10] This need not be an ideal world, but it does bear upon the issue of coercion. All outcomes are ambiguous, and people do of course often make mistakes about rationality. We are still in a human world, and folly arises no less in reasoning than in desiring. But that is merely another reason why it is wise to limit the power of coercion. Nevertheless, we are moving into a new world in which very considerable effective consensus will be possible among peoples sharing a common culture.

It is the differences within the common culture which make it desirable that these nations should also be competitive. Each of them has its own unique character, and each is likely to adopt different forms of social organisation, different ways of dealing with the problem of the poor, responding to new social developments, and so on. The genius of Europe has long consisted in the passionate localism with which it has resisted attempts to unify it, from Charlemagne to Adolf Hitler. Competition is very different from conflict. It draws the best from people, and it is entrenched in the very bones of a games-playing people like Europeans.

I hope that my argument is not merely a lament for an international vision which can never be. The dead hand of corporatist rationalism already powerfully grips the institutions of Europe, and the likelihood that the national states in the near future will be able to reassert their control over the powerful bureaucracy of the Berlayement is not great. I write, therefore, with a sense that the immediate future presents us with the doom of a new oligarchy. But the future is unpredictable, and the passion for power self-destructive. In the end, the most important thing is never to be confused about what *ought* to happen.

NOTES

1.   For a similar argument see Richard Body, *Europe of Many Circles: Constructing a Wider Europe* (London: New European Publications, 1990).
2.   For one version of this argument – that from which the quotation is taken – see 'Cry Havoc' in *New Statesman and Society*, 9 November 1990, pp. 16–17. Mr Wallace is a Fellow of St Anthony's College, Oxford.
3.   Neal Ascherson, *The Independent on Sunday*, 18 November 1990, p. 23.

4. See T.C. Hartley, *The Foundations of European Community Law*, 2nd edn. (OUP, 1988), p. 241.

5. James Buchanan, *An American Perspective on Europe's Constitutional Opportunity,* paper presented in the Mt Pelerin Society meeting in Munich, August 1990.

6. Peter Bernholz, *Constitutional Proposals for Europe*, prepared for the Frankfurt Institute, and developing Buchanan's ideas in European terms.

7. In remarks made to the Bruges Group in 1990.

8. Body, op. cit.

9. Mancur Olsen, *The Rise and Decline of Nations* (New Haven, Conn.: Yale University Press, 1982).

10. Kenneth Minogue, 'Loquocentricity, Society and its Critics', *Government and Opposition*, Vol. 21, No. 3, Summer 1986, pp. 338–61.

3 Federalism with a Bureaucratic Face

Wayne Hunt

> I don't want to make a long speech because the most important principles can be briefly expressed.
>
> The Lord's Prayer has 56 words; the Ten Commandments has 297; the American Declaration of Independence has 300; but an E.E.C. directive on the import of caramel and caramel products requires 26,911 words.
>
> The moral is obvious.
>
> Sir Frank Hartley, Vice-Chancellor,
> University of London, 1976–1978.

Ours is an age of ideas. Why this is so has much to do with changes in the world order and with the exhaustion of the attendant 'isms' that gave rise and sanction to the great wars, both hot and cold, of this century. It was said that in 1989 peace broke out throughout the world. Like all engaging generalities this was not quite true. War had been banished to the inner cities and to the developing world. The calming of the cold war loosed a whirlwind of ideas about the reordering of societies in the new global order.

Ideas move nations. This was made dramatic in 1989 in *Mitteleuropa*. For the scholarly community the year of peace, 1989, also brought drama in the form of Francis Fukuyama's (in)famous article entitled 'The End of History?' which appeared in the summer 1989 edition of *The National Interest* (No. 16). Fukuyama opined that history had ended or was coming to an end, in Hegel's sense of the term, because of the ineluctable spread of a western, consumer culture that had gathered all into a global 'common marketisation'. Communism and fascism had offered the twentieth century's only comprehensive alternatives to this end and these master plans for reassembling the heavens on earth had been thoroughly discredited. But at what cost was victory purchased? Fukuyama sadly acknowledged that 'the world-wide ideological struggle that called forth daring, courage, imagination and idealism' was 'replaced by economic calculations, the endless solving of technical problems, environmental concerns and the satisfaction of endless consumer demands.' The human spirit which showed itself greatest in times of adversity had no place here, for this was a world of neither pervasive darkness nor penetrating light; neither heroes, nor villains; neither saints, nor satans. Only caretakers. Grey, monotonous caretakers. Or as Fukuyama put it: 'In the post historical period there will be neither art, nor philosophy, just the perpetual caretaking of the museum of modern history.' The Hegelian pretenses of this analysis were easily and readily dismissed but the invective raised by what the author had to say suggested something far more telling: that he had hit the mark. Indeed few bothered to dispute the substance of his argument, the view that he had captured the reality of an emerging world; that was taken as given.

And taken it was! For Fukuyama had created a vortex, and countless other arguments were swept within. One such argument was that presented by Jacques Attali. Attali is a media guru, economic philosopher, literary lion, sometime confidant of France's President Mitterrand and, in his latest role, is President-designate of the European Bank for Reconstruction and Development. He envisions the Bank's projects leading toward 'the progressive economic and cultural homogenisation of the European Region' and the concomitant emergence of the United States of Europe. A superpower. The world's newest, in fact. The older superpowers, he asserted in a recent article 'slouch toward relative, if not absolute, decline' because the 'Order of Force has been supplanted by the Order of Money'. By this he meant the reign of the market. But where Fukuyama sounded the pessimistic note, Attali rose to optimism; where Fukuyama spoke to reality, Attali spoke to idealism. Repeatedly the Bank's President-designate called for a 'new political imagination' which would accommodate this Order of Money by allowing Europeans to 'draw new boundaries and invent new institutions that are supra-national, yet democratically accountable'. This United States of Europe would be, it was to be assumed, rid of the entrapments which rent the American dream, domestic violence at home and foreign intrigues abroad, for (here the optimism reaches a crescendo!) it was only a milestone on the road to a 'planetary political power'.

The catch? That 'politicians and statesmen accept the unpopular abandonment of sovereignty'.[1]

If politicians could shed outdated concepts of sovereignty and embrace the greater notion of a federal Europe, all would be for the best in the best of all possible worlds. There was a historical ring to these comforting illusions about a society of managers and caretakers[2] or alternatively about possibilities of an earthly paradise. They would have come unstuck of their own accord in the 1990s had not the ugly reality of Saddam Hussein and the Gulf Crisis intervened first. Did Europe respond as a superpower? No. Anything but. Britain's special relation with America allowed it to deploy its naval and air forces and, as war by other means, its diplomacy to considerable advantage. The French responded in kind with a sizeable contribution of naval and ground forces but the commitment of other European powers ranged from low farce to high comedy. Germany's preoccupation – or more to the point, obsession – with internal problems made for partisan dithering over whether Germans could be sent to the Gulf as part of a UN force (being as they are constitutionally restricted to the NATO area). In the end Chancellor Kohl told the American Secretary of State, James Baker, that Germany would give a hugely generous sum of DM 3.3 billion (US\$2.1 billion) as its share of the burden. Of this amount DM 1.6 billion was to help pay America's military expenses and the rest was directed toward Egypt, Turkey and Jordan. Yet each of these responses points toward something more profound. When the chips are down, when duress threatens, it has always been the nation-state that has commanded first loyalty, a distinguished scholar noted a generation ago, and his insight remains tellingly pertinent.[3]

The notion that Europe must inevitably evolve into a federal form of government has just as inevitably evolved into a convenient fiction: convenient in that it allowed politicians to read their own domestic political agendas into bigger events; a fiction in that it was always based too heavily on fleeting and politically expedient calculations. That economic forces were going global there could be no doubt. But regional trading blocks in the Pacific, the Americas and Europe meant that Fukuyama's common market was in fact driven (and potentially riven) by three competing versions of capitalism, from a neo-mercantilist version in the Pacific to a social democratic version in Europe which sacrificed some political sovereignty in order to create economic opportunities across borders.[4] Attali and many other commentators assumed that to make political structures accord with changed economic realities there could be but one route to follow: federalism.[5] But the assumption that political structures must follow the dictates of economic forces makes for bad logic, and worse public policy.[6]

In Britain, the leadership of the Labour Party has been in search of a replacement for grand Keynesian thinking about the role of the state, for what the social sciences all-too-pretentiously call a 'new paradigm' and for what Hugo Young all-too-rightly calls a 'big idea'. For them, as for the Liberal Democrats, there is one 'big idea': Europe. Ditto for the socialist governments of France and Spain, which avail themselves of the same contingency by imagining that 'Europe' is a way to revive their intellectually tattered 'market socialism'. (Emphasis is falling more and more on the market, rendering their socialism obsolete.) For German politicians of all political stripes, integration of Germany was ineluctably tied to European integration. Meanwhile Thomas Mann's exhortation to work 'not for a German Europe, but a European Germany' has so unthinkingly and so often been invoked by policy-makers in Bonn that it has come, paradoxically, to suggest the exact opposite. (A 'European Germany' is pointedly calculated to placate nationalists within Germany with visions of a German-dominated pan-European nationalism, just as it is calculated to placate uneasy neighbours outside their borders and, most of all, the restive superpowers with the opposite vision.) For Italian politicians of all partisan colourings Europe is an expeditious way to supersede the rigidities of Italy's own incestuous bureaucracy, a feudal fiefdom widely perceived to be the exclusive preserve of Italians from the south. (The prime minister, Giulio Andreotti is supposed to have said 'Someone has to govern Italy'.) All the continental countries entertain warm memories of the European Community if for no better reason than their association of this institution with the prosperity of the 1950s when they joined. It need not be added that Britain's entry in the 1970s in a period of austerity affords it no such collective memory.

Closer inspection reveals more flaws in the federal design. Experience from other nations is richly instructive and can place this debate in a proper perspective. For the segmentation of the world economy into the present regional blocks has limited the freedom of manoeuvre for politicians at the national level, and the incremental ceding of national policy instruments to supranational authority has rendered the range of political manoeuvrability smaller still. Britain's entry into the European Exchange Rate Mechanism is a case in point. The economic imperatives which dictate such a move weigh more heavily than the corresponding loss of political sovereignty. Yet again it must be asked, at what cost has this managerial victory been purchased? Other nations drawn into the embrace of supranationalism have found that the hard truth behind the rhetoric about the need for political restructuring was that it was never the economic giants who were obliged to restructure; restructuring, it seems, has turned out to be a one-way street.[7] There is little doubt at which end of the street Britain is situated.

Talk of a European federation is much like what Lord Bryce called, in a parallel context half a century ago, a 'bloodless abstraction'. By this he meant that theories had to be put to the practice. In practice federalism makes for additional layers of bureaucracy and for the accompanying evils of big government.[8] In practice most, if not all of the world's great federations have been moving toward centralisation, but it is centralisation of a special kind, a domination by a central bureaucratic elite. Reacting against this there has been a counter-surge of an autochthonous democracy at the state, provincial or *Länd* level.[9] As nations become locked into a network of global interdependence and as nation-states become more circumscribed in their freedom of action (federalists read this as obsolete), citizens turn to regional institutions as a matter of course.[10] And of course this leads to what John Kenneth Galbraith noted some time ago, a movement of economic forces toward larger units, and a political movement in the opposite direction, toward smaller units. To absorb these latter tendencies the European Community has seized upon and made fashionable the concept of subsidiarity, a term adapted from late nineteenth-century papal bulls. It allows for decisions to be made at the lowest possible levels – whenever appropriate. But the church heritage shows through and it remains to be seen how the invocation of this holy cant can transform Welsh nationalists and Basque separatists into Euro-enthusiasts. That requires an article of faith in the new Europe.

Federalists see themselves at the end of history. The leaders of France and Germany, Mitterrand and Kohl, see it as their historic mission to cement the Franco-German partnership into the foundations of a glorious and magnificent centre of world power. Such monumental *hubris* can only be appreciated as theatre. Like the transmogrification that befell the hapless politicians in Pirandello's famous play they seem to be turning into statues. Or statutes. For Europeanisation has been translated into harmonisation which in turn has been translated into bureaucratisation.

Margaret Thatcher took issue with this at Bruges when she asserted that:

> We have not successfully rolled back the frontiers of the state in Britain only to see them reimposed at a European level, with a European superstate exercising a new dominance from Brussels.

Almost two years later, at Aspen, she made common cause with the Eastern and Central European democratic movements. Of these people she said:

> They have not thrown off central command and control of their own countries only to find them reincarnated in the European Community. With their new freedom, their feelings of patriotism and national identity are flooding out again. Their newly restored parliaments are full of vitality.

And recently at her Bournemouth party conference she emphatically rejected European measures that would undermine Britain's national independence. She stressed that:

> Europe cannot be built by ignoring or suppressing this sense of nationhood, by trying to turn us into regions rather than nations.

The Iron Lady thereby aligned herself and Her Majesty's Government with a patriotic tradition that found its most elevated expression in Edmund Burke's eloquent insistence that British institutions of law and government were an ancestral trust weighted far beyond the vicissitudes that moved a public's opinion and a continent's fashions; for these, he proclaimed, were the promulgations of 'sophisters, economists and calculators'.[11]

And it was a tradition as well that found less elevated expression in Nicholas Ridley's impolitic outburst of last summer(!).

By holding steadfast to this ancestral trust the British Prime Minister allied herself with what the most brilliant Germanic minds have thought the best of British institutions and customs, and conversely she arrayed herself against what was thought the worst of theirs. Consider Max Weber. Irresponsibility, shallow posturing and an ineptitude in times of crisis: all were marks of the post-Bismarck legacy of weak parliaments and strong administrations Weber felt; and the great sociologist was at one with continental eminences like Montesquieu and Voltaire in his express admiration for English arrangements.[12] Consider also Karl Mannheim. Mannheim extended his predecessor's analysis to show, from the German example, that it was a characteristic of bureaucratic thought to transform all political problems into problems of administration.[13] Consider finally Franz Neumann. Almost forty years ago Neumann pointed out that federalism cannot be considered abstractly and he took to task those who poured 'unrestrained adulation' upon the idea of a European federal state.[14]

Thatcher's battle is not just with European Commission president Jacques Delors and/or current Council president Gianni DeMichelis who seek for a so-called deeper Europe (their federalism is a code word for socialism); it is equally with the various and sundry 'sophisters, economists and calculators' who seek to place their market orthodoxies and the Order of Money upon the world (their 'federalism' is a code word for privatisation). By the logic and logistics of the latter ideology Big Ben could wind up on a Nevada desert. Or the Houses of Parliament could grace a California theme park.

The point is that limits must be set. Nationalism does not enjoy a good press at present, but national pride is essential if we are to restore faith in the efficacy of democratic action and to inspire honour in public affairs. This lies at the centre of western civilisation. It is salutary to recall that Aristotle declared politics to be the master science, not because it explained or included every other human endeavour, rather it had to be the master science because it gave order and priority to the competing claims made upon society.[15] This classical balance has been upset in the present rush toward Europeanisation. Economics has displaced history and replaced politics.

The federalists foresee Europe expanding in concentric circles. In their view a federal type of government will inevitably take form in what might be called the first circle, among the original founders of the EC (which is to say Germany, France, the Benelux countries and Italy). Britain will have to decide whether to form a confederal association with the outer ring(s), in Churchill's phrase, to be 'with Europe but not of it' – or to go whole-hog federal. To stay outside is to be removed from the centre of decision-making. As is so often the case, common sense rests with Sir Ralf Dahrendorf. He has proposed a policy menu that nations like Britain may opt in and out of instead of being shackled to either a federal or a confederal form of government.[16]

The choice will be placed before the British electorate by 1992. Commentators are looking back a century and a half to the Corn Laws and saying that the most fundamental realignment of British politics since then may well take place. They could also look sideways, to Canada, to Mexico.

The 1988 Canadian General Election turned on the issue of free trade with the United States. (The other United States.) Parliamentary sovereignty and political sovereignty were much debated. In their perfervid lust for electoral advantage the major political parties abandoned their principles and reversed their historic standing as continentalists or as nationalists. The pressure cooker atmosphere nearly tore the parties apart from the inside. It left a rot upon the whole political process which helped to debase the following discussions over Quebec's constitutional future in Canada and the rot lingers to this day.

Mexico is currently undergoing a similar catharsis in its dealings with the United States over the Free Trade issue, and its political process is being similarly debased. In future a furious swell of populism and nationalism may well destroy the present agreements.

Is there a lesson here?

Only that Europe is an idea whose time has yet to come to Britain.

NOTES

1. Jacques Attali, 'Lines on the Horizon: A New Order in the Making', *New Perspectives Quarterly* (Spring, 1990), pp. 4–11. These assertions carry a long history in the 'idealist' school of international relations. For a recent critique, not of Attali, but of many of the key assumptions that his argument is built upon, refer to Eliot Cohen 'The Future of Force and America's Strategy', *The National Interest*, No. 21 (Autumn 1990), pp. 3–15.

2. In an earlier era James Burnham had written of a managerial revolution in which the world divided into three superstates, ruled by a caste of managers, scientists and bureaucrats. George Orwell took powerful exception to what Burnham was saying on the grounds that his 'realism' led to a fascination with power, a glorification of those who hold power and an easy acceptance of the status quo. Refer to Orwell's classic essay 'Burham's View of the Contemporary World Struggle' in S. Orwell and I. Angus (eds) *The Collected Essays, Journalism and Letters of George Orwell*, Vol. IV: *1945–1950* (London: Secker & Warburg, 1968), pp. 313–26.

3. Rupert Emerson, *From Empire to Nation: The Rise to Self-Assertion of Asian and African Peoples* (Boston: Beacon Press, 1960), pp. 95–6.

4. Robert Reich, 'The American 80's: Disaster or Triumph', *Commentary*, Vol. 90, No. 3 (September 1990), p. 16. A more extended treatment can be anticipated in Robert Reich, *The Work of Nations: Capitalism in the 21st Century* (New York: Knopf, forthcoming 1991).

5. See David Marquand, *Faltering Leviathan: National Sovereignty, the Regions and Europe* (London: Wyndam Place Trust, 1989), p. 43.

6. Refer to K. Minogue *et al.*, *Is National Sovereignty a Big Bad Wolf?*, Bruges Group Occasional Paper No. 6 (London: Paris Publishing, 1990).

7. Herbert Schiller, *Culture Inc.* (New York: Oxford University Press, 1989), p. 120.

8. See the survey in D.V. Smiley, *The Federal Condition in Canada* (Toronto: McGraw-Hill Ryerson, 1987), pp. 18–19.

9. Samuel Beer, in specific reference to the United States, has styled this a 'technocrat' vs. 'topocrat' fight. He composed the term 'topocrat' from the Greek 'topos' or place or locality and 'kratos' or authority. Topocrats refer, then, to state or local government officials. See his 'Federalism, Nationalism and Democracy in America' in the *American Political Science Review*, Vol. 72, No. 1 (March 1978), pp. 18–19. A parallel point is made by Sydney Tarrow, 'Introduction' in S. Tarrow *et al.* (eds), *Territorial Politics in Industrial Nations* (New York: Praeger, 1978).

10. Richard Simeon, 'Considerations on Centralization and Decentralization', *Canadian Public Administration*, No. 29, Vol. 3 (Autumn 1986), pp. 445–61.

11. They think that government may vary like modes of dress, and with as little ill effect; that there needs no principle of attachment, except a sense of present convenience, to any constitution of the state. They always speak as if they were of opinion that there is singular species of compact between them and their magistrates which binds the magistrate, but which has nothing reciprocal in it, but that the majesty of

the people has a right to dissolve it without any reason but its will. Their attachment to their country itself is only so far as it agrees with some of their fleeting projects; it begins and ends with that scheme of polity which falls in with their momentary opinion. These doctrines, or rather sentiments, seem prevalent with your new statesmen. But they are wholly different from those on which we have always acted in this country.

Edmund Burke (ed. T. Mahoney),
Reflections on the Revolution in France
(New York: Bobbs-Merrill, 1955), pp. 86–100.

In the twentieth century, F.A. Hayek has taken the Burkean insistence that law and the institutions of society should grow out of experience, a 'social evolutionism', and fused it with an enthusiasm for the market, for 'spontaneous order'. Refer to F.A. Hayek, *The Constitution of Liberty* (Chicago: University of Chicago Press, 1960) and *Law, Legislation and Liberty*, Vol. 1 (Chicago: University of Chicago Press, 1973), *Law Legislation and Liberty* Vol. 2 (Chicago: University of Chicago Press, 1976) and *Law, Legislation and Liberty* Vol. 3 (Chicago: University of Chicago Press, 1979). Burke and Hayek provide the philosophical landmarks which guide Thatcher's position on Europe.

12.   Weber contrasted Germany's 'negative politics' and underdeveloped parliamentarianism with the opposite condition which prevailed in England. Refer to 'Parliament and Government in a Reconstructed Germany. (A Contribution to the Political Critique of Officialdom and Party Politics)' in M. Weber, *Economy and Society,* Vol. 2, G. Roth and C. Wittich (eds) (Berkeley: University of California Press, 1968), pp. 1381–1420.

13.   This Mannheim labelled 'bureaucratic conservatism'. He wrote that: 'The fundamental tendency of all bureaucratic thought is to turn all problems of politics into problems of administration. As a result the majority of books on politics in the history of German political science are *de facto* treatises on administration' Karl Mannheim, *Ideology and Utopia* (London: Routledge and Kegan Paul, 1936), p. 105.

14.   Franz Neumann, Chapter 8, 'On the Theory of the Federal State' in F. Neumann, *The Democratic and The Authoritarian State,* H. Marcuse (ed.) (New York: Free Press, 1957), p. 229. The article originally appeared in the *Columbia Law Review,* Vol. 57, No. 7 (November 1953), pp. 901–35.

15.   The point is elegantly taken in Bernard Crick, *In Defense of Politics* (London: Weidenfeld & Nicolson, 1962). For an incisive critique of philosophic 'foundationalists' who seek to give philosophic precepts a sovereignty over politics see Benjamin Barber, *The Conquest of Politics: Liberal Philosophy in Democratic Times* (Princeton: Princeton University Press, 1988).

16.   Ralf Dahrendorf, *Reflections on the Revolution in Europe* (London: Chatto & Windus, 1990).

4 Why Sovereignty Matters
Gavin Smith

It has become fashionable in the debate over Britain's role in the next phase of EC integration to dismiss the concept of sovereignty as either outmoded or a theoretical abstraction that hinders discussion of the practical issues. This paper argues that this approach is misguided, and that sovereignty is central to the debate.

Sovereignty matters because it defines a state's relationship with other states and the source of ultimate authority within a state. In the European Community a proper understanding of national sovereignty is becoming increasingly compromised. The member states' external competence is gradually being diminished. Legislation is being initiated and influenced by an unelected body, the European Commission, which seeks both to enlarge the Community's competence and to exploit the legislative process in pursuit of its own, often narrow, view of the European interest. The contribution of national parliaments to Community legislation is minimal. Majority voting, once the exception, is now set to become the rule. Community directives, once passed, can now in many cases be enforced in national courts even where the state in question has voted against the legislation and failed to implement it in its own law.

The ultimate arbiter of questions of EC law is the European Court, whose decisions can only be reversed by amendment of the Treaties and are thus for practical purposes beyond challenge.

Those who advocate transferring sovereignty to Community institutions claim that national influence will thereby be enhanced. Indeed, Sir Geoffrey Howe defines sovereignty as a state's capacity to maximise its influence in the world, a 'resource to be traded rather than guarded'.[1] What he and others overlook is the cost of this influence in terms of loss of accountability and self-determination. Moreover, they fail to appreciate that retention of sovereignty and closer cooperation with other states are not mutually exclusive.

It is true that argument over sovereignty has often been obscured by a failure to distinguish between a number of different senses in which the term is used. A number of recent contributors to the debate have recognised this. The House of Lords Select Committee on the European Communities refers in its recent report[2] to three meanings, while Sir Geoffrey Howe, in a wide-ranging study, identifies four.[3]

The starting point for any discussion of sovereignty must be state sovereignty or independence in international law. This is bound up intimately with the idea of statehood itself. The qualifications for statehood are threefold: the occupation of territory, the possession of a population, and a government capable of exercising effective control over its territory and of conducting international relations with other states.[4] (Recognition by other states is considered by some to be a further condition, by others merely to be evidence that the first three have been fulfilled.)

Clearly, the EC member states satisfy the conditions of state sovereignty or independence, at least at this stage in the development of the Community. The very act of making the Treaty of Rome (and acceding to it in the case of the states which joined subsequently) was an exercise of that independence. As the International Court of Justice declared in 1923.[5] 'The right of entering into international engagements is an attribute of state sovereignty.' The member states continue to enjoy and exercise treaty-making powers in many fields, most importantly foreign policy and security. Nevertheless, the Commission and some Member States envisage substantial transfer of these powers to the Community institutions.

What is equally indisputable, however, is that as a result of their Community membership, the member states agreed – under Community law – to restrict their right to make treaties on subjects falling within the purview of the EC institutions. Three provisions of the Treaty give the Community the express power to conclude agreements. First, Article 113 gives the Community the right to enter into agreements with non-member states ('third countries' in EC parlance) on such matters as tariffs and trade protection measures, in pursuance of the EC's common commercial policy. Second, Article 229 stipulates that 'it shall be for the Commission to ensure the maintenance of all appropriate relations with the organs of the United Nations, of all its specialised agencies and of the General Agreement on Tariffs and Trade', and that it shall 'maintain such relations as are appropriate with all international organisations'. Finally, Article 238 empowers the Community to conclude association agreements with other states, unions of states or international bodies. These three provisions are quite specific and limited in their scope. The Treaty contains no provision conferring a more general treaty-making power on the Community. Moreover, Article 228, which lays down the procedure to be followed for the conclusion of Community agreements, begins with the words 'where this Treaty provides'. This implies that the EC's treaty-making powers are confined to the three categories of agreement set out in the Treaty referred to above.

Nevertheless, the Community's competence in the external field has been progressively extended by the European Court of Justice, which held in 1971[6] that this was justified because it was to be implied both from the Treaty as a whole and from the Community's power to take internal action in specific fields. Indeed, the Court went so far as to hold that wherever the Community agrees on a common internal policy, the member states are prohibited from entering into their own bilateral agreements with third countries to the extent that such agreements might conflict with the common policy: 'As and when such common rules come into force . . . the Community alone is in a position to assume and carry out contractual obligations towards third countries affecting the whole sphere of application of the Community legal system.'

The range of policy areas in which the member states' own treaty-making powers have been severely restricted by the European Court's interpretation of Community law – invariably in the face of national opposition – is extensive: agriculture, fisheries and some aspects of transport are the most important examples. Environment, broadcasting and financial services are likely to follow.

It is not suggested that the statehood of the Twelve is seriously jeopardised by this encroachment on their external competence. It may properly be regarded as a self-denying ordinance which is effective only for so long as they remain members of the Community. It is also true that treaties made in breach of Community law would nevertheless be recognised under international law according to normal principles. Experience shows, though, that powers that have once been transferred are hard to regain, and in practice the restriction will surely be permanent.

It is unsatisfactory that decisions going to the heart of the external sovereignty of the member states should be made by the European Court, itself a creation of treaty, and not by the member states themselves. The issue is not so much whether certain treaty-making powers should reside with the member states or with the Community, but who should decide. The obvious solution to this problem would be an amendment to the Treaty listing those policy areas in which external competence was to be transferred to the Community – with perhaps a procedure for adding to the list – and stating expressly that in other fields competence remained with the member states. There seems, however, to be little chance that this issue will be addressed by the recently convened Intergovernmental Conferences on Political Union.

Turning to the internal sphere, it is probably the doctrine of parliamentary sovereignty that has given rise, in the United Kingdom, to the most heated discussion in relation to the European Community. The classic statement of this, the fundamental doctrine of the British constitution, was made by the great Victorian constitutional lawyer A.V. Dicey:

> Parliament has under the English constitution the right to make or unmake any law whatever; and . . . no person or body is recognised by the law of England as having a right to override or set aside the legislation of Parliament.

The origins and evolution of the doctrine do not matter in the present context. What is of central importance is the corollary of Parliament's legislative omnipotence, namely that no Act of Parliament has a status superior to any other. Parliament cannot bind itself. Entrenchment of Acts, even of those with constitutional implications, is not possible, and in the event of a conflict between two Acts, the later in time will prevail, according to the doctrine of implied repeal. This is as true of the European Communities Act of 1972 as of any other statute.

On the one hand, therefore, Parliament is supreme. But by the time the United Kingdom joined the Community, the European Court of Justice had already declared that Community law took precedence over national law in areas within the Community's competence.[7] It is worth pointing out that there is no supremacy clause in the Treaties; and it is paradoxical, to say the least, that a system of law created by treaty should prevail over its parent system. Moreover, had the treaty draftsmen intended this they would surely have armed the Court with effective sanctions. The Court cannot, notably, annul national legislation, but only declare a state to be in breach of a Treaty obligation. (It does, however, have the power to order a member state to suspend a national measure pending determination of the issue of its compatibility with Community law.)

Parliament had also to accommodate another substantially judge-made principle of crucial importance, the doctrine that Community law could in principle be directly effective in national court proceedings. Sir Geoffrey Howe is right in stating that it is this aspect of Community law that is truly 'revolutionary'. What he does not point out is that the principle is largely judge-made. It is true that the Treaty explicitly provides that certain Articles could take effect in national law, notably Articles 85 and 86 which relate to competition policy. Yet, far from supporting the case for direct effect, these and a small number of other Articles ought rather to be regarded as exceptions that prove the general rule that the Treaty was intended to govern only the relations between states. This was certainly the view of three of the original member states that made submissions in the historic case in which the direct effect doctrine was established, where the Court held that any provision of the Treaty that was clear, unconditional and capable of being enforced as a rule of law could take effect in national proceedings.[8]

It is important to note that each member state has had to incorporate its obligations under the Community Treaties – if not the Treaties themselves – into its domestic law according to its own constitutional practice. Some countries, such as Ireland, have had to amend their constitutions in order to do so. Others, such as Germany and Italy, do not need to pass implementing legislation to give effect to treaties.

The position in the United Kingdom is simple. It is a long-established constitutional principle that treaty-making powers are vested in the Crown (that is, the government of the day), but that legislation must be passed in the ordinary way for a treaty to have effect in national law. Thus the executive can bind the state *vis-à-vis* other states in international law, but the agreement will be ineffective internally unless implemented by Act of Parliament. In the case of the Community Treaties, this was accomplished by the European Communities Act of 1972.

The two doctrines of the supremacy and direct effect of Community law, whatever the doubts over their legal status, had therefore to be taken into account in the European Communities Act, without offending the doctrine of parliamentary sovereignty.

The 1972 Act is a subtly drafted piece of legislation. It does not seek to entrench itself and could, in theory, be repealed or amended like any other statute. However, it seeks to avoid conflict between national and Community law by introducing a rule of interpretation to be applied by the British courts. All Acts of Parliament passed before or after the 1972 Act are to 'be construed and have effect' subject to such EC law as is directly enforceable in national proceedings, including rulings of the European Court. The practical consequence is that where national law and EC law are in conflict, the latter will prevail, in all cases save those where Parliament clearly evinces the intention to override Community law. In such cases as these – an instance of which has not yet arisen – the courts would surely be obliged to give effect to the later Act, as representing the will of Parliament. The United Kingdom would almost certainly be brought before the European Court by the Commission and would have to decide whether to introduce legislation to bring our law into conformity with the Court's ruling. The final decision would thus be Parliament's, and constitutional orthodoxy would have been observed. Nevertheless, this interpretation is open to question following a ruling of the European Court in 1978 (thus after the United Kingdom's accession) that Community law takes precedence even over national law passed subsequently.[9] The Court held that:

> . . . a national court which is called upon, within the limits of its jurisdiction, to apply provisions of Community law is under a duty to give full effect to those provisions, if necessary refusing of its own motion to apply any conflicting provision of national legislation, even if adopted subsequently, and it is not necessary for the court to request or await a prior setting aside of such provisions by legislative or other constitutional means.

If the British courts applied this ruling literally, should an appropriate case arise, it is hard to see how the will of Parliament could prevail. Since, however, as explained above, our courts can only give effect to EC law though the medium of the 1972 Act and that Act has no special status, the later Act of Parliament would take precedence.

What is clear, though, is that the European Court regards Community law as having a status superior even to the constitutional law of the member states.

It is also doubtful whether Parliament could have imagined, when it passed the 1972 Act, that the Court of Justice would deliver a ruling enabling the House of Lords (acting in its judicial capacity) to suspend the operation of certain sections of an Act of Parliament, while awaiting a decision from the Court on their compatibility with Community law. Yet this occurred last year, in relation to the Merchant Shipping Act 1988.[10]

The combination of direct effect and the supremacy of Community law is already a powerful instrument of European integration. They are, moreover, essential prerequisites for the fully federal system of law that many wish to see established. Indeed, the achievements of the European Court in this regard have been described by one European judge as 'fashioning a constitutional framework for a federal type structure in Europe'.[11] According to this member of the Court, the Court has endeavoured to remove or reduce the features of the Treaty that differentiate it from a constitution.

It is perhaps political sovereignty – the ability of the electorate to influence decisions that affect it – that has been most impaired by our membership of the Community. An unelected European Commission has the exclusive right of proposing legislation. It decides whether and if so whom to consult before drawing up its proposals. It decides – subject only to scrutiny by the European Court – what legal base is appropriate to the proposal, that is whether it should be passed by majority or qualified majority vote. It has a disproportionate influence over the course of legislation, owing to its right to withdraw the proposal at any time and to incorporate amendments made by the European Parliament into its revised proposals.

The accountability of the Council of Ministers to their national Parliaments, save in the most theoretical sense, has been rendered nugatory by the practice of majority voting.

The European Court of Justice is at liberty to interpret the Treaty as it sees fit, and its rulings have particular force as a result of the direct effect and supremacy of Community law.

The European Parliament is at present only a consultative body, as far as its role within the legislative process is concerned. Any increase in its powers, however, would inevitably reduce still further the accountability of Ministers and present an unacceptable threat to the sovereignty of Parliament. The consequence has been that electors are increasingly removed from Community decision-making.

A solution surely lies in the model offered by other treaty organisations. The United Kingdom belongs to a whole host of international bodies, dealing with matters ranging from defence to human rights, from space research to economic cooperation. Indeed it probably plays as active a role in these organisations as any other nation state. Our membership of these bodies perceptibly enhances our influence in the world and enables us to learn from the experience of other countries. But – and this is crucial – it does not compromise our sovereignty. This is for three reasons: first, the purposes and powers of these bodies are strictly delimited. Second, decision-making is invariably by unanimity. Third, their institutions do not create law which must be directly applicable in and which purports to take precedence over the laws of their member states.

NATO and the Council of Europe are two examples of international organisations that achieve the purpose for which they were established – international cooperation in their respective fields – efficiently and without encroaching on national sovereignty. Certainly, this cooperation can entail member states entering into binding obligations. But such international obligations are an expression, not a restriction, of sovereignty.

It is still not too late for the European Community to abandon its pretensions to be anything other than the classic treaty organisation it was always intended to be. The true cause of Europe and of democratic government can only be advanced by its doing so.

NOTES

1. 'Sovereignty and interdependence: Britain's place in the world', *International Affairs*, vol. 66, 1990, no. 4, p. 675.
2. 27th Report, 1988–1990 Session, Volume I, para. 12.
3. 'Sovereignty and interdependence: Britain's place in the world', *International Affairs*, 1990, p. 675.
4. M. Akehurst, *A Modern Introduction to International Law*, 6th edn (London: Allen & Unwin, 1987) p. 53.
5. SS *Wimbledon* case PCIJ 1923, Series A, no. 1, p. 25.
6. *Commission* v. *Council* (Case 22/70) [1971] ECR 263.
7. *Costa* v. *ENEL* (Case 6/64) [1964] ECR 585.
8. *Van Gend en Loos* v. *Nederlandse Administratie Belastingen* (Case 26/62) [1963] ECR 1.
9. *Simmenthal* (Case 106/77 [sic]) [1978] ECR 629.
10. *Factortame* (Case 213/89) [1990] 3 CMLR 1.
11. G. Mancini, 'The Making of a Constitution for Europe', *CMLR*, Vol. 26, p. 596.

5 Conservatism and the Paradox of Europe

Conrad Black

One of human nature's most popular impulses is to eat your cake and still have it in front of you. This is especially true in politics, where persuading everybody that you are keeping them happy can mean the difference between office and obscurity. In Britain we are seeing the crucial debate over the future of the European Community and our participation in it develop in these terms.

I had better explain at the start what I mean by 'the paradox of Europe' as it affects Conservatism. On the one hand we, as Conservatives, want to be in the European Community because we believe in Free Trade and cooperation with our geographical neighbours. We want to be in a large manufacturing and commercial area without political restraints that can pursue to the zenith the Cobdenite ideal of the most efficient division of labour. We want a large trading bloc in which market forces encourage the competition that allows the growth of participating nations to be maximised. Whatever the wider concerns about defence and other foreign policy cooperation, or the more personalised desire to move about Europe on business or pleasure with a minimum of inconvenience, that was the economic impulse that attracted so many Conservatives to the idea of a European Economic Community.

However, the philosophy of Europe has moved on since then. What began as the European Economic Community is now just the European Community; centralisation of policy affects far more than just trade. It has become a vehicle for removing much of our ability to govern ourselves as an independent sovereign nation. And, at the moment, the next stage of that debate is about whether we should make the most important sacrifice yet: whether we should give centralised, unaccountable institutions in Brussels the power to run our economic policy.

Most Conservatives, myself included, were happy to join the Exchange Rate Mechanism, once most of the conditions enunciated by the Prime Minister at Madrid last year had been met, especially the abandonment of exchange controls by France and Italy. We all seem to seek to arm ourselves with Germany's legendary resistance to inflation, but many of us have serious reservations about definitions of European integration that take us much beyond the point Britain has already reached.

Here the paradox presents itself. Conservatives have been basically free traders ever since the arcane debate about Imperial Preference went to the grave with Joseph Chamberlain and my rather dreary countryman, Andrew Bonar Law. Many of our efforts as Conservatives over the past seventy years have been to secure free trade as a way of achieving the economic aims I have just outlined. Yet the majority of our European partners now tell us that if we wish to participate fully in this attractive free-trading enterprise we must be prepared to make further and much greater sacrifices of sovereignty. Although the Conservative party has always, first and foremost, upheld and defended the British constitution, many Conservatives see the surrender of our sovereign powers as acceptable in the name of the emotive and nebulous concept of 'European Unity'.

Europe has been the site of three of recent history's most important and welcome developments: the *rapprochement* of ancient foes – especially France and Germany – the implosion of Communism, and the reunification of the Germans. Even before the last two events, the concept of Europe had become contemporary history's greatest fad, the wave of the future, the future that we saw and that worked, to borrow some platitudes from our friends on the Left. To the tepid and the unconvinced, Europe was a phenomenon which, since it was an incumbent fashion, Britain should be a part of. It is a powerful, though usually an implicit orthodoxy in Europe, that the World Wars and the barbarities of the Third Reich require nothing less from us than the complete submergence of European nationalism.

The facts that I am a Canadian who was raised in the august imperial twilight of the late Churchillian era and am today a part-time resident of both Canada and the United States perhaps strengthen my conviction that the continental Europeans, whether they realise it or not, are also partly motivated in their effort to dragoon Britain into an exclusive Europe by a desire to sever Britain's connection with the Commonwealth and the United States. Often in its history Britain has had to choose between Europe and the world and no one should minimise the difficulty of reconciling these alternative orientations now. Many Europeans are inexpressibly resentful that Western Europe has not been, these past fifty years, the political centre of the world, and Britain is being asked, in effect, to prove its loyalty to Europe by renouncing its long, profound and benign association with the rest of the English-speaking world.

Europeans purport to hold Britain responsible for strengthening democracy by throwing its lot in with an assimilationist European community and undergirding Euro-democracy from within. Who among us does not admire the success of most Western European political institutions, especially as the four principal western continental countries, Germany, France, Italy and Spain, have all been fascist dictatorships within living memory (albeit very involuntarily in the case of France)? Of course we respect and admire these great and allied nations, but not, I suspect, to the point of betting centuries of our political maturity on the efficient and democratic constitutional aptitudes developed since 1949 by the Germans, since 1958 by the French, since 1975 by the Spanish, even more recently at the European Commission, and whose effective emergence in Italy we are still awaiting.

If I seek to achieve anything this evening, it will be to remind those Conservatives who support European integration of their inherently Tory responsibility to safeguard the constitution of this sovereign nation. To affect a Churchillian resonance, this Conservative government has not been elected to preside over the dissolution of British sovereign power. I hope to show that Britain is not only not ready for such a sacrifice, it is not suited for it; and, indeed, in order to maintain and improve the free-trading union of which we are all in favour, such a sacrifice is not desirable and probably not necessary.

Moreover, those Conservatives who would make this sacrifice should recall not just what the Prime Minister said at Bruges two years ago, but what she said at Aspen last August. Europe does not involve just the twelve nations of the EC, and maximising our economic growth and trading performance does not involve just Europe. We must consider ways of moving closer to

America in trading terms, and we must consider, with even greater urgency, ways of bringing the newly-liberated countries of Eastern Europe into our trading system as the Prime Minister recently said in Hungary and Czechoslovakia, and of helping the Soviet Union to embrace the market economy and become a more active trading partner.

These are the issues that should now engage the attention of the Western European nations. Bureaucratic obsessions with common currencies, economic, monetary and political unions and – dare I say it – with the creation of a European superstate are not strictly relevant to what the world's leading nations should be seeking to do now. Moreover, if I may be provocative, I should remind those Conservatives who still feel this fervour for union that the blueprint they are being offered is essentially one of 'market socialism', embodying all the evils of intervention, centralisation and unaccountability that have no place in our Conservative philosophy. It is not necessary to be a little England humbug to have serious misgivings about both the jurisdictional appetite and ideological tenor of the European Commission.

ANCIENT HISTORY

A short diversion into the past would perhaps be germane. Charles II, William III and George I, on arrival here from different parts of Europe to assume the throne of this country, all objected to British Tory insularity. George I complained of the fallacious 'old Tory notion that England can subsist by itself whatever becomes of the rest of Europe'. I do not recommend or feel myself any respect, or even nostalgia, for that parochial and rather xenophobic view of the world.

When the future of Europe was considered at the Congress of Vienna in 1814 and 1815, Britain eschewed the sort of meddling, centralising role that, then as now, our European neighbours found so attractive. Our only concerns, rightly, were freeing up trade, and maintaining a balance between the great powers and between the conservative and liberal forces of Europe. The Quadruple Alliance of 1815 that formed the Concert of Europe was as far as we would go. Castlereagh was happy to enter into an accord that policed the settlement of frontiers, and which pledged to keep a Bonaparte off the French throne. He would not, though, back intervention in the internal affairs of any other state. Without revolution, though not without difficulty, Britain abolished slavery, emancipated Catholics, repealed the Corn Laws, and reformed elections, while Metternich and the restored French Bourbons and their cousins ignored or misjudged democratic forces until they were swept away by them. In his public career of over half a century, Palmerston was alternately the delight and terror of the radicals.

Britain recognised that the economic advantages conferred on it by its Empire made trade with Europe less imperative than it might otherwise have been. Britain is a maritime nation conditioned through the centuries to have a vastly different outlook on the world, and on our role in it, than some of our neighbours. Though there is no longer a British Empire, this strategy of market diversification still makes sense, provided the whole world is not segregated into exclusive trading blocs, in a scramble for markets slightly reminiscent of the nineteenth century's pursuit of colonies.

More to the point, Britain refused to join the 'Holy Alliance' of Russia, Prussia and Austria, being rightly sceptical about this invention of a Christian union of love, peace and charity – not unlike the blessed Social Charter. Metternich called the Holy Alliance 'a high sounding nothing', Talleyrand 'a ludicrous contract' and Castlereagh, unduly charitably, 'a piece of sublime mysticism and nonsense'. It is an example of cooperation overreaching itself.

In effect, the Alliance was a Trojan horse that allowed unbridled interference by the great powers in the affairs of the Christian European countries that were duped into signing up to its aims. That, too, could be a lesson for today.

Britain has been notably resistant to pan-European institutions, especially those identified with the hegemony of foreign culture or arms. Even those European countries that have shared or succumbed to some of these forces have distinct characteristics borne of being in a Europe of nations. All this background may make integration harder than the Community's idealists imagine and it is this Europe of nations, with all the cultural and philosophical advances made by the interaction of so many different traditions, that is the true Europe. Nor would it be right to pretend that Britain is the only country to be worried about protecting sovereignty. For this reason, federation on an American basis is a fantasy. There are not, and never have been in civilised times, the conditions in Europe that there were in America in the era of Washington, Jefferson, Hamilton and Franklin. Nor, despite the merits of some of the advocates of European unity, is a cast of such arresting personalities in evidence.

THE TORY IMPULSE

Conservatism – or, in this case, its Tory progenitor – has always been concerned with protecting our nationhood. What made us shrink from the Holy Alliance was our difference of outlook, embodied by the Tory Castlereagh, but upheld by the more liberal Canningites and Whigs as well, between constitutional and autocratic states. The autocracy with which we are now faced in Europe is that of socialist centralism, the political force that has (in one form or another) dominated Europe since 1919, but which we in Britain cast off in 1979. Castlereagh complained that the Holy Alliance cared much about the divine right of monarchs and little about the rights of subjects. That, too, is true of the unaccountable and insufficiently democratic race towards European federation. At least Castlereagh could move Britain away from the Quadruple Alliance when its absurdist tendencies became too pronounced. There is no sign that any such escape route would be available from European federation.

In modern times Conservatives have wavered back and forth about the EEC. Indeed, since the European Coal and Steel Community was initiated in 1950 there have been few who could match the consistent, blinkered, febrile passion for the Community of, let us say, Edward Heath. Many have been down that road, seen what lay at its end, and decided that their Tory impulses compelled them to turn back. The most famous is Enoch Powell, who is still the Tory High Priest of the Anti-EC movement. It is not necessary to subscribe to Mr Powell's misguided anti-Americanism and assorted other quixotries, to judge his views of the European Community worthy of consideration. He wrote in 1971:

I was not an opponent of British membership of the EEC in 1961–62. I was prepared to accept it, on the grounds of trade, as the lesser evil, compared with being excluded. But we were excluded; and the events of the years which followed convinced me that this judgment had been mistaken. Meanwhile it became clear that the community, if indeed it survived at all, would be something quite different from a free-trade area, and something to which Britain could not belong. It also became clear that the sense of forlornness produced by realisation that the Empire and Commonwealth no longer, for practical purposes, existed, was the real cause which underlay the rationalised case for British entry. Hence the anxious doubt, so misleadingly expressed: 'surely we cannot go it alone?'

WHAT SOVEREIGNTY MEANS

We should be in no doubt that the Eurosocialist-led direction of Europe is aimed squarely at federation, at the submergence of our distinctiveness and the marginalisation of our institutions. And we should, equally, be in no doubt that federation is viscerally unacceptable to the British. But what loss of sovereignty are we talking about? Does not Sir Leon Brittan base his true case for union on the fact that our sovereignty consists of the 20 minutes of power we enjoy between the Germans putting up their interest rates and our following?

Sir Leon exaggerates, but like a good lawyer he does so from a scintilla of truth that makes his contention harder to repudiate. What economic and monetary union would mean, as we all know, is a common currency; and a common currency means a common economic policy. We would have almost no control over that policy. To paraphrase Mr Nicholas Ridley, those British electors aggrieved by the effects of that policy – which could well mean spiralling unemployment – would be told to take their complaints to the unelected (and, by this stage, almost certainly unelectable) Chairman of the European Central Bank. The British government would have lost all power over the currency, and all the ramifications of that power. Moreover, the British people would not be able to call to account those who wield that power. We must dispel any fog of illusion – or delu-

VIRGIN MEGASTORE   VAT NO. 278 5548 76

46 :T/0 ID   0810 0409 102

MAN DONT GIVE A F% QTY 1   .99
                  TOTAL   .99

CASH   5.00
        CHANGE   4.01
    WE ARE OPEN 7 DAYS

4/12/96 15:05

sion – that has come to surround the forthcoming Intergovernmental Conferences. So far their import is not being spoken of
in polite company. What Britain will ultimately be asked to do
at those Conferences – let us not deceive ourselves – is to send
such a plan to Parliament for ratification. That ratification
would be the last properly sovereign act of our Parliament: it
would find itself called upon to approve its own forthcoming
impotence. Is Westminster really prepared to meet, like the last
parliament of the French Third Republic at the Vichy Casino,
albeit in more majestic surroundings and infinitely kinder circumstances, to declare itself effectively superfluous?

I contend that the only serious arguments in favour of European Monetary Union are transactional cost savings which would
be largely offset by implementation problems and price
stability which monetary union would not, in fact, guarantee.
For much of the 1980s Britain and Switzerland had lower levels
of inflation than the EMS average. Our mistake was not
standoffishness about monetary union; it was taking our eye off
monetary targets and placing unjustified hopes in shadowing
the deutschmark. We should look much more carefully than
many seem disposed to do before taking the leap from the
voluntary EMS to the inflexible EMU with its attendant and
irretrievable surrender of sovereignty.

This government has, of course, brought this state of affairs
largely on itself. The Single European Act, which it somewhat
recklessly ratified five years ago, commits us to eventual union.
It commits us to surrendering to other nations effectively to
decide how we are to be governed, and to removing from the
British people the right to elect those who will govern them.
Even a beefed-up European parliament, to which the economic
institutions might be made more accountable, would be no
proper substitute for what we would have lost. I see no evidence
that Britain is really ready, much less eager, for this.

I doubt that the Conservatives, at least, knew what they were
getting into with the Single European Act, or even with the
1972 European Communities Act. We as Conservatives must
not be careless of our constitutional system. We must recognise
the starkness of the choice facing us on economic and monetary
union and its political sequels, and we cannot pretend that
some miraculous diplomatic finesse is going to make that choice
any less stark. The issue should not be the pace at which we

proceed inexorably toward ceasing to be a sovereign nation. The issue should be the point at which we end our descent toward loss of sovereignty without, for that, ceasing to be conscientious participating Europeans by all but the most assimilationist standards.

ENDING CONSERVATIVE DELUSION

Enoch Powell put the question to his party twenty years ago: 'Will you, or will you not, continue to be governed by the Queen in Parliament?' Mr Heath knew the importance of this choice to the British people. He told them in 1970 that Britain's entry to the EEC would proceed only 'with the full hearted consent of Parliament and people'. After its initial stages, consent has been rather more half-hearted than full-hearted, with the result that dissension has not died down in the intervening two decades. We are not whole-hearted for absorption into a common European political system, and only a fantasist would pretend that we ever will be.

Why, though, should Conservatives fight to preserve what we have as a constitutional heritage, rather than commit themselves to a fresh, pan-European start as part of a federation? Well, it all depends on what one understands to be the guiding principles of British Conservatism. I apologise for quoting Enoch Powell one last time. However aberrant or even bizarre some of his views, he remains an authentic, as well as a fearless, Conservative:

> I was born a Tory, am a Tory, and shall die a Tory. It is part of me, an inborn way of apprehending human life and society and the history and character of my own country. It is something I cannot alter . . . I never yet heard that it was any part of the faith of a Tory to take the institutions and liberties, the laws and customs, which his country has evolved over centuries, and merge them with those of . . . other nations into a new-made artificial state and, what is more, to do so without the willing approbation and consent of the nation.

If he were not burdened with a demonological misconception of the United States, Mr Powell would be equally righteous

about the Tory duty to preserve the overseas option and aptitude which this country uniquely possesses.

What he does say is rather mystical stuff, but then however
physical it seems, our nation and all nations are essentially at
heart a metaphysical concept; part of the 'faith' Mr Powell talks
of. Was not, though, this the sentiment that underpinned, in
less emotional but no less direct terms, Mrs Thatcher's speech
at Bruges two years ago? And, indeed, at Aspen two months ago
when she advocated 'a Europe based on willing cooperation
between independent sovereign states; a Europe which is an
expression of economic freedom . . . which rejects central control and its associated bureaucracy . . . which does not resort to
protectionism . . . and of supreme importance for Britain, a
Europe which always seeks the closest possible partnership with
the United States?'

MRS THATCHER'S CHALLENGE

It should be clear to all but the most ostrich-like idealist that the
institutions the interventionist bureaucrats at Brussels are
planning for Europe's future are likely to be largely useless to
that future. Mrs Thatcher has issued them the challenge to stop
their introspection and to take practical steps to bring the
newly capitalist countries of Eastern Europe into the Community. These countries will not want their new independence
compromised by the European superstate. Mrs Thatcher has
made it clear that to involve these countries, to build links with
the reforming Soviet Union and to develop crucial trading
arrangements with North America, the centralising institutions
as presently envisaged are no use, and should not be persisted
with. As she said at Aspen, freedom should be redefined in
Europe not only to include the elements generally defined by
Mr Churchill and Mr Roosevelt in the Atlantic Charter of 1941,
but also 'freedom of the market-place, freedom . . . to own
property, freedom to maintain nationhood, and freedom from
fear of an over-mighty state'.

To try to suppress nationhood and concentrate power at the
centre of a European conglomerate would be highly damaging
and would jeopardise the objectives we seek to achieve. Like
the economies of the respective European states, their respec-

tive objectives do not, of course, converge. Ours, as I have stated, are of unbridled free trade, deregulation and fair competition; those of Brussels, and the socialist governments (of whatever colour) in most of Europe's capitals are of unbridled centralised interventionism. This brings us back to the most shining beacon in the Bruges speech, the clearest expression of our brand of Conservatism: 'We have not successfully rolled back the frontiers of the State in Britain, only to see them reimposed at a European level, with a European superstate exercising a new dominance from Brussels.' It is not reassuring to hear M. Delors describe himself as 'Le Président de l'Europe' or to say, as he did to the Trilateral Commission in Washington in April, 'I can manage 12 countries, but not 16 or 24.' Does anyone who heard his address to the TUC conference two years ago with his promise to give back to the unionised British worker from Brussels what he implied Mrs Thatcher had taken away, or who remembers his performance as M. Mitterrand's finance minister, want him to manage anything to which Britain adheres?

THE DELORS REPORT

Mrs Thatcher spoke at Bruges before the Delors report on economic and monetary union was published. She spoke, though, after the European Council meeting in Hanover in June 1988 had noted that 'in adopting the Single European Act, the Member States of the Community confirmed the objective of progressive realisation of economic and monetary union.' She will have remembered that the final stage of this union does, in the words of the Report, mean 'irrevocably fixed exchange rates between national currencies and, finally, a single currency'. And that, as the report goes on, 'This, in turn, requires a high degree of compatibility of economic policies and consistency in a number of other policy areas, particularly in the fiscal field.'

One of the principal purposes of our sovereign Parliament has been to raise and disburse revenues. Fiscal compatibility will mean that our taxation policy will be regulated. A key part of sovereignty – one of the policies that wins or loses elections, and which influences the way people vote – would, therefore, be sacrificed to Brussels. Delors talks of 'a transfer of decision-making power' to the centre from individual governments. The confidence-trick of 'subsidiarity' – the principle by which nothing is carried out centrally that can just as easily be discharged by national governments – counts for little here. The transfer of decision-making is, as Delors says, necessary 'to avoid unsustainable differences between individual member countries in Public Sector Borrowing Requirements, and place binding constraints on the size and the financing of budget deficits'. The annual ritual of the Budget, one of the most profound exercises of power of our national government, would be emasculated. Our Chancellor of the Exchequer and our First Lord of the Treasury would lose control of the fundamentals of economic policy.

SOCIALIST EVILS

The cold language of Delors, however logical it might or might not be in economic terms, pays no regard to the human nature of the citizens of democratic countries in Europe jealous of their constitutional rights and privileges, indeed of their independence. Delors' view is, in the most literal sense, politically ignorant, yet is argued by apolitical economists and socialists with an astonishing flippancy and even negligence. Britain, now a nation, would be relegated to the status of a region, governed by people whose ideological acceptability, cultural amenability and competence, if not goodwill, would require, but might not successfully withstand, serious scrutiny.

What is more, our economic efficiency could be penalised by subsidising the inefficiencies of others. We have seen this all too clearly in the iniquity of the Common Agricultural Policy, whereby our efficiency raises resources that buy for other governments the votes of peasant farmers on smallholdings all over Europe – notably in France and Germany. How long will it be before Europe takes the advice and follows the example of President Bush, and helps create a proper non-interventionist market in agricultural produce?

Delors presents further evidence of the move to interventionism that we, as Conservatives, should reject out of hand. He says that 'wage flexibility and labour mobility are necessary to eliminate differences in competition in different regions and

countries of the Community. Otherwise there could be relatively large declines in output and employment in areas with
lower productivity. It might be necessary in certain circumstances
to provide financing flows through official channels.' That is
what you and I know, without the benefit of euphemism, as
subsidy.

Delors, as he said in his egregious speech to the TUC in 1988
and on many other occasions, seeks to undermine the basic
ideology of the Right. Elsewhere, he says that 'the constraints
imposed by market forces might either be too slow and weak or
too sudden and disruptive. Hence countries would have to
accept that sharing a common market and a single currency
area imposed policy constraints.' Thus we, as Conservatives, are
being asked not just to countenance centralised interference,
but to do so in the unashamed desire to subvert the basis of the
new Conservative creed of the predominance of market forces.
Remember, too, that we do not believe in market forces for
their own sake, but because they maximise economic efficiency
and pay the most regard to the freely determined wishes of the
individual consumer. Such philosophy is anathema to Jacques
Delors.

As my fellow *Daily Telegraph* director, Sir James Goldsmith,
remarked in the address last June in which he proclaimed the
'unbundling' of the Soviet Union 'as the European self-adjusting
mechanisms, among them devaluation, are blocked, a further
system of bureaucratically controlled regional transfers would
develop so as to attempt to equalise the standards of living of
those who run their economies well and those who do not.' He
added that the 'two apparently harmless words, 'tax harmonisation', signify the desire of certain governments not to have to
compete.'

It is our duty here to call things by their rightful names, and,
where necessary, to affront Euro-complacency. Europe itself,
for all its greatness and current virtue, requires demystification.
Except for Thatcherite Britain, almost every European country
has too great a public sector share of GNP, an unbearable over-
commitment to social spending, and an unsustainably high
level of unemployment. The European fear that absence of a
generous social safety net leads to mob rule and political ex-
tremism is comprehensible, but it contrasts with the American
view, enunciated by former president Reagan, that 'the only

welfare system we ever had that worked is a job'. In the eight Reagan years, the United States created 19 million net new jobs, or eighteen million more than the entire EC. The United States has re-emerged as the world's largest exporter and has a growing trade surplus with the EC. Even the Federal Republic of Germany, Europe's undoubted powerhouse, has a larger public sector debt as a percentage of GNP than the USA even before paying the reunification bills, and, without America's racial problems or defence commitments, has less than three-quarters of the American standard of living and barely a sixth of the US GNP. Despite the almost universally cherished Euro-mythology and the tremendous success of German engineered products, there is very little evidence that Europe as a whole can compete externally with the Japanese or the Americans. Narcissism is no substitute for competitiveness.

FEDERATION BY STEALTH

What Jacques Delors seeks is federation by stealth. All the policies of economic union add up to political union: indeed, they are unworkable without it. Nor, of course, will political union confine itself to controlling political economy: it will seek to formulate a common foreign policy too. Where would that have left Britain, for example, at the time of the Falklands War? The ludicrous, if sometimes hilarious, fiasco of our EC partners' military response to the Gulf Crisis can hardly be reassuring on this point. While Germany brandished its foreign non-intervention constitution and Italy and Spain sent token forces while renouncing any military initiative, France went from an 'embargo civilisé' to an 'embargo fort', to the despatch of an aircraft carrier with no airplanes on it. Canada, and even Argentina, seemed more purposeful than most of our brothers in the Community. In broader terms, what role would be left for the British government? What would be the significance of the British monarchy? These are all constitutional issues of which the bureaucratic planners in Brussels take no account, but which we, as Conservatives, should care passionately about, for we are their political guardians. At the moment, though, we are being drawn into federation mainly because the French fear the power of a resurgent united Germany and wish to

dilute it, the Germans have yet to overcome their embarrassment at their resurgence and understandably wish to reassure
their neighbours, and the Italians have made such a shambles
of government, despite great success in other fields, they are
ready to embrace any plausible alternative to the status quo.
Many others, including many in this country who should know
better, are mere political surfers riding a wave.

THE INTERGOVERNMENTAL CONFERENCES

All this drama will be played out at the Intergovernmental
Conferences, starting in December. Just as I have argued that
we should be under no illusions about the starkness of the
choice that will face us there, so too should we be under no
illusions about the strength of our bargaining position. Our
friends are just starting to emerge from the woodwork.

Ever since Cardinal Wolsey's time, Britain has cultivated and
been popular with the secondary states of continental Europe.
She remains so today. We have a vital European role that
consists first of all in championing the maximum convenient
level of national distinctiveness.

Mrs Thatcher is often spoken of as isolated in the Cabinet.
This is not true. Many ministers share her concerns about
European centralisation. In a speech in July the Chancellor of
the Exchequer said: 'The more I examine the present proposals,
the more I feel that they would lead us away from common
objectives, rather than towards them.' He admitted to the
prospect of 'severe effects on jobs and output in some regions'
if economic and monetary union were proceeded with on the
Delors model. But that is what our partners seem to want. In
Brussels, too, there is a mixed reception for the Chancellor's
idea of the Hard ECU. On the one hand they congratulate us
for making a constructive suggestion; on the other, they say it is
too late. In fact, with our eyes on the newly liberated countries
to the east and America to the west, it is their idea that is 'too
late'. Everyone in Europe, including the Germans and the
Russians, acknowledges the desirability of a continued alliance
with the United States. What could be more implausible than to
exclude the North Americans from commercial Europe while
urging the retention in Europe of American and Canadian

expeditionary forces. What could be less appropriate to the vitality of Western Europe and the power of its message than to slam the door on our Canadian and American allies, kindred nations and tested friends, while refusing to offer all the encouragement we can to the Eastern Europeans who yearn to join us? Mrs Thatcher is not a little Englander. M. Delors is a little European.

NOT JUST A CONSERVATIVE PROBLEM

It will take immense courage, and immense resolve, for the British government to defend the constitutional rights of the British people against this benign onslaught from Europe. But defend them it must, in the interests of our national autonomy. It must convince our partners that, with the introduction of much more fresh blood into the Community, this huge free-trading system can flourish and maximise its potential far more efficiently without centralisation than with it, far more efficiently while retaining the nationhood of at least some of the individual states than by homogenising them all. This is the duty of the Conservative party if it wishes to preserve not just its ideology, but also to preserve the rights of the British people to choose the government and the policies that they wish to see implemented in Britain. It is also, as growing numbers of Europeans are coming to realise, the best course for continental Europe as well.

In defending these rights, and standing out against airtight economic and monetary – and therefore political – union, the Prime Minister should know that she has the backing of more than her own party. Parliament, when given the chance to vote on the principle of union, has never supported it. The Labour party, which longs to use economic policy for the purposes of social engineering, is now realising the danger of the ideal of European Unity. While in many of its aspects it may be too socialist for the Conservative party, in many others it is not socialist enough for Labour. As Peter Shore said in July: 'If the Delors version of economic and monetary union comes into effect, we shall say goodbye to democratic self-government, for we shall no longer be able to make the key economic decisions that affect our life.'

No Conservative could have put it more succinctly. We need all the allies we can get in the battle to retain the right of the British people to elect the government it wants for Britain, and the right of Europe to flourish in cooperation and not stifle itself in oppressive homogeneity. The Euro-masquerade of the Labour party's image-managers has not convinced the Shadow Cabinet or the party executive. It is unlikely to impress the voters.

Before I finally subside, I must ensure that I have not short-changed the Europeans. The achievements of the European unifiers, including Jacques Delors, are great and admirable. Germany's reconciliation with France and peaceful reunification, in particular, are among the great political triumphs of human intelligence of this century. They were achieved by outstanding statesmen acting on behalf of great nations. The desire of many Europeans to regain political influence in unity is compre-hensible and perhaps not altogether unrealistic. Britain can provide a stabilising influence and a powerful commercial participation in Europe, but if present trends continue we will be asked to choose between assimilation in Europe and virtual abstention from it.

It is not too late to press for more flexibility. Partisans of European political integration should not be denied it because of us. We and other less perfervid joiners should not be made the villains of a Manichean drama. An inner Europe of full political adherents probably based on the original six should be formed in close association with an outer Europe of common marketeers practising a more restrained political participation. The emerging democracies of Eastern Europe could join this group relatively soon, a group which M. Delors could be assured that he would not be called upon to 'manage'. Dr Karl Otto Pohl has already envisioned such an arrangement. Britain could lead both echelons of Europe in ensuring an uninterrupted and amplified economic and strategic alliance with the useful elements of the Commonwealth and more importantly the United States. This would doubtless cause Enoch Powell's Philippics about Europe to be succeeded by Jeremiads and glottal stops over America. In furtherance of so desirable and urgent a cause, I even promise the personal sacrifice of enduring Enoch Powell's easily foretold reflections in quiet, if not in silence.

The great achievement of Europe must not be doubted or jeopardised, neither by scepticism nor an excess of misguided zeal. Like other great prime ministers, including Palmerston, Disraeli, Salisbury, Churchill, and even Lloyd George, Mrs Thatcher too will be able to strike an appropriate balance between Europe and the world. All Conservatives should play their part in resolving this historic, perennial paradox.

The British people have the right, if they are so myopic, to choose a government (such as a Labour government) that is allowed to implement policies that we here would regard as wrong and harmful. Shortly after the 1945 election, Mr Churchill exclaimed, from his bathtub, 'If the people want Attlee, they can have him. That's why we fought the War.' Mr Churchill referred to the privilege of democracy. It is a privilege that we as Conservatives must do everything to ensure remains with the British people.

Part Two
Money, Competition and Price Stability

6 An Introduction to European Monetary Union

Geoffrey E. Wood

The EC has since its inception been committed to achieving 'economic and monetary union'. All the papers in this section of the volume are prompted by that latter objective. In this brief introductory essay, the background to the current discussion of monetary union is set out; this will provide the context for the debate to which the following papers contribute. This is followed by a short guide to the main points of the papers.

THE HISTORY

The current European Monetary System is the latest of several efforts to peg exchange rates within Europe. In contrast the scepticism with which it was generally viewed at its inception, it now seems popular. Why the change?

The early scepticism is certainly easy to understand. For interest in pegging exchange rates within Europe dates back certainly to the 1950s, when six countries signed the Treaty of Rome. Although the immediate objective of the Treaty was to establish a customs union and a common market for cereals (which latter turned eventually into the CAP) the longer term objectives were much more extensive. In particular, the signatories agreed to 'regard exchange rate policy as a matter of common interest'. The Monetary Committee of the EC dates from 1958.

Why this concern? Several factors lie behind the particular continental European aversion to floating exchange rates. The first is recent European history. In the 1920s, competitive devaluations – beggar thy neighbour policies, in Joan Robinson's vivid term – were extensively used in Europe as a defence against external shocks. These policies are by many European policy-makers believed to have been responsible first for the disruption of international trade and economic activity of these years, and then for the subsequent collapse of European democracies. (See Nurske (1944) for an account which sets out this view in detail.) This view of the experience of the 1920s and 1930s has been one motivation for the search for a pegged exchange rate system in Europe.

Secondly, the countries of Europe are very open with regard to each other – more so than they are with the rest of the world. Even before the EEC was formed, imports formed 30 per cent of GDP in Belgium and the Netherlands, and 16 per cent in Germany. These ratios have risen to around 60 per cent and 25 per cent respectively in the years since the EEC was formed. (Of course openness is not the only relevant factor. Canada is even more open with regard to the US but, perhaps because of the historical volatility of the US economy, has never contemplated monetary union and was, indeed, an early floating currency.)

A third and very important factor was one of the institutions set up by the Treaty of Rome. The survival of the CAP depends on exchange rate stability. Consider French and German corn – a commodity essentially identical and readily transportable, and therefore one which must have the same price in both markets. But the same is not true of the imputs to that corn – of labour in particular. Exchange rate changes can thus produce large shifts in agriculture's profitability across Europe, and thus big shifts in agricultural trade patterns.

To prevent these shifts, countries resorted to tariffs and subsidies for agriculture in the wake of exchange rate changes. This interfered with the basic principles of the EEC, and also contributed to the growth of expenditure on agriculture. It proved easier to remove tariffs by letting prices rise in the devaluing countries than to remove subsidies by cutting prices in the strong currency countries. With every realignment, therefore, expenditure on subsidies rose and so did agricultural production.

There were thus three sources of the pressure to establish pegged exchange rates within Europe; this helps explain the persistence of these efforts, despite the repeated failures before the EMS.

ESTABLISHMENT OF THE EMS

The system was launched on 13 March 1979, following planning and discussion initiated by Roy Jenkins in his 1977 Jean Monnet memorial lecture. The year 1979 was a particularly favourable time for the launch, for the dollar was in a period of turbulence, and there was widespread desire to be insulated from that. Giscard d'Estaing and Helmut Schmidt seized an opportune moment.

Initially the system was in fact not particularly stable, but it has in recent years settled down.[1] Why, in view of this recent stability, has there been the recent urge for change? There are three reasons. Before one of them can be understood, a very brief outline of the existing system is required. There were a set of pegged exchange rates, a system of credit facilities to defend these pegged rates, and a proposed 'European Monetary Fund'. That was of course very much like the Bretton Woods System. And the similarity is further emphasised by the existence of the European Currency Unit – the ECU – which was used as a unit to quote exchange rates, a unit of account for the credit facilities, and it was intended also to be the 'currency' of denomination of deposits at the European monetary cooperation fund. It was, in fact, very much like the SDR in the Bretton Woods System.

The features of that description which produce pressure for moves to monetary union are, first, that just as the SDR was not intended to become a currency in general circulation, and there was no mechanism for it to do so, the same was true of the ECU. It could not evolve to a 'European currency'.

Why the pressure in 1990 in particular? First because there were widespread fears for the continued stability of the system when exchange controls were removed, as they were due to be soon; the Bretton Woods experience of fixed but adjustable parities without exchange controls had not been encouraging in this regard. And second, because German reunification raised the distinct possibility of a DM revaluation – to reduce Germany's capital outflow – this would be both disruptive in itself, and in addition alert markets to the possibility of changes once more, a possibility that had over the preceding two or three years become less and less of a possibility.

In response to this, three proposals were advanced.

PROPOSALS FOR UNION

There has so far been one proposal for monetary union, and two proposals which could, but not necessarily would, lead to union. The Delors Report leads directly to monetary union; the 'hard ECU' plan, itself a development of Nigel Lawson's competing currency proposal,[2] could but would not necessarily do so. These are considered in turn, as they provide the background and stimulus to the papers in the present volume.

The Delors Plan[3] sees Europe moving to a common currency by means of first *fixing irrevocably* (as opposed to pegging with the option to shift) exchange rates. Central banks would coordinate monetary policies to hold these rates, and at some point would 'pool' authority in a European central bank, and convert national currencies to one European currency.

The difficulties with this are as follows. First, it presumes it is appropriate for Europe to have one currency. Second, it presumes the central bank which supplies that currency will make it stable in value. Third, it ignores the transition problems – the new central bank would have neither credibility nor experience. The 'Lawson Plan' dealt with the first of these; the hard ECU with the first and third.

The reason it may not be appropriate for Europe to have one currency is that by ruling out exchange rate changes, it rules out a possible response to disturbances which affect different European countries in different ways – for example a dramatic oil price increase. In the absence of the possibility of exchange rate changes, adjustment would have to take place through wage rate changes, labour mobility, capital mobility, or some combination of all three.

Competing currencies address this difficulty in two ways. First, when currencies have stopped fluctuating, shocks affect all European economies identically (see Vaubel, 1990). Second, if people wish to use a common currency they can. (And it has also been argued it would produce low and stable inflation – see Wood (1989).)

Two difficulties arise from that competing currency proposal. First, there is the possible political one that a national currency become the European one – some could find that unattractive on political grounds. Second, if it is decided on these grounds to create a European currency, its issuers would have neither credibility nor experience.

The hard ECU deals with this by being issued in parallel with national currencies, and its issuing authority gains credibility by keeping it stronger on the foreign exchanges than existing national currencies.

That, then is the background against which the four following papers are written. None of the papers requires elaboration or clarification. What the following remarks do is set out their main features.

THE PAPERS

Tim Congdon's paper is in two parts. The first points out that convergence to monetary union has as a prerequisite convergence of inflation and of inflation expectations. Without such convergence, interest rates would differ at long-term maturities, and union, by suddenly moving Europe to one common set of interest rates, would produce large and arbitrary transfers from creditors to debtors in some countries, and from debtors to creditors in others. This is an important and generally neglected point. The second part of his paper raises the question of legal tender. Will the hard ECU be legal tender? If not, he argues, it will not be accepted. And if it is, if all currencies are legal tender, then there is the possibility that one European national government would gain revenue from all of Europe by inflation.[4]

Professors Martino and Neuman are both concerned to ensure that the European money is stable in value. They do, however, differ in the route they choose to follow. Professor Martino argues that monetary policy be guided by a rule; Professor Neuman argues that it be guided by a central bank independent of political pressure. Both of these routes have appeal. (It is, incidentally, noteworthy that while no independent central bank formally follows a rule, they all generally pursue policies under which the rate of growth of money changes only slowly.) Professor Martino's route would avoid major mistakes in policy; Professor Neuman's attempts to manipulate the economy by politicians to their electoral advantage.

There is not really much conflict between these two apparently divergent proposals. For if a central bank were independent and committed to price stability, then if a rule turned out to be the best way to conduct policy (as many have argued) then it would adopt a rule *voluntarily*.

Finally to Professor Salin. He argues for competition among central banks – in the Hayek and Vaubel tradition. This, he argues, would let us use the market to discover whether Europe was an optimal area for a currency, and would also ensure the kind of low and stable inflation that the consumers of money want. It defers pressing on to a common currency by law on the grounds that, although independent central banks have all delivered better inflation performance than those which are not independent, there may nonetheless be special factors at work in each case. We are, in his view, not yet very experienced in the design of satisfactory monetary institutions.

CONCLUDING OVERVIEW

It will be clear from the above overview of history and proposals that the subject of Monetary Union in Europe is of great and immediate importance. The present European Monetary System can not stay as it is, and 'official' proposals for change are unsatisfactory. The following four papers deal with weaknesses in official proposals, and advance recommendations of their own. They are important contributions to an important debate.

NOTES

1.   For an assessment of the early years, see Wood (1983), and of the recent performance, Giavazzi and Giavannini (1990), pp. 313–22.
2.   The origins of this plan can certainly be traced to Hayek (1976) and are developed further in Vaubel (1979) and Wood (1989).
3.   See Wood (1990) for a detailed discussion; the summary here deals only with what is essential for subsequent discussion.
4.   An interesting brief discussion of the legal tender doctrine can be found in Hayek (1978), pp. 29–30.

REFERENCES

Giavazzi, F. and Giavannini, A., 'Can the European Monetary System Be Copied Outside Europe?' in Bransen, W.H., Frenkel, J.A. and Goldstein, M. (eds), *International Policy Coordination and Exchange Rate Fluctuations* (Chicago: University of Chicago Press for NBER, 1990).

Hayek, F., *Denationalization of Money*, Hobart Special Paper No. 70 (London: IEA, 1976; 2nd edn. 1978; 3rd edn. 1990).

Vaubel, R., *Choice in European Monetary Union*, 9th Wincott Memorial Lecture, Occasional Paper No. 55 (London: IEA, 1979).

Vaubel, R., 'Currency Competition and European Monetary Integration', *Economic Journal*, Vol. 100, No. 402, September 1990, pp. 936–40.

Wood, G.E., 'The European Monetary System', in Jenkins, R. (ed.), *Britain and the EEC* (London: Macmillan, 1983).

Wood, G.E., 'Banking and Monetary Control After 1992: A Central Bank for Europe?' in Veljanovski, C. (ed.), *Whose Europe?* (London: IEA, 1989).

Wood, G.E., 'One Money for Europe? A Review Essay', *Journal for Monetary Economics*, Vol. 25, 1990.

7 European Monetary Union: Is There a Halfway House?

Tim Congdon

INTRODUCTION: THE PARALLEL CURRENCY VS. 'BIG BANG' APPROACHES TO EUROPEAN ECONOMIC AND MONETARY UNION

The pressures on the British government to accept European Economic and Monetary Union (EMU), including an eventual move to a single European currency, are intensifying. Indeed, according to many observers these pressures have built up such a momentum that they are irresistible. Since – in their view – the final destination has already been decided, the only remaining question is to choose the best route to it.

European Commissioners Delors and Christopherson were reported in *The Wall Street Journal* of 23 September 1990 to be urging that EMU be accomplished in a 'short' period. Although the precise meaning of this word was not spelt out, the general intention according to the *Journal* was that there be 'a one-year transition from so-called Stage 2, during which time the EC central bank would be set up, to the final stage 3, when national currencies would be replaced by the ECU'. Moreover, 'Stage 2 would begin in 1993 and Stage 3 in 1994'. This would be a 'Big Bang' or 'Big Leap' approach to EMU, with an abrupt replacement of the existing national monies by a single European money. (The suddenness of the change would be similar to that in London stock exchange practices in the Big Bang of October 1986.) More recently, a meeting of European leaders in Rome found a majority of EC member states in favour of setting a timetable for Stages 2 and 3. Although the timetable was less demanding than that suggested by Delors and Christopherson, with January 1994 set as the start of Stage 2 and 1997 for Stage 3, it was a clear political endorsement for imposing a single currency.

These ideas are flatly opposed to the gradual and evolution-ary approach favoured by the British government, and distilled in the 'hard ECU' proposal. Despite a genuine British attempt to be conciliatory in recent months, a gulf has emerged between the British position and the so-called 'Big Bang' solution sup-ported by other European governments. In essence, Britain favours the idea of a parallel (or common) currency which might become a single currency by an evolutionary and voluntary process possibly lasting many decades. By contrast, the rest of the EC (and, of course, the European Commission) wants a single currency to be imposed on a particular date. (The Delors Report's reference to 'stages' is perhaps rather misleading, in that it does not identify the substance of the changes being contemplated. It makes observers think in terms of the chro-nology of the process rather than the content.)

The purpose of this paper is not to bridge the distance between the two sides. Rather it is to clarify some key points about the nature of 'money' and 'monetary policy' which are essential if those taking part in the debate are to have a meaningful discussion. Too often in recent months meetings on EMU have broken up with participants puzzled about what the other side really meant. The gap in understanding seems to arise because certain fundamental attributes of 'money' have either been forgotten or never elucidated. One outcome of the paper will be to cast doubt on the analytical coherence of the Hard ECU proposal and so on the intellectual integrity of the British government's position. This should certainly not be taken to establish the case for the 'Big Bang'.[1] The aim is rather to tighten the logical and conceptual basis of the debate in order to highlight what is really at stake.

THE IMPORTANCE OF A CURRENCY'S STATUS AS LEGAL TENDER

Our starting point is to note, uncontroversially, that a currency is not a 'money' in the usually understood sense unless it is both a unit of account and a medium of exchange. Many things can serve duty as units of account, including a host of durable commodities and various price indices. Contracts can be ex-pressed in terms of precious metals, a sum of money indexed to retail prices or producer prices, and so on. But such units of account are not money. A money must also be generally acceptable in payments in a particular geographical area; it must be a valid medium of exchange.

If a currency is a valid medium of exchange, people and companies hold some of it in reserve in order to ease the process of buying and selling. In modern circumstances, when virtually all money is paper, two types of monetary asset need to be distinguished. The first are monetary assets which are claims on the private sector, nowadays almost exclusively on the banking system. The face value of such claims may not be repaid in full, if the private sector institution which issued them makes losses and goes bankrupt. Bank deposits are the dominant form of private-sector money. The other type of monetary asset is legal tender, issued almost exclusively by a central bank. The central bank may be 'independent' in a constitutional sense, but it is commonly owned by the state and has invariably been created by legislation. Legal-tender money is accepted in transactions because of its special legal status, not because of its intrinsic worth. People must take it in payment whether they like it or not. Bank notes are the main form of legal tender, although coin also needs to be mentioned for completeness.

This distinction raises a key question. People know that they must accept legal tender in payment. But why do they also accept cheques written against bank deposits? They appreciate – or rather should not have entirely forgotten the possibility – that banks may be unable to meet their obligations in full. So why is the value of transactions completed by cheque a multiple of the value of transactions in legal tender? Why are people so relaxed about writing cheques to each other? What justifies the universal faith in the soundness of the banking system?

The explanation is that everyone believes that their bank deposits can be changed into legal-tender notes and coin at full value. Even when there is a notice period, hardly any doubt arises about the ultimate convertibility of deposits into cash. Because of this convertibility, the value of a sum of money in the bank is (practically) as certain as the value of notes and coin. Decades of safe banking have convinced people that they can treat deposits as equivalent to notes. There is even a tendency to call deposits held by companies and financial institutions their 'cash'.

It cannot be emphasised too strongly that, although almost everyone thinks they are equivalent, deposits and notes are different assets. Notes are legal tender and are always worth their face value; deposits are not legal tender and may not be worth the value stated in bank accounts. Two questions then arise: 'Why are people so confident that deposits will in fact be fully convertible into cash?' and 'Why does no one doubt that legal tender will be worth its face value?'

The answer to the first question is that banks retain a certain amount of cash in their assets and so are able to meet requests for them to convert deposits into cash. In the British context, cash is to be understood as coin, Bank of England notes and bankers' balances at the Bank of England. (A cheque drawn on the Bank of England may not be legal tender, but the point hardly matters because Bank of England balances are obviously convertible on demand into its notes.) Requests for the conversion of deposits into cash take three main forms:

1. *Deposit withdrawals over the counter.* When depositors withdraw cash, they reduce banks' liabilities (deposits) and assets (cash).
2. *Instructions to make payments (e.g. tax payments, payments for government debt issues) to the government.* The reduction in banks' cash due to tax payments is the result of certain institutional arrangements. The government's most important account is the Exchequer account at the Bank of England. When someone writes a cheque to pay taxes, he instructs his bank to make a transfer from his account to the Exchequer account at the Bank. The bank's liabilities fall because its customer's deposit is down and its assets fall because it has a lower balance at the Bank of England. The drop in the balance at the Bank is, of course, a reduction in its cash holdings.
3. *Instructions to make payments to other banks.* When someone writes a cheque to another private-sector agent, he is instructing his bank to make a transfer of cash from his account to the account of the other agent. If one bank receives a great many instructions of this kind, its cash would run out. In practice, banks receive a host of instructions both to debit and credit accounts every day. These largely cancel out for each individual bank and cancel out entirely (apart from timing discrepancies) for all banks taken together. But any shortfall by an individual bank at the clearing of the debits and credits

has to be made good by a drop in that bank's cash. The result is a fall in its Bank of England balances. (The bank with an excess of debits over credits instructs the Bank to pay the deficiency from its balance into other banks' balances.)

The various factors influencing the size of the economy's total cash holdings are listed each day in the money market report in the *Financial Times*. The various operations can seem complicated, but the report merely describes the transactions that enable the banks to have enough cash to maintain the full convertibility of their liabilities into legal tender. Very similar arrangements are found in all other industrial countries.

Our second question was 'Why does no one doubt that legal tender will be worth its face value?' The answer is very straight-forward. The state is prepared to use its law-enforcement powers to make people accept that the bits of paper (i.e. bank notes) issued by the Bank of England are worth their stated face value. In the last resort legal tender has value because of the state's law-enforcement role and its monopoly of coercion (i.e. control over the army and the police) within certain geographical boundaries.

Some important consequences flow from the connection between legal-tender money and the state. Two points are obvious, although the recent debates on EMU suggest, rather surprisingly, that they need to be spelt out. First, there is a simple reason that a particular currency circulates as a medium of exchange in one country but not in neighbouring countries. This reason is not to be sought in people's currency preferences. Instead currency areas coincide with political units because national boundaries define where a state's laws cease to apply. Secondly, where legal tender is a paper asset which is costless to produce, the right to issue legal tender cannot be granted to a private sector agent. If a particular company or individual were empowered to issue legal tender, they could print enormous quantities of paper and force other people to give up real goods and services in return. This would be an extremely profitable activity! In effect, the right to issue legal tender is akin to the right to levy taxes. If someone in the private sector is given this privilege, he can rob other people almost at will. A third point follows from the second. The only logical customer for the central bank is the government, since the government is the fitting recipient of the resources (known as 'seigniorage') made available by the issue of legal tender.

These points help in analysing various monetary proposals made in recent years. Last year the Treasury suggested at a meeting of European Community finance ministers in Antibes that the best way to proceed to EMU was currency competition, with the currencies of every EC nation given the status of legal tender in every EC nation. Our argument shows that this idea is based on a rather disturbing *naïveté* about how governments and central banks would respond. If the Italian lira were legal tender in the UK, the Banca d'Italia would be able to extract resources from the UK economy; if the pound were legal tender in Italy, the Bank of England would be able to extract resources from the Italian economy; and so on. Every central bank would have an incentive to over-issue in order to capture resources from other countries. Furthermore, over-issue of pounds and lira would affect aggregate demand in Germany and France, and, hence, increase the German and French inflation rates. Finally, currency competition is conceivable only in a regime of floating exchange rates. If exchange rates were fixed, the temptation to over-issue would not be constrained by the risks of depreciation and inflation. The urge to capture resources from other countries by printing money would become overwhelmingly attractive. At best, currency competition would therefore be incompatible with the European Monetary System as it is now constituted; at worst, it would degenerate into total instability.

The distinction between bank deposits and legal-tender notes – or, in effect, between private and state money – is crucial also to defining the meaning of 'monetary policy' in a modern context. Indeed, it is essential to understanding why central banks can conduct monetary policy in the usually recognised sense. We have seen that the complete convertibility of deposits into notes is essential to the banking system. If banks did not have legal tender as part of their assets, they could not remain in business. We have also seen that the banks and the central bank meet every day in the money market, where the various influences on the banks' (and the economy's) cash holdings intersect. The money market therefore presents the central bank with an opportunity for exerting power over the banks. By keeping the banks fairly continuously 'short' of cash and setting the interest-rate terms on which the shortages are to be relieved, the central bank can regulate interest rates for the entire financial system. The central bank's position as the monopoly supplier of legal tender explains its ability to determine short-term interest rates and so to decide monetary policy.

The argument so far can now be summarised. The standard monetary arrangements of today – with every country having a single legal tender issued by one central bank, which is banker to the government – have not grown up haphazard. There can be only one legal tender in a particular national jurisdiction, for much the same reason that there can be only one law, one police force and one army. The one legal tender has to be issued by a public (or semi-public) authority, since private issuance of a legal tender would enable the issuer to obtain resources unjustly from the rest of the population; and, since there is room for only one legal tender, only one institution – the central bank – can issue it. Private money can nevertheless be issued in the form of bank deposits. Monetary policy, which consists essentially in the central bank exerting influence over the behaviour of private banks, can be made effective precisely because such private money is subordinate to the legal tender.

A government economist recently suggested in the official *Treasury Bulletin* that legal tender 'is often believed to have more relevance in this area than it really has.' He amplified the point by saying, 'What matters from the point of view of the monetary authority . . . is that it be regarded as the ultimate source of primary liquidity for the currency concerned. In turn, this means that its own monetary liabilities must be entirely free from risk of default. Because it would be a Community institution, backed by the Community itself, the EMF would enjoy this unquestioned status.'[2]

But the fact that an institution's liabilities are backed by the EC does not make them 'a source of primary liquidity'. The liabilities of the European Investment Bank are undoubtedly backed by the EC, but they are not 'primary liquidity', let alone a 'currency'. So what does this phrase, 'the ultimate source of primary liquidity for the currency concerned', mean? It evidently implies a distinction between 'primary liquidity' and the rest of 'the currency', presumably between the liabilities of 'the monetary authority' and the banking system proper. If the key differentiating characteristic of the liabilities of the monetary authority is that they are 'entirely free from default risk' whereas those of privately-owned banks are not, the question arises 'why are they free from default risk?' If the uniqueness of the monetary authority (i.e. the central bank) rests on its backing from government and the law, 'primary liquidity' is equivalent to 'legal tender'. The Treasury's point is semantic and irrelevant, and the putative distinction between primary liquidity and legal tender collapses.

CONSUMER RESISTANCE TO PARALLEL CURRENCIES

The argument of the last section is hardly very abstruse. Indeed, it merely recapitulates certain long-familiar features of our own and every other modern monetary system. But its message for the parallel-currency approach to EMU is very damaging. The parallel-currency approach proposes that a new currency should, in some sense, be introduced in order to coexist with a national currency. In other words, two (or perhaps even more) currencies would circulate at the same time. This raises several difficulties in the logical design of the new monetary order.

The first is simply why anyone should want to switch from the existing national currency into the new currency. It is all very well to say a parallel currency is to be established on a particular date in a particular year. But what does that mean in practical terms? Currencies are issued by banks. Which banks are to issue them? Are they to be issued in response to demand or irrespective of demand? And, crucially, are they to be legal tender or not?

In fact, Europe has had a parallel currency of sorts for over a decade. The ECU was born in 1979 at the same time as the EMS, with its value based on a weighted basket of the various national currencies. It was a development of the 'European unit of account' which had been used for EC public accounting since 1975. The ECU has subsequently developed into a popular currency of denomination in the international bond market, apparently from a wish to diversify and reduce currency risk. But it is striking that the ECU has not been widely adopted as a unit of account within European countries and nowhere is it a recognised medium of exchange. The ECU may be a 'parallel currency'; it is certainly not a currency. Advocates of another parallel currency need to be asked: 'Why has the ECU failed to become a currency?' and 'Why should your alternative do any better?'

The ECU's failure is due partly, no doubt, to the deadweight of tradition, the tendency for people to adhere to the currency with which they are familiar because all prices have previously been expressed in terms of it. But, surely, the dominant reason is that its legal position is unclear and inferior. Without legal-tender status it cannot compete against existing national currencies. That is the gravamen of our argument about the connection between money, law and the power of the state. (It should be emphasised that some countries, notably West Germany, have in the past officially discouraged the private use of the ECU.)

So supporters of a parallel currency have to add some spice to the idea if they are to be persuasive. This is the function of the word 'hard' in the 'hard ECU' proposal. One of the reasons the Germans dislike the ECU is that its inflation performance is the average of all European countries', not the best, which is Germany's itself. Suggestions that the ECU become the single European currency are therefore likely to be rejected by the Bundesbank. But the word 'hard' means that the hard ECU cannot be devalued against the deutschmark or any other European currency. According to Mr Paul Richards of Samuel Montagu & Co., writing in the *Financial Times*, 'The hard ECU would not be the same as the deutschmark; the deutschmark's central parity in terms of the hard ECU could never be revalued, although it could be devalued.'

Here is the key innovation in the hard ECU plan. It is the added ingredient which, apparently, is judged to make the idea so worthwhile. To quote from one of Mr Richards' papers, 'If there was a realignment in the ECU central parities of national Community currencies, the central parity of the strongest national Community currency in terms of the ECU would not change as a result of the realignment. In other words, the hard ECU would be as strong as the ECU central parity of the strongest national Community currency.' Let us consider whether the hard ECU, thus defined, could ever become a 'currency' or 'money' in the usually understood senses of these terms.

First, would it be accepted as a medium of exchange? This seems to be the official intention. In his speech 'Beyond Stage One' on 20 June 1990 Mr John Major, the Chancellor of the Exchequer, urged two steps – first, an initial issue of ECU bank notes against deposits of national notes and, secondly, once the idea had been agreed, an issue of hard ECU bank notes also against deposits of national notes. (According to Mr Major, people and companies would go to a new institution, a European Monetary Fund, to convert national notes into ECU or hard ECU equivalents. The EMF's note liabilities would thus be fully backed by national notes.)

The problem here is that the new (ECU) and old (national) notes would be exactly stable in value – and therefore virtually equivalent for practical purposes – only if exchange rates between currencies were locked irrevocably. If exchange rates still varied a little, ECU notes would fluctuate in value against those of any individual currency. Businessmen would know this and would be reluctant to incur the extra costs involved in transacting in both kinds of notes. Hard ECU notes would be particularly awkward, because the hard ECU plan has meaning only if exchange rate variation is explicitly envisaged.

This kind of difficulty would be particularly serious at the cheque clearing in any of the EC member states. Advocates of the hard ECU plan presumably want to end the differentiation between clearing in domestic currencies and the inter-bank settlement of intra-European foreign exchange transactions. They may hope that, in short order, banks would treat debits and credits in ECU or hard ECU in exactly the same way as debits and credits in national currencies, and that the two types of debits and credits would become indistinguishable. But that would clearly not be possible. Since the hard ECU would be revalued from time to time, the banks could suffer arbitrary losses or profits at the clearing after such revaluations, depending on the balance of their customer business between national currencies and hard ECUs. They would have to separate payments in hard ECUs and national currencies, as they do now.

The very notion of a parallel currency is a contradiction in terms. People use a currency because – in the well-defined political unit of the modern nation-state – it is the only currency. The usefulness of a currency rests on this uniqueness. People and companies want to standardise on one currency because it reduces transaction costs and provides a common standard of value, and they standardise on that unit which has legal recognition and government backing. The familiar monetary and political arrangements of the modern age – with each nation having one law, one government, one central bank and one currency – have not evolved accidentally. Except in cases of severe monetary dislocation (such as Latin American hyperinflations), no significant counter-examples to this pattern exist.

WOULD A HARD-ECU 'MONETARY POLICY' BE POSSIBLE?

The hazy legal status of the hard ECU would give rise to further problems, notably the difficulty of operating – and, indeed, even of defining – a meaningful 'monetary policy'.

We have already seen that the money market – the market where banks settle imbalances in their cash receipts and payments – is the arena in which central banks enforce monetary policy decisions. If the hard ECU plan were adopted, the prospect of occasional revaluation would require that there still be several national money markets and, hence, a need to retain the existing national central banks. The European Monetary Fund would not have primacy over these banks. On the contrary, if ECU (or hard ECU) notes were not legal tender but the national notes were, the banking systems of the various EC countries could ignore the EMF. In deciding where to set interest rates, they could continue to take the lead from the national central banks.

In his speech on 20 June Mr Major nevertheless suggested the EMF 'would set interest rates on hard ECU'. Initially this would be confined to large interest-bearing deposits from commercial banks. Later, 'the EMF could move to setting interest rates by the normal central banking techniques, namely through the creation of money-market shortages which would then be relieved at the chosen interest rate.'

One is reminded of the general who, when asked how he would move his troops, replied 'by land, by sea and by air'. Again, it is essential to delve into the practicalities. As we have explained, the 'normal central banking techniques' are successful only because the note liabilities of central banks are legal tender. It is this which gives central banks their cutting-edge against the commercial banks in setting interest rates. Nowhere in this speech (or others) does Mr Major spell out what legal-tender status he foresees for the hard ECU. The whole notion of 'money market shortages' is meaningless unless there is a legal-tender 'money' which can be in short supply.

Of course, if the hard ECU notes were legal tender and the EMF had the right to lend to governments, the hard ECU proposal would be in deep water. It would involve as massive a transfer of sovereignty to a European monetary authority as anything implied by the Delors Report. To grant the right to issue legal tender to the EMF would be a clear encroachment on the British Parliament's fiscal prerogatives. But let us make the discussion as favourable to the hard-ECU scheme as possible. Assume that Britain does plunge in at the deep end, and that the government overcomes its reservations about monetary sovereignty and allows Hard-ECU notes to become legal tender. Would the EMF then be able conduct 'normal central banking techniques' to influence interest rates, as Mr Major claims?

In national money markets as now constituted central banks relieve shortages by purchasing interest-bearing instruments (Treasury or commercial bills, mostly) from the banking system. Of course, the central banks take them onto their balance sheets. But – according to Mr Major's 20 June speech – the EMF is supposed to be 'a currency board', with its ECU notes backed only by its own holdings of the various currencies which make up the ECU. The EMF is meant to abstain from 'new money creation'. It follows that the EMF's assets would consist only of national notes and balances with national central banks. By definition, they could not include interest-bearing instruments. As a matter of logic, the EMF could not determine hard ECU interest rates, because its operations would be confined to currency transactions between the ECU and national monies. The EMF could determine hard ECU interest rates only by purchases and sales of hard ECU interest-bearing instruments. But, if it did purchase such instruments, it would be straight into the business of money creation.

In short, the Treasury's description of the EMF's balance sheet and its account of hard ECU monetary policy are logically incompatible. If the EMF denies itself the ability to create money, it cannot determine European monetary policy; if it is to determine European monetary policy, it has to have the ability to create money. It cannot be both a blameless and inactive observer of national central banks' propensity to print money and an all-powerful umpire superintending their monetary policies.

CONCLUSION: THE IDEA OF A PARALLEL CURRENCY IS NOT VIABLE

To summarise, our argument is that the hard ECU plan cannot be reconciled with certain necessary and essential characteristics of any 'money' and any known structure of 'monetary policy'. The difficulties are not unusual with parallel-currency proposals, which in the past have tended to have rather murky intellectual pedigrees.

The Bundesbank – which pro-EMU British politicians usually profess to admire – is very clear that it dislikes this route. In a clear attempt to distance itself from the British position, it has insisted in recent months on the indivisibility of monetary policy. Dr Pohl, president of the Bundesbank, was particularly emphatic about this in a speech he gave to a conference at the London School of Economics on 9 November. Noting that the hard ECU would be issued by a newly-established European Monetary Fund coexisting with central banks, he charged that the parallel-currency approach has 'the disadvantage that an indeterminate area of monetary policy responsibilities might emerge'. It followed that 'we are unable to support the proposal to create a new monetary institution because this could lead to a grey area in monetary policy.' The Bundesbank's preferred approach to EMU would be to set a European central bank with powers similar to its own and to mimic the process of German monetary unification completed in recent months. In its June *Monthly Report* the Bundesbank published the regulations and ordinances required to implement the Treaty on German monetary union. The first article reads as follows:

> With effect from 1st July 1990 the deutschemark shall become the currency of the GDR. As from 1st July 1990 the banknotes denominated in deutschemark issued by the Deutsche Bundesbank and the Federal coins denominated in deut-

schemark or pfennig issued by the Federal Republic of Germany shall be the sole legal tender.

Note that the phrase, 'sole legal tender', is used at the very outset of the document. The strategic importance of legal-tender status is clearly well-understood by the Bundesbank. The transfer of the legal-tender role from the ostmark to the deutschmark was vital to the change in monetary regime. Indeed, it virtually defined GMU. The Bundesbank was not so silly in early 1990 as to set out proposals for GMU which were inconsistent with basic defining features of any viable monetary system. Unless the British Treasury pays more attention to such features in the coming debate on EMU, it will be overwhelmed intellectually by the Germans at the December IGC.

This does not mean that other European countries have all the answers. They certainly have not worked out in detail all the ramifications of the Big Bang route to EMU. Some of them, particularly the smaller countries, are likely to have a shock when they realise the scale of the hijack of national sovereignty implied. But other European governments are probably right that the Big Bang route is the only one that would 'work', in the sense of actually introducing a single European currency. The Big Bang introduction of this new currency would be a very definite, once-for-all event. Either a country joins or it does not join. No intermediate position can be imagined. Equivocation and trimming would be no different from a flat refusal to participate.

If Britain does not want to participate in EMU, it will have to stop dithering. The answer has to be 'yes' or 'no', not 'perhaps', 'sometimes' or 'later'. Attempts to evade a clear-cut response – like the competing currencies idea and the hard ECU plan – cannot be sustained. They are little better than elaborate word games and merely forfeit intellectual respect for Britain in other European capitals. The British government must decide whether it is for or against EMU, and say so.

NOTES

1. The author has criticised the Big Bang approach in a recent pamphlet *EMU now? The leap to European money assessed*, published by the Centre for Policy Studies, November 1990.
2. 'The UK Proposals for a European Monetary Fund and a "Hard Ecu"', *Treasury Bulletin*, Autumn 1990.

8 A Monetary Constitution for Europe?

Antonio Martino

> The most savage controversies are those about matters as to which there is no good evidence either way.
>
> (Bertrand Russell)

The discussions on European monetary unification appear to confirm the wisdom of Bertrand Russell's insight. Both supporters and opponents of the idea are forced to resort to essentially *theoretical* arguments, as there is no *specific* empirical evidence on the merits of the various alternatives. In what follows, after looking at some advantages of a common currency for Europe and at the objections that are being raised against it, I'll say something about the transition process as currently envisaged.

The argument of this paper is that a common European currency may be desirable or undesirable (feasible or unfeasible) depending on the kind of monetary constitution (or lack of it) that will be adopted.[1] A monetary rule appears to be a necessary precondition for moving toward a common European currency. If, on the other hand, money continues to be used as an instrument of (discretionary) *policy*, monetary unification is unlikely to be achieved. Agreement on the need for a monetary rule is far more important than the choice of the actual monetary constitution. Therefore, little will be said about the type of rule to adopt.[2]

ADVANTAGES OF A COMMON CURRENCY[3]

> Monetary union in Europe is capable of being good, bad or indifferent. All depends on precisely how it is done.
>
> (*The Economist*, 1989)

Would Europe benefit from a common currency? if, for the

moment, we ignore both the difficulties of achieving that result and the preoccupations with the conduct of monetary policy after the establishment of a common currency, the answer is positive: Europe and the world would probably benefit a great deal from a common European currency.

Interestingly enough, most commentators seem convinced that the *only* advantage of a common currency for Europe would be that of reducing uncertainty in foreign exchange markets. For example, the Governor of the Bank of England has recently stated:

> [I]n what circumstances would the benefits of a single currency exceed the costs?
>
> The benefits are fairly easy to identify. Where prices within an area are quoted in a common currency, uncertainties arising from unpredictable exchange rate fluctuations within the area are removed. In consequence, business decisions are not complicated by a need to take account of possible exchange rate changes within the currency area, which would help to improve confidence, particularly in relation to investment decisions with long time horizons. Furthermore, there would no longer be any transactions costs associated with exchanging one currency for another or with trying to hedge against changes in rates.[4]
>
> (Leigh-Pemberton, 1989, p. 12)

I do not wish to deny the importance of reduced uncertainty in foreign exchange markets and of a saving in transactions costs, but first of all I think it's reductive to see no other advantage in a common currency for Europe: as I shall try to show, there are other, possibly more relevant, advantages. Second, I believe it is this reductive interpretation of the benefits of a common currency that has led to the fallacious identification of monetary unification with fixed exchange rates, which is responsible for some of the absurdities in the various political proposals. Let me first start to list what I consider to be *some* of the main advantages other than the reduction in transactions costs.

International Stability

A common European currency could provide an alternative to

the US dollar as an instrument of international liquidity. The 'national' currency of such a large market could achieve the same degree of acceptability presently enjoyed by the dollar. The competition between the two major international currencies would result in some kind of 'Gresham's law' in reverse, because the more stable currency would be preferred in international transactions. The overall stability of the international monetary system would increase.[5]

In particular, Europe would benefit in that it would be able to use its own currency, rather than the US dollar, as a reserve asset.[6] Needless to say this would not be a minor advantage, and, by itself, might in fact be as important as (if not more important than) the saving in transactions costs. The US would also benefit to the extent that a monetary system based on two currencies would make the external value of the dollar less volatile.

Balance of Payments Equilibrium

Inside Europe, a common currency would eliminate balance of payments problems, making the 'adjustment process' smooth and automatic. There would be no balance of payments problems between, say, England and France because both countries would be using the same currency. National economic policies would, therefore, be relieved of one of their present worries. Finally, scarce resources presently dissipated in the collection, analysis and discussion of intra-European balance of payments statistics could be diverted to more productive uses.

Internal Stability

With a common European currency, provincial considerations would play no role in monetary decisions, which would aim at overall stability rather than respond to 'local' pressures. As a result, for example, there would only be one rate of inflation rather than twelve. This is a very important consideration indeed: I know of no economist willing to argue that a proliferation of *regional* currencies within a given country would increase overall monetary stability on a *national* level.[7]

Freedom and Efficiency

A common currency would make the liberalisation of capital movements within Europe automatic and irreversible, with all the known advantages in terms of personal liberty and economic efficiency. It would be as difficult to restrict capital movements in an area using the same currency as it is within a given country.

These are not necessarily all of the benefits from a common currency for Europe, but it seems to me that they are possibly more important than the advantage of reduced uncertainty in foreign exchanges and of savings in transactions costs. Furthermore, while the smoothness of the adjustment process and the elimination of balance of payments problems could also be achieved by a system of freely floating exchange rates among European national currencies, all the other advantages can only be attained by a single currency for Europe.[8]

OBJECTIONS TO A COMMON CURRENCY

Several objections have been raised to the idea of adopting a single European currency. While some are undoubtedly well-founded (if not insurmountable), others are, in my view, definitely dubious. Here are some of the major objections:

1. The most common objection is that *money does not manage itself*: discretionary monetary management requires political control. Europe's present political institutions are inadequate for that kind of task. A variation on this theme is that the surrender of monetary sovereignty is unjustifiable at this point, since the existing European political institutions could not guarantee member states that the common currency would be managed in a way of which they would approve.
2. Another objection is that a common currency would be premature, given the present heterogeneity of the various European national economies. Monetary unification, according to this view, should follow, not precede, 'economic integration' (whatever that means).

3. A third objection states that monetary unification would be beneficial to 'high-inflation countries' and harmful to 'low-inflation countries'. The idea here is that with a common European currency inflation in Europe would settle at some kind of average of the existing national inflation rates.
4. Finally, there is a problem which is seldom explicitly stated: money creation is an important source of revenue for national governments, and they are not ready to give it up easily.

ARE THE OBJECTIONS VALID?

None of the preceding objections is insurmountable. Some are totally false: for example, different regions of the same national economy are often very heterogeneous, yet this does not prevent them from using the same currency. As previously mentioned, no one has advocated the introduction of separate *regional* currencies as an instrument to reduce *national* heterogeneity.

A different version of this argument draws on Keynesianism: a monetary union would prevent 'individual member countries from each attaining their optimum combination of inflation and unemployment on the so-called Phillips curve' (see Vaubel, 1979, p. 20). However, as Vaubel pointed out, the 'trade-off between inflation and unemployment has disappeared,' and few economists today believe that much good can result from monetary instability. From this point of view, therefore, Vaubel's conclusion seems as valid today as it was ten years ago: 'If national monetary policy can no longer be used to raise employment, the economic cost of joining a monetary union must be small indeed.'

Also, there is no reason to suppose that a common currency would result in an inflation rate equal to the average of today's national rates. If Europe would adopt a common currency, it would have one rate of inflation (rather than twelve), which would be 'high' or 'low' depending on whether the rate of growth of the money supply at the European level was 'high' or 'low'. The classification of countries in 'high inflation' and 'low inflation' is highly misleading because it suggests that somehow the degree of monetary stability/instability of a country is determined by some 'inevitable law of historical destiny', and it has nothing to do with the country's actual monetary policy.

Monetary history provides irrefutable evidence that this is not the case.

It seems to me that there are only two valid objections to a common currency. One is that related to the use of money as an instrument of discretionary policy; the other is connected with its use as a source of revenue by European national governments. But, before discussing these, I shall make a few remarks on the transition process and the Delors Report.

THE DELORS REPORT

> Does all this mean that European monetary union, let alone European political integration, is not an aim worth striving for? In my view, such a conclusion would be premature. It may very well be that European monetary union would be a great achievement, but that the road by which we are trying to reach it is conducive to serious breakdowns and accidents and, indeed, does not lead to its ultimate destination. What must worry all advocates of European integration is precisely that the choice of an unworkable strategy will – again, and this time fatally – discredit the whole idea of a united Western Europe.
>
> (Vaubel, 1979, p. 19)

Vaubel was right: even today, much of the discredit surrounding the idea of a common European currency is due to the clumsy political attempts at planning a strategy for the transition process. This is true of the earlier efforts as it is of the latest sample of these ill-conceived political attempts: the Delors Report. This remarkable document has recently prompted Professor Patrick Minford to express the following judgment:

> The Delors Report is a monstrous conspiracy of centralism, mounted by an *ad hoc* alliance of central bankers and bureaucrats whose interests wonderfully coincide in this assault on consumer choice and democratic rights.
>
> (Minford, in Leigh-Pemberton, 1989, p. 28)

These are strong words. There is no doubt, however, that the Report lends itself to public choice analysis (Vaubel, 1989), and offers no small amount of entertainment to those of us who are inclined to question the superior wisdom of bureaucrats and politicians.

It is true, as Professor Minford has stressed, that the Report marks a departure from the liberal philosophy of the European ideal, as most recently reconfirmed by the Single Act, and that it embraces a 'statist' approach to European money.[9]

The 'statist' bias is probably a consequence of the Report's original sin: that of identifying monetary unification with fixed exchange rates.[10] It is an old mistake: it was the basic assumption of the Werner plan of 1970, of the 1972 'snake', and of the present European Monetary System. As for the Delors Report, it believes that 'irrevocably fixed exchange rates between national currencies' and 'coordination of policy between separate national authorities' are necessary (and sufficient?) first steps toward monetary union. Once fixed exchange rates are attained, the Report maintains, monetary unification will be completed.

Despite the experience of the Werner plan, the belief that fixed rates are (1) almost indistinguishable from monetary union, and (2) a necessary step toward that goal, is still widely held. Such view is unacceptable. In the words of Professor Milton Friedman:

> The basic fact is that a unified currency and a system of freely floating exchange rates are members of the same species even though superficially they appear very different. Both are free market mechanisms for interregional or international payments. Both permit exchange rates to move freely. Both exclude any administrative or political intermediary in payments between residents of different areas. Either is consistent with free trade between areas, or with a lessening of trade restrictions.
>
> On the other hand, national currencies linked by pegged exchange rates, whether or not through the mechanism of gold, and a system of variable exchange rates, controlled and manipulated by governmental bodies, either through an adjustable peg or day-to-day market operations, are also members of the same species. Both are interventionist standards. Neither, in my opinion, is consistent with a permanent lessening of barriers to international trade, but

only with oscillating barriers as nations shift from surplus to deficit.

(Friedman, 1968, p. 271–2)

Furthermore, while a single European currency *automatically* implies a single monetary *regime* and is, therefore, immune to balance of payments problems,[11] a system of fixed exchange rates among different national currencies does not. It can survive if, and only if, it succeeds in imposing coordinated patterns of behaviour on all member countries. This last possibility – witness the fate of the Werner plan – is rather remote.[12]

Finally, it isn't true that fixed exchange rates would bring Europe closer to monetary unification. In fact, the opposite might very well be true.[13] This is so because under fixed exchange rates domestic policy goals are at times incompatible with external balance. When such a dichotomy arises, the alternative to a change in the exchange rate is that of imposing the burden of the adjustment process on domestic macrovariables. Balance of payments equilibrium is then achieved without any change in the exchange rate parity but at the cost of sacrificing domestic stability.

Such a choice is neither desirable or likely to be made: should a country find itself forced to choose between pursuing domestic policy goals or adhering to 'irrevocably fixed rates', it would most likely let the exchange rate adjust to a new equilibrium. The arrangement suggested by the Delors Report is, therefore, unlikely to succeed. Needless to add, the failure of the authorities to maintain their 'irrevocably fixed rates' for an indefinite period of time would result in frustration and it would discredit the idea of monetary unification.

The crucial error of identifying fixed exchange rates with monetary unification is probably the result of a mistaken concept of gradualism. Gradualism is a very useful political tool, but it can be applied only to problems which have a *divisible* solution, it certainly cannot be used for problems with an *indivisible* solution (of the all-or-nothing type). A common European currency is indivisible: we either have it or we don't, but we cannot have just a bit of it.[14] It has been possible to liberalise trade gradually, because tariffs are divisible, and can be reduced progressively. But I don't see how a common currency can be divided into separate allotments to be incrementally added to the existing bundle. And, in any case, fixed exchange rates do not represent the 'partial' creation of a common currency.

WOULD A EUROPEAN CURRENCY BE PART OF A FISCAL CONSTITUTION?

> . . . money can be a potent tool for controlling and shaping the economy. Its potency . . . is exemplified . . . by the extent to which control over money has always been a potent means of exacting taxes from the populace at large, very often without the explicit agreement of the legislature.
>
> (Friedman, 1962, p. 174)

A major obstacle in the introduction of a common European currency – one that indeed lends credibility to the view of the Governor of the Bank of England that 'the establishment of a single currency area in Europe . . . remains distant' (Leigh-Pemberton, 1989, p. 26) – is the obvious one that money creation is an important source of revenue for national governments, and we must assume that they are reluctant to give it up.

On the other hand, this would also be one of the main advantages of a common European currency. Some supporters of a united Europe, in fact, saw this as the major reason for having it (Einaudi (1944), 1985, pp. 102–3).

If Europe had a common currency, this would in and of itself represent a significant change in the existing fiscal constitution of national governments, as they would have to forego the use of inflationary finance, the 'inflation tax', debt monetisation as a means to finance public spending. As Luigi Einaudi maintained, it would be a substantial improvement over present fiscal procedures. Of course, it is an open question whether national governments can be persuaded to give up such a source of revenue. This problem is not explicitly discussed in the Delors Report, which does not address the question of whether a *constitutional* framework is needed. We are, however, reminded that there must be a 'system of binding rules governing the size and the financing of national budget deficits.' But the unresolved question is: how are national governments going to be persuaded to give up such a source of revenue?

A EUROPEAN MONETARY CONSTITUTION?

> The main costs [of monetary union] arise from the loss of autonomy over domestic monetary policy ...
>
> (Leigh-Pemberton, 1989, p. 12)

> Who would control such a central bank?
>
> (Minford, in Leigh-Pemberton, 1989, p. 28)

Money Matters

The preoccupations with the issue of monetary sovereignty are entirely justified: money matters and, as Milton Friedman has often repeated, it is too important to be left to central bankers. The reasons that make us worry about monetary management by national central bankers are even more valid when referred to a single currency for Europe. Monetary mismanagement on a national level can be a disaster; on a European level it would be a catastrophe of unbearable proportions.[15] Moreover, the argument against binding rules that they are 'undemocratic' because they prevent 'elected officials from responding as best they can to the wishes of the electorate' obviously does not apply to the case of Europe.[16]

The problem arises because, with the end of the gold standard, money, in addition to its traditional functions, has become an instrument of discretionary policy to an extent that was inconceivable before. Discretionary manipulation of monetary aggregates on the part of 'independent' central banks can produce pro-cyclical rather than anti-cyclical consequences. Instead of achieving a higher degree of stability, monetary policy becomes an autonomous source of instability.[17]

This in no way implies *incompetence* on the part of the monetary authorities: even the most competent central banker does not possess all the knowledge that would be required to make a discretionary anti-cyclical monetary policy succeed. Information about the working of our macroeconomic systems are inadequate; short-term predictions are seldom sufficiently reliable; decisions may be untimely, and lags in the effects of monetary changes are largely unknown in advance.[18]

In any case, the outcome of discretionary monetary policy in terms of increased economic instability, already harmful at the national level, would be disastrous at the European level. It's hardly surprising, therefore, that so many people consider that risk unacceptable, and oppose a common currency for Europe altogether.

A European Monetary Constitution?

The need to constrain discretion in the conduct of monetary affairs has long been recognised. From the pioneering, classic paper of Henry C. Simons (1936) – arguing that 'an enterprise system cannot function effectively in the face of extreme uncertainty as to the action of monetary authorities' – to contemporary times, several economists have supported the view that monetary policy should be entrusted to rigidly specified rules rather than to the discretion of 'authorities'.[19]

For public choice theorists, for example, only a constitutional set of rigid rules can prevent the ordinary working of political incentives from resulting in monetary instability.[20] For them, 'the absence of an explicit monetary constitution is unacceptable' (Brennan and Buchanan, 1981, p. 65).

As is well known, the main proponent of a monetary rule has been Milton Friedman:

> If . . . we cannot achieve our objectives by giving wide discretion to independent experts, how else can we establish a monetary system that is stable, free from irresponsible governmental tinkering, and incapable of being used as a source of power to threaten economic and political freedom?
>
> A . . . possibility is to try to achieve a government of law instead of men literally by legislating rules for the conduct of monetary policy. The enactment of such rules would enable the public to exercise control over monetary policy through its political authorities, while at the same time preventing monetary policy from being subject to the day-to-day whim of political authorities.[21]
>
> (Friedman (1962), 1968, p. 190)

What Kind of Rule?

A common currency for Europe would be desirable if its adoption meant an end of discretionary short-term policy. Should European nations agree on some kind of monetary constitution, making discretionary manipulation of monetary aggregates impossible, a common currency for Europe would greatly increase overall stability both in Europe and in the world. One could think of a rule fixing the rate of growth of some monetary aggregate to a predetermined level and mandating its continuation for an extended period of time (say, three to five years).[22]

The adoption of a monetary rule would be highly desirable *per se* if it would eliminate the variability of monetary growth, with its accompanying economic instability and uncertainty. But it would also be the solution for the creation of a common currency for Europe. All the justified worries about the surrender of national monetary sovereignty to a (politically irresponsible) European central bank would lose meaning if money was entrusted to predetermined (and agreed upon) rigid rules rather than to the whim of policy-makers possessing discretionary power. Furthermore, all the advantages of a common currency for Europe, referred to before, could be attained.

The problem is that even among those who believe in rigid monetary rules, there is no general agreement on the *specific* type of rule to adopt.[23] This is, however, less important than the decision to have a rule at all. Once the principle of a discretionary manipulation of monetary aggregates by an 'independent' European central bank is rejected, and the opposite one of a rigid monetary rule is introduced, the specifics of the rule can be progressively improved upon, as experience dictates.[24]

What I mean is that the main point to be made about rules is that there is no such thing as 'the ideal' rule, because, among other things, as our knowledge progresses new devices are thought of which can replace older arrangements.[25]

Once the principle of entrusting money creation to a rule is accepted, in other words, the choice of the best possible rule will be determined by accumulation of experience and analytical progress.[26] What is essential, regardless of the kind of rule adopted, is that the target rate of growth of the chosen monetary aggregate is adhered to for several years (so as to favour stable expectations). The concrete design of a European monetary constitution would also have to consider the problem of enforcement, so that it should contain the principle of accountability of the person(s) in charge. The bill presently (1989) under discussion in the New Zealand Parliament provides an inspiring example, as it makes the Governor's salary inversely related to inflation.[27]

CONCLUSION

A common currency for Europe could provide a good chance for introducing the kind of constitutional discipline monetary economists and public choice theorists have advocated for years. It's hard to tell whether politicians and central bankers will in the end become convinced by this argument, but one thing seems clear enough: the Delors Report approach does not seem likely to bring about a common currency for Europe. Since it does not solve (in fact, it does not even address) the problem of the shift of monetary sovereignty, it will lead nowhere. Furthermore, committed as it is to the enforcement of fixed exchange rates among European currencies, it is likely to promote political conflict and disagreement rather than the harmonisation it attempts to achieve.

If Europe does not get a common currency, it will not reap its great advantages and monetary policy will continue to be in the hands of 'independent' central bankers. Money will remain exposed to the temptations of politicians to use it as a way to purchase consent, and monetary stability will exist only if governments consider it in their own self-interest.

Unless European countries are prepared to give up discretion in the conduct of monetary policy (which means giving up money as an instrument of policy), the only kind of monetary unification that can be achieved is that which will spontaneously arise from the liberalisation of markets. As the Delors Report indirectly recognises, 'full freedom of capital movements and integrated financial markets' would discipline 'incompatible national policies'. Stable currencies would be preferred in international transactions, and some kind of competition among national currencies would be established. Countries with a high degree of monetary instability would see their national currency rejected by increasingly competitive markets, and would, as a result, be forced to change their policy. Therefore, even if a common currency for Europe is not introduced Europe might still get some kind of discipline in monetary affairs thanks to the 'filter mechanism' inadvertently introduced by the Single Act.[28]

NOTES

1. By monetary constitution I mean a regime 'in which the discretion of policymaking authorities is constrained, at least in the short run' (Leijonhufvud, 1987, p. 130).

2. As pointed out by J.M. Buchanan, agreement on the need for a monetary constitution should take precedence over that on the specific kind of rule to be adopted:

    > I think that this debate-discussion [on monetary reform] is prematurely joined when we start referring to the advantages and disadvantages of this or that rule, this regime or that regime ... Debates about which of the alternative regimes is to be preferred must take place. But, prior to this discussion, we should try to attain consensus on the need for *some* alternative regime that will embody greater predictability than the unconstrained monetary authority that describes that which now exists. The familiar analogy is with the traffic chaos that would exist if there were no rules. The first requirement is that there be some rules of the road. Whether or not these rules require driving on the left or the right is of secondary importance to the requirement that there be a rule.
    >
    > (Buchanan, 1983, 1987, p. 124)

3. What follows draws on my 1989 paper, and, to a lesser extent, on previous work; see Martino, 1971a, 1971b, 1976, 1977, 1978a, 1978b, 1986, 1988.

4. Apparently, this has also been the consensus among professional economists and public opinion:

    > There is little disagreement among economists about the *benefits* of monetary union, i.e. of a system in which exchange rate risks, exchange control risks, payments restrictions, the costs of information about exchange rates and exchange market prospects, and hopefully the costs of money-changing are eliminated. Monetary union defined in this way intensifies competition and international integration of product as well as factor markets.
    >
    > (Vaubel, 1979, p. 19)

There would also be a big saving in transaction costs. The story goes that somebody setting out of Britain with £1,000 to visit each of the EEC countries, changing his money into local currency every time but buying nothing, would arrive back with only £500. Monetary union would be such a blessing to people like that. And to everybody else.

(*The Economist*, 24 June 1989, p. 20)

5. For the analysis of currency competition, see, for example, Hayek (1976), Vaubel (1986), and Dowd (1988).

6. If Europe had a common currency, there would be one central bank rather than twelve. This, in and of itself, might result in a considerable saving if the European Central Bank would cost less than the present twelve national central banks. (This is, however, not clear, considering the rather lavish way Eurocrats tend to treat themselves.) Even more important, the dollar reserves presently used by the national central banks would become unnecessary and, if the common currency was allowed to float freely in international markets, the European Central Bank's reserve requirement would be very small.

7. It is in the light of this argument that one should read *The Economist's* point: 'simply ask whether America would be better off with separate currencies for each of its states' (op. cit.). Strangely enough the only problem that the authoritative publication sees in having the USA use 50 different currencies is that of the cost of converting one into another!

8. If these potential advantages are taken into consideration, the evaluation of the performance of the European Monetary System becomes less favourable. Even granted that the 'European Monetary System has not failed', because 'the potential for an inflationary bias predicted by many economists has not materialised', and because it 'has achieved lower exchange rate variability' (Fratianni 1988, p. 489), it is also true that none of the advantages of a common currency mentioned above has been achieved. Thus, Fratianni's conclusion that it is not clear whether the EMS has been a success is probably too benign.

9. The Single Act had elicited the following accolade from Victoria Curzon Price:

> For those of us who believe in markets, the Single Market based on the White Paper and the Single Act is a fantastic dream, a pure exercise in deregulation, the devolution of power to the market and economic federalism. It is perhaps one of the best, most market-oriented blueprints for economic cooperation that has ever been devised. It says: give a maximum of say to markets, a minimum to Brussels and it will even get national governments off our backs . . .
>
> (Curzon Price, 1988, p. 41)

The Delors scheme, by contrast, would require a centralised network of regulations (even on the decisions of national governments and monetary authorities): it is an interventionist's dream and a liberal's nightmare.

10.   'The adoption of *a single currency*, while not strictly necessary for the
        creation of a monetary union, might be seen – for economic as well
        as psychological and political reasons – as a natural and desirable
        further development of the monetary union.'
                                        (Delors Report, April 1989, p. 10.)

        Strangely enough this identification of monetary union with a system
        of fixed exchange rates is explicitly accepted even by *The Economist*: 'A
        fully fixed system would eliminate the bands within which the curren-
        cies are allowed to fluctuate. Monetary union would then go one step
        further by adopting a single currency.' (*The Economist,* op. cit., p. 18.)

11.   Professor Milton Friedman has repeatedly argued that the two necessary
        and almost sufficient conditions for disequilibria in the balance of
        payments are fixed exchange rates and autonomous national central
        banks.

12.   In the words of Roland Vaubel:

        The snake approach, the monetary-harmonization approach and the
        combined money-supply and exchange-rate approach all belong to
        one family: they are all coordination strategies. They do not lead to
        the creation of a common currency. The crucial defect of all coor-
        dination strategies is that they rely on discretion instead of automa-
        ticity. . . . Since the coordination approach lacks automaticity, it fails
        to make exchange rates predictable. If it involves the fixing of pari-
        ties, it may indeed lead to more errors and uncertainty than exchange-
        rate flexibility and the pre-announcement of definite rates of national
        money-supply growth which exchange-rate flexibility makes possible.
                                                        (Vaubel, 1979, p. 25)

13.   As Sir Alan Walters has argued:

        Compared with a floating system, the EMS entails a considerable
        politicization of exchange rates. The occasion for realignments in-
        volves a great political bargaining session rather than an occasion on
        which to review the fundamentals of real exchange rates. . . . If the
        ultimate objective is the monetary integration of Europe through a
        European Central Bank in a single currency area, then the EMS
        seems to be hardly a step in the right direction. It creates too many
        tensions, both economic and political.
                                                    (Walters, 1988, pp. 505–6)

14.   Of course, this does not imply that *its introduction* cannot be gradual, as
        Vaubel recommends. (See Vaubel, 1979, pp. 28–30.)

15.   'In a monetary union the design of the central authority is crucial. It
        must be the anchor against inflation that gold was in the gold standard
        and the D-mark is in the present EMS. An EMU under a badly run
        European central bank would be much worse than the EMS under the
        well-run Bundesbank. In setting up the new central bank a balance
        would have to be struck between accountability and independence.'
        (*The Economist*, 1989, p. 20.)

16. See Leijonhufvud (1987) for a criticism of such an argument.
17. It is not enough, in other words, to say that empirical evidence does not support the view that stabilisation policies have in fact had a stabilising effect on the economy (Romer, 1986), the problem is that empirical evidence suggests that they may have had a *de*stabilising effect. According to Friedman:

> Anna Schwartz and I have examined the cyclical behavior of the quantity of money in the United States for the whole period since 1867. Throughout that period monetary growth has risen and fallen not with but before economic activity. The cyclical peak of monetary growth regularly precedes the cyclical peak of economic activity by an interval that varies a great deal, but on average is something like six to nine months; the cyclical trough of monetary growth regularly precedes the cyclical trough of economic activity by an average interval of roughly the same length. Moreover, sizable monetary accelerations and decelerations tend to be followed by sizable expansions and contractions in economic activity; modest accelerations and decelerations, by modest expansions and contractions. . . . The evidence is clear: variability in the rate of monetary growth is associated with variability in economic growth. High monetary variability accompanies high economic variability, and vice versa. . . . The Federal Reserve has sought to use monetary policy to stabilize the economy – that is, to vary monetary growth in order to offset forces introducing disturbances into the economy. Had it succeeded, high monetary variability would have been associated with low economic variability, not with high economic variability. The correlations between the moving standard deviations that we have calculated would have been negative or zero, rather than systematically positive. The implication is again that monetary variability has been a source of economic variability, not an offset.
>
> (Friedman, 1984, pp. 33–4)

18. A common criticism of policymaking is that economists and policymakers do not know enough about how the economy functions to have a model that describes accurately the behavior of macroeconomic variables like real GNP and the price level. In this case, it has been argued that policy action based on a flawed or incomplete model might cause more harm than good.
     (Bradley and Jansen, 1989, p. 37)

As a result, 'one cannot be confident that relaxing . . . constraints on discretionary policymaking will bring a net social benefit' (Leijonhufvud, 1987, p. 131).

19. For example:

> The monetary authorities of the United States – that is, the Administration, the Congress, and the Federal Reserve System – do not obey *any* reasonably well defined set of policy rules that would tend to produce some particular, reasonably predictable path of the price

level over the long haul. There is no monetary constitution in effect that limits the short-run options of the authorities for the purpose of providing long-run stability ... none of these uncertainties would matter very much if some set of constitutional constraints were in force that would prevent the rapid cumulation of moves in one direction.

(Leijonhufvud, 1984)

20.   For example:

For many of these politicians, 'doing good' comes down to the spending of public monies. Hence, even for the most benevolent of politicians, revenue becomes a goal to maximize, an instrument through which they can promote public happiness and well-being. Would it not then follow that, for such well-meaning politicians, revenue-*increasing* policy is to be preferred to revenue-*decreasing* policy? Would it not follow that, for such agents, inflation might still offer a very tempting source of gain?

(Brennan and Buchanan, 1981, p. 58)

Which leads Kevin Dowd to the pessimistic conclusion:

Whenever the government is involved in the monetary system, monetary policy becomes an inherently *political* matter determined by the interplay of political (and to some extent, bureaucratic) interests. There is no mechanism to ensure that this non-market incentive structure delivers a desirable outcome.

(Dowd, 1988, p. 21)

21.   See also:

Proponents of stable monetary policy have studied the quality of specific rules. If central banks would concentrate on keeping the money supply on the path they have committed themselves to they would provide a public good: price level stability. Such a predictable policy would, as empirical evidence shows, contribute to a stable development of overall demand, a result which has not been achieved by the discretionary policies actually pursued in industrial countries. It would eliminate a great deal of the price variations on financial markets about which many observers complain so much.

(Langfeldt, Scheide and Trapp, 1989, p. 40)

22.   A monetary constitution would also impose fiscal responsibility on national governments, thereby achieving two goals at once. In this case, Jerry Jordan's opinion, according to which a fiscal reform is needed in order to achieve the desired monetary reform, would not apply: the monetary reform would achieve both:

... meaningful monetary reform cannot precede reform of the fiscal regime. ... Reform of the fiscal regime is a necessary, but not a sufficient condition for reform of the monetary regime. Reform of the monetary regime is neither necessary nor sufficient for reform of the fiscal regime.

(Jordan, 1986, p. 741)

23.   Personally, I agree with the view of Langfeldt, Scheide and Trapp:

An important element in a policy rule is that the central bank uses a monetary aggregate that it can control with sufficient precision. Broader aggregates (M1, M2 or M3) can be influenced through changes in the monetary base, but the links seems to become weaker the broader the measure is. So it appears best to use the monetary base which reflects precisely the actions of the central bank.

(Langfeldt, Scheide and Trapp, 1989, p. 40)

24.   See Buchanan's opinion quoted above.
25.   This has always been explicitly recognised by Milton Friedman:

I should like to emphasize that I do not regard this proposal as a be-all and end-all of monetary management, as a rule which is somehow to be written in tablets of gold and enshrined for all future times. It seems to me to be the rule that offers the greatest promise of achieving a reasonable degree of monetary stability in the light of our present knowledge. I would hope that as we operated with it, as we learned more about monetary matters, we might be able to devise still better rules which would achieve still better results.

(Friedman (1962), 1968, pp. 193–4)

26.   As is well-known, in the light of the American experience, Milton Friedman has recently changed his proposal of stating the rule in terms of M1 (Friedman (1962), 1968, p. 193), and has suggested instead that 'the quantity of high-powered money – non interest-bearing obligations of the U.S. government – be frozen at a fixed amount' (Friedman, 1984, pp. 48–9). This clearly illustrates the need for 'trying out' proposed rules in order to ascertain how well they work in practice, and formulating alternative proposals when the 'experiment' is not as successful as it was hoped. No matter what rule is chosen, however, it seems to me that it must conform to the principles spelled out by Langfeldt, Sheide and Trapp (1989, p. 43).

27.   The need for a monetary constitution governing the common European currency would be reduced, but not eliminated, if it was introduced through a competitive process of the kind advocated, for example, by Vaubel (1979) and Minford (in Leigh-Pemberton, 1989). For, if the competitive process would lead to a monopoly in money enjoyed by either the 'European' or a national currency, the need for some kind of monetary constitution would again present itself. The mere *possibility* of creating an alternative to the dominant currency would not be sufficient to constrain the inflationary tendencies of the monetary monopolist. This is why, though I agree with the parallel currency

approach to the introduction of a common European currency, I still believe that a monetary constitution is needed.

28.   As Victoria Curzon Price has recently pointed out:

> It is often said, and rightly so, that creating a single European currency would represent such a loss of sovereignty that were we to get there, we would not be far off full political integration. And yet, if EMS governments stick to their stated commitments . . . they will have tied their hands as firmly as if they had actually created a European central bank . . . Even if they retain the right to vary their exchange rates within the EMS, the need to compete for their citizens' savings will force them to behave with extreme fiscal and monetary caution.
>
> (Curzon Price, 1989, p. 37)

REFERENCES

Bradley, M.D. and Jansen, D.W., 'Understanding Nominal GNP Targeting', *The Federal Reserve Bank of St Louis Review*, Vol. 71, No. 6, November/December 1989, pp. 31–40.

Brennan, H.G. and Buchanan, J.M., *Monopoly in Money and Inflation*, Hobart Paper No. 88 (London: Institute of Economic Affairs, 1981).

Buchanan, J.M., 'Monetary Research, Monetary Rules, and Monetary Regimes', *The Cato Journal*, Vol. 3, Spring 1983, pp. 143–6, reprinted with revisions as 'Constitutional Strategy and the Monetary Regime', in Dorn, J.A. and Schwarz, A.J. (eds), *The Search for Stable Money: Essays on Monetary Reform* (Chicago and London: University of Chicago Press, 1987), pp. 119–27.

Committee for the Study of Economic and Monetary Union, *Report on Economic and Monetary Union in the European Community* (Delors Report), 12 April 1989, mimeo.

Curzon Price, V., *1992: Europe's Last Chance? From Common Market to Single Market*, Occasional Paper No. 81 (London: Institute of Economic Affairs, 1988).

Curzon Price, V., 'Three Models of European Integration', in *Whose Europe? Competing Visions for 1992* (London: Institute of Economic Affairs, 1989), pp. 23–38.

Dowd, K., *Private Money, The Path to Monetary Stability*, Hobart Paper No. 112 (London: Institute of Economic Affairs, 1988).

Einaudi, L., *I problemi economici della Federazione Europea* (Lugano, 1944), reprinted in *Europa Padri e Figli, Gli antesignani italiani dell'europeismo* (Rome: Editrice Europea, 1985), pp. 100–53.

'European Monetary Union', *The Economist*, 24 June 1989.

Fratianni, M., 'The European Monetary System: How Well Has It Worked?', *The Cato Journal*, Autumn 1988, pp. 477–501.

Friedman, M., 'Should There Be an Independent Monetary Authority?', in

Yeager, L.B. (ed.), *In Search of a Monetary Constitution* (Cambridge, Mass.: Harvard University Press, 1962), reprinted in *Dollars and Deficits: Inflation, Monetary Policy and the Balance of Payments* (Englewood Cliffs, NJ: Prentice Hall, 1968) pp. 173–94.

Friedman, M., 'The Political Economy of International Monetary Arrangements', in *Dollars and Deficits: Inflation, Monetary Policy and the Balance of Payments* (Englewood Cliffs, NJ: Prentice Hall, 1968), pp. 266–79.

Friedman, M., 'Monetary Policy for the 1980s', in Moore, J. (ed.), *To Promote Prosperity: U.S. Domestic Policy in the Mid-1980s* (Stanford University: Hoover Institution, 1984).

Hayek, F.A., *Denationalisation of Money*, Hobart Paper Special No. 70 (London: Institute of Economic Affairs, 1976).

Jordan, J.L., 'Monetary Policy as a Fiscal Instrument', *The Cato Journal*, Winter 1986, pp. 733–41.

Langfeldt, E., Scheide, J. and Trapp, P., 'The Case for Money Supply Rules', *Geld and Währung/Monetary Affairs*, Vol. 5, May 1989, No. 2/3, pp. 30–47.

Leigh-Pemberton, R., *The Future of Monetary Arrangements in Europe*, with a Commentary by Patrick Minford, Occasional Paper No. 82 (London: Institute of Economic Affairs, 1989).

Leijonhufvud, A., 'Inflation and Economic Performance', in Seigel, B.N. (ed.), *Money in Crisis* (Cambridge, Mass.: Ballinger, 1984), pp. 19–36.

Leijonhufvud, A., 'Constitutional Constraints on the Monetary Powers of Government', in Dorn, J.A. and Schwarz, A.J. (eds), *The Search for Stable Money: Essays on Monetary Reform* (Chicago and London: Chicago University Press, 1987), pp. 129–43.

Martino, A., 'La politica monetaria e il piano Werner', *Rivista di politica economica*, May 1971a, pp. 605–12.

Martino, A., 'Il problema monetario internazionale', *Nuovi studi politici*, May 1971b, pp. 77–81.

Martino, A., 'L'unificazione monetaria europea: problemi e prospettive', *Quinterni Economici della Cassa di Risparmio di Roma*, October 1976, pp. 11–17.

Martino, A., 'Verso una moneta europea?', *Quinterni Economici della Cassa di Risparmio di Roma*, October 1977, pp. 10–17.

Martino, A., 'Un nuovo ordine monetario europeo?', *Quinterni Economici della Cassa di Risparmio di Roma*, July 1978a, pp. 9–14.

Martino, A., 'L'unificazione monetaria europea: verso una soluzione intermedia?', *Thema*, No. 2, October 1978b, pp. 68–72.

Martino, A., 'La Comunità Economica Europea, a trent'anni dalla Conferenza di Messina', *Economia delle scelte pubbliche*, anno IV, Nos. 1–2, January–August 1986, pp. 103–7.

Martino, A., 'Riflessioni in tema di unificazione monetaria europea', *La Comunità Internazionale*, Vol. XLIII, No. 2, Second quarter 1988, pp. 181–91.

Martino, A., 'A Common Currency for Europe or Monetary "Union"?', in *A Citizen's Charter for European Monetary Union*, Occasional Paper No. 5 (London: The Bruges Group, 1989), pp. 15–19.

Romer, C.D., 'Is the Stabilization of the Postwar Economy a Figment of the Data?', *American Economic Review*, June 1986, pp. 314–34.

Simons, H.C., 'Rules Versus Authorities in Monetary Policy', *Journal of Political Economy*, Vol. 44, 1936, pp.1–30, reprinted in Lutz, F.A. and Mints, L.W. (eds), *Readings in Monetary Theory* (Homewood, Ill.: Irwin, 1951), pp. 337–68.

Vaubel, R., *Choice in European Monetary Union*, Occasional Paper No. 55, (London: Institute of Economic Affairs, 1979).

Vaubel, R., 'Currency Competition versus Governmental Money Monopolies', *The Cato Journal*, Winter 1986, pp. 927–42.

Vaubel, R., 'A Public-Choice Interpretation of the Delors Report', Statement at the Conference on the Political Economy of International Economic Organizations, Claremont, November 1989 (unpublished).

Walters, A., 'A Critical View of the EMS', *The Cato Journal*, Autumn 1988, pp. 503–6.

9 Central Bank Independence
Manfred J.M. Neumann

THE EUROPEAN AGENDA

Europe is in the midst of a historically unique process of fundamental reform. The driving vision in European politics apparently is to develop a European Union which will be both, economic and political union. While the debate on the political structure has hardly begun, the basic microeconomic principles of Economic and Monetary Union (EMU) have been set by the Single European Act and the macroeconomic principles will be fixed in the revision of the EC treaty.

At the present time the predominant vision of EMU is eventually to replace national currencies by a single European currency and to have it controlled by an independent European Central Bank. In the political domain it is often argued that the completion of the single market requires a single currency. To be sure, the free movement of people, of goods and services, of companies and of financial assets does not require a single currency. Nevertheless, the eventual acceptance of a single European currency promises the benefit of reducing the citizens' information and transaction costs and of promoting the integration of European markets. But this gain from currency standardisation is to be evaluated in the light of a possibly reduced internal stability of the European currency. At least in Germany sentiments are that a single European currency will be acceptable only if it is likely to be at least as good as Europe's anchor currency, the deutschmark.

The quality of a currency depends on the monetary constitution of a country. Therefore, the European Council is right in insisting on fixing the specifics of the institutional structure for the final state of EMU within the new EC treaty. But the question is whether this is the most urgent task for 1991/92. I am going to argue that it is preferable to shift the emphasis from final EMU towards concentrating instead on the question what measures should be taken in the immediate future at the level of each nation-state, in order to set in motion an automatic process of increasing convergence of the member countries' economic performances during the 1990s.

According to the official Delors philosophy, the only promising approach of making headway towards EMU is to fix the future final state as soon as possible and then enforce convergence towards that state by subordinating national policies to centralised coordination. This is an end-state approach. It is rather technocratic and interventionist in nature and violates the principle of subsidiarity. Moreover, the approach rests on entrusting the Committee of EC Central Bank Governors with the coordination of national monetary policies. But the problem is that most members of this committee are government-dependent figures who have to take orders from their own governments. For this reason, policy coordination à la Delors will always be liable to political opportunism, implying that convergence of national inflation rates at a level close to zero is unlikely to be secured. Consequently, the danger with this approach is that it may either lead to a split into a two-speed Europe or eventually force member countries into a big final jump, hence turn out very costly to the citizens of Europe.

The alternative approach towards EMU is preparing member countries for a peaceful competition for internal stability. It is based on the idea that an EMU-guided reform of national macro structures is an indispensable prerequisite for making headway in stability towards EMU, hence must not be postponed until the date of entrance into the final stage of EMU. The cornerstone of the approach is doing away with the politicians' power over monetary policy as soon as possible by providing national central banks with a status of true independence from governments. The traditional dependence of central banks on government is the source of excessive money growth which enforces permanent inflation.

The envisioned reform of national monetary constitutions is a liberal programme, as it is designed to limit government in the interest of the people. After all, it is not the people who are interested in inflation but government. As history shows, any government is tempted to exploit the state monopoly of base money creation as a convenient source of hidden taxation and as a means of artificial stimulation of the economy in pre-election time. It is for this reason that no government can credibly pre-commit to price stability if the national central bank is kept as a subordinated institution. Pre-commitment cannot be achieved by a declaration of good intent but only by constitutional change. Providing independence by a constitutional bill amounts effectively to tying the hands of the current government as well as of future governments.

If the alternative programme of reforming the monetary constitutions of EC member countries already during the current Delors stage 1 were accepted, Europe's central banks would no longer be prevented by governments from delivering what the citizens are entitled to receive: a stable currency. Once achieved, Europe's citizens would be better off. Moreover, with stable national currencies the necessary precondition would be met for making the final step towards EMU at minimal adjustment cost.

CONSTITUTIVE ELEMENTS OF CENTRAL BANK INDEPENDENCE

An incentive-compatible status of independence from government requires a central bank law based on the following principles:

1. prohibition of lending to public-sector authorities;
2. independence of instructions from other authorities;
3. exchange rate sovereignty;
4. provisions for the personal independence of central bank council members;
5. constitutional rank for the central bank statutes.

The first principle, prohibition of lending to public-sector authorities, appears to be widely accepted already in Europe as an indispensable element of central bank independence. It is less recognised that what needs to be prohibited is not just direct lending but any type of public debt acquisition by the central bank. Note that the principle will not hinder central bankers from indirectly facilitating deficit finance by providing faster money growth, should they wish so. The point is to protect them from having to comply with such demands.

The second principle, independence of instructions from other authorities, may be self-evident. But note that taking this principle seriously requires more than most governments are likely to accept. They must do without an explicit legal obligation of the central bank to support general economic policy. The German experience with a similar clause in the Bundesbank law is not encouraging. Unavoidably, such an obligation invites politicians to press for monetary over-expansion any time they feel they have to fight for their political survival.

The third principle is to transfer exchange rate sovereignty to the central bank. Typically governments keep the right to decide on exchange rate parities for themselves and ask central banks to support the rates chosen. But monetary policy cannot guarantee both stable prices and fixed exchange rates. Therefore, if the domestic value of the currency is to be preserved, the central bank must have the undivided power to decide on intervention and exchange rate matters. The experience with the EMS indicates that most governments value nominal exchange rate stability higher than domestic price stability and, moreover, tend to delay, if not to refuse, realignments. Therefore, it is interesting to observe that the president of the Federal Association of German Industries, Mr Tyll Necker, has recently joined forces in demanding that European governments transfer the sovereignty of deciding on exchange rate matters to central banks.

With respect to the fourth principle, provisions for personal independence of central bankers, conditions should be set such that upon appointment central bankers free themselves from former political ties and accept the objective of safeguarding the internal value of the currency as their personal leitmotif. To achieve this 'Thomas-Becket' effect, central bankers must receive long-term contracts which rule out the practice of re-appointment. Otherwise a banker may have the incentive of lobbying for another term by serving special political interests. A flexible scheme to achieve a sufficiently long term of office by means of a single contract is to combine a uniform retirement age with limits for appointment age. For example, retirement age might be set at 70 and appointment age at 45 to 55 years. Depending on the age of the appointee this would secure a contract length of 15 to 25 years. To be sure, the numbers chosen are arbitrary. What counts is the general design of the procedure.

A closely related question concerns the appointment of the president of the central bank. The traditional procedure of having government selecting and appointing the president fits the fact that in most countries the appointee is not supposed to be a policy-maker but just a compliant executor of the government's intentions. The traditional selection procedure is in conflict with the concept of central bank independence. A more congenial procedure is to have the members of the central bank's policy-making body, the central bank council, electing the president. Advantages of this solution over current practice are, first, the person chosen for president is not imposed from the outside, hence will not be the product of any specific political constellation; secondly, the central bankers are likely to choose from their ranks the one person they consider to be the true *primus inter pares*. Thus the president will not be an inexperienced freshman but an old hand. In passing, note that the term of presidency should be of shorter duration, say five to ten years, with the possibility of repeated re-election.

Taken together, the discussed elements make up for a central bank constitution that provides central bankers with more independence and power than any existing central bank law does. In comparison to this blueprint even the Deutsche Bundesbank is a relatively dependent bank. Indeed, the internal value of the deutschmark has not been fully maintained since the creation of this currency in 1948, though with an average inflation rate of less than 3 per cent this currency has remained much more stable than most others.

Central bank independence is sometimes charged with violating the principle of democratic accountability. But it seems that this charge is without force. The independent bank is committed to just one objective: monetary stability. This implies that the central bank council does not decide on a political trade-off, a decision that would have to be defended in parliament. The central bank's objective is fixed. All it needs is technical decisions with respect to implementation, matters which are better not politicised.

A SIDE-GLANCE AT THE PLANNED EUROPEAN CENTRAL BANK

It goes without saying that the sketched blueprint of central bank independence applies to both the national and the European level. It may be used as a benchmark to evaluate some characteristics of the currently discussed model of a 'Eurofed'.

To judge from the Commission's recent publication *One Market, One Money,* as well as from what has been leaked to the press, the current design of Eurofed conflicts with at least three of the principles outlined above.

First, Eurofed will have to support the general economic policy objectives defined at Community level and will be held democratically accountable for its actions. Second, Eurofed will not receive the right to decide on the exchange rate regime *vis-à-vis* third currencies or to negotiate international monetary agreements. And it is not in the least clear whether Eurofed will be entrusted with the decisions on intervention. Third, the members of the central bank will be appointed for the relatively short period of eight years and reappointment will not be ruled out. Moreover, the president of Eurofed will be selected by the European Council.

On these accounts Eurofed will certainly not be an independent central bank. And it will be interesting to observe whether the currently discussed set-up will survive the intergovernmental negotiations. One can only hope that Eurofed will not turn out to be a topcross of the Bundesbank with, say, the Banque de France.

PEACEFUL COMPETITION FOR INTERNAL STABILITY

Suppose Europe's national authorities would accept concentrating now on reforming national monetary constitutions along the lines of the blueprint of central bank independence sketched above. This would open up Europe to an evolutionary process of peaceful competition for internal stability.

The status of independence would provide each national central bank with the incentives, the means and the power to set in motion an irreversible process towards lasting internal stability at home. This drive for stability would not be at the expense of other countries because all central banks would move in a parallel, quasi coordinated fashion. There would be no explicit central coordination because each central bank would decide on its own what actions to take in order to stabilise the internal value of its currency. But the Committee of EC Central Bank Governors would continue to meet as the central bankers would wish to cooperate by exchanging information and discussing the exchange rate implications of their measures. Therefore, it would be a peaceful process which would not generate any major upheaval in foreign exchange markets or destabilise nominal exchange rates.

To be sure, the envisioned competition for internal stability is not to be equated with the Darwinian concept of currency competition where weak currencies are crowded out by strong currencies. The Darwinian concept is a matter for textbooks rather than for European reality. After all, the empirical evidence indicates that for the obverse of Gresham's law to work (good money drives out bad money) requires much larger inflation differentials than we have experienced in Western Europe in the postwar period.

The concept of peaceful competition for internal stability is fundamentally different from the Delors approach to the transition towards EMU. First, in accordance with the principle of subsidiarity the concept assigns the responsibility for monetary stability to the national level instead of to a supranational committee for the years of transition towards EMU.

Second, the concept offers a solid solution to the anchor problem by relying on fundamental changes of national monetary constitutions, hence the economic order in each member country, instead of on the coordination of national policies or processes. In contrast to the policies of independent central banks, policy coordination among government-dependent central banks is subject to political opportunism. Therefore, it cannot guarantee lasting convergence in stability.

Third, the concept provides an open, evolutionary approach towards EMU, as any European country can join the emerging zone of stability by executing the necessary reform of the domestic monetary constitution.

Fourth, as the reform work in each country would be guided by EC-wide recommendations but not be closely harmonised, the experiences of the countries with central bank independence at home would provide useful, new information for the final design of an independent European central bank. It is useful to recall that there is no need to fix the final set-up as soon as possible, given that a European central bank serves no function during the period of transition towards final EMU.

CONCLUDING REMARKS

It is beyond doubt that the proposed liberal concept is very demanding. After all, it requires politicians to bind the hands of government with respect to monetary policy and exchange rate matters, once and for all. But the liberal has no stake in defending the power of government, be it European or national government, if there is sufficient reason and evidence to suggest that this power is not used in the true interest of the citizen.

Declaring national central bank reform a matter of top priority for the immediate future has two major advantages over simply continuing along the lines sketched by the Delors Report.

First, it will provide a test for the national governments' seriousness with respect to transfering monetary sovereignty to a European institution at some future date. Europe's politicians use every occasion for publicly demanding that further headway is to be made towards an EMU in stability. Let them take the test. Any government which is not prepared to hand over monetary policy to the national central bank is unlikely to accept later on that an independent European central bank will eventually take over.

Second, if put through, the reform will initiate an irrevocable process towards lasting internal stability in each country. No longer will a country have the need to borrow credibility from another country through the exchange rate mechanism of the EMS, because national monetary policy will be committed to stability not by rhetoric but by structure. Consequently, it will be credible to the citizen. In comparison to today's situation, this would be a lasting achievement, even if it should happen that the final decision of replacing national currencies by a single European currency will never be taken.

To be sure, it will be no surprise to learn that most politicians are not really prepared to transfer sovereignty to their central banks now, if ever. But, if they are not ready for that, they must realise that the choices they will be left with are either to subordinate to the European rule of a possibly painful exercise of centralised coordination à la Delors, or to pay the price of instability in isolation.

10 A European Central Bank?

Pascal Salin

Most people interpret monetary integration in Europe as a system of fixed exchange rates which may pave the way towards the establishment of a single currency and a single central bank to replace present national currencies and central banks.[1]

This traditional approach is inadequate because it stems from a frequent confusion between the different possible meanings of the word 'integration'. Over the short history of European integration, there has been a shift of emphasis from the creation of a large common and competitive market to the elaboration of common policies and regulations.

In fact, economic *integration* should imply the possibility for markets to play their role, which means that people should be free to choose the goods they prefer regardless of the nationality of the producer. Competition increases the welfare of consumers and the efficiency of producers in such an integrated area.

Common policies aiming at harmonisation of taxes, regulations and interventions are often common policies to avoid or to limit free competition. Therefore, they can mean forced cartelisation and not integration of markets.

According to the Delors Report, the internal market calls for a single currency, a European competition policy, a regulation of takeovers, common policies on research, technologies, regional development etc. and strong coordination of macro-policies.

The traditional approach to monetary integration in Europe thus aims at constituting a cartel of central banks and monetary authorities and, ultimately, a European public monopoly, instead of increasing the freedom of choice for producers and consumers.

THE ULTIMATE GOAL: A SINGLE CURRENCY
FOR EUROPE?

European citizens do not especially need a single currency, but what they do need are good currencies, which means that they should be non-inflationary.

It is true that exchanging several currencies for a single currency decreases transaction and risk costs. But it also implies an increase in the degree of monopolisation of money production in Europe. The existence of more or less competing currencies in Europe has put a brake on the willingness of some monetary authorities to inflate. This discipline is likely to become looser with a single currency: public authorities will no longer fear potential competition with more stable currencies.

All over the world monetary authorities are inclined to adopt inflationary policies, either to finance public deficits or to offer voters the illusion of short-term prosperity. It is clear therefore that a sound monetary system would require institutional arrangements in order to impose a discipline on monetary authorities. Competition – i.e. freedom of entry into a market and freedom of choice – is the best possible discipline. Just imagine, however, the existence of a central bank in Europe with representatives of the different member states on the Board. Monetary policy would be the outcome of painful negotiations between diverging views from governments which are more or less in favour of inflation.

Drafting plans for monetary union, with a single currency, without specifying the rules for monetary management is frivolous and may lead to unwelcome events. The Delors Report on Economic and Monetary Union does not say a word about the institutional arrangements which could put a brake on money creation. As such, it is significantly deprived of much interest.

Far more important is the need to secure free movement of currencies and capital than to aim for a single currency and the harmonisation of banking regulations. An important role for European institutions would be to secure this freedom.

Fixed exchange rates (or the existence of a single currency) are not the norm according to which monetary arrangements can be evaluated. The main problem in money production is not the plurality of currencies, it is the public monopoly. The

Delors Report also suggests that a European system of central banks should be an independent institution, one which would be free from political interference. However, once more, the fact that it would be a monopoly is problematic, since most independent organisations work better in a competitive environment.

Let us imagine, for example, the case of a single European currency unit in the process of rapidly depreciating. The freedom of European citizens to select a different currency would have been removed, especially if ECU is protected against competition from 'non-European' currencies. Events are unpredictable, and if ever a single currency were to be created in Europe, it may happen that we have to face a situation similar to the present one in Brazil, for instance. Instead of having to use one single and very bad currency, would it not be better for Brazilians to have the choice of several competing currencies – issued, for instance, in the different states?

We should also consider lessons from the past. For example, in the United States, the states of New England, which benefited from less regulated banking systems, did not import the 1837 and 1857 monetary crises which developed in the more regulated systems of New York and even Great Britain. The diversification of banking regulations and of currencies may help parts of Europe to protect themselves from disturbances which may occur elsewhere. Those who suffer from such occurrences may learn from the experiences of others.

INTERMEDIATE STEPS

Following traditional lines of reasoning, the Delors Report calls for fixed exchange rates and reinforced 'cooperation' between European monetary authorities as a way towards a single currency. In fact, the fixity of exchange rates cannot be considered a legitimate goal for economic policy, any more than a single currency.

Fixed Exchange Rates

It is normally assumed that monetary integration means fixed exchange rates, and the traditional question in literature on the subject or in policy forums is the following one: How to increase the fixity of exchange rates between countries in order to improve monetary integration? However, this approach to monetary integration is similar to the general approach to economic integration which we have criticised, namely the one according to which integration does not mean a better functioning of markets – and, therefore, a high degree of diversity between competing goods – but a (forced) homogenisation of products between different producers.

There is a well-established principle according to which, under a fixed rate system, there cannot be an independent monetary policy. Unhappily, monetary authorities are largely ignorant of this principle. When choosing a fixed rate system, they cling to a symbol of stability, but they pretend, meanwhile, to embark into 'active' monetary policies. The inconsistencies which result from such behaviour are the real cause of numerous 'monetary crises'. Under such conditions, flexible rates would be preferable: perfect substitutability between various national currencies cannot be imposed, and it is not sufficient to pretend the contrary by occasionally fixing prices. Thus, there is a need to question whether monetary integration necessarily implies fixed rates and therefore cannot correspond to a regime of flexible rates.

Meanwhile, when monetary authorities adopt fixed rates without accepting the corresponding monetary policies, imbalances appear. Thus, a lot of technocratic and harmful devices are invented every year to protect badly-managed organisations, such as short-term or long-term monetary support between European central banks.

Monetary Cooperation

In the EMS all countries participating in the system are supposed to be on an equal footing. There are two ways to describe this system in operation. The first case is where there is no coordination of monetary policies between countries. If the member countries are implementing independent – and, therefore, inconsistent – monetary policies, the system is imbalanced and necessarily leads to 'monetary crises'.

The second case occurs when there is 'monetary coordination'. Clearly, the working of such a cooperative system is not easy to determine, since all monetary authorities should agree in advance on a common target for the amount of money circulating in Europe, and then determine consistent growth rates in the quantity of money in the member states. However, such a decision process is necessarily founded on insufficient information. *Such a system therefore cannot work without cooperation, but cooperation is nearly impossible.* This is the case with the EMS. In other words, cooperation is not good *per se*, as is too often considered in discussions about European integration, probably because integration is understood to mean 'integration of policies' and not 'integration of markets'. If it is agreed at the outset that integration implies the creation of public cartels, cooperation is necessarily thought of as being desirable. The EMS is just one example of this cartel approach.

It is very difficult to manage a *symmetrical* exchange rate system, as is the case in the EMS, especially when there are no explicit rules about the respective responsibilities of participants. What are the tools for adjustment? Which country has to adjust? These are some of the questions which are not explicitly answered in the EMS. This means that whenever exchange rate and monetary policies of some member countries are incompatible, solutions have to be found through difficult and lengthy negotiations. The reason, therefore, that cooperation is necessary and difficult is because it is a system based on discretion and not on rules: policy answers to difficulties born of inconsistencies in previous policies have to be negotiated each time they appear.

Whenever there is such a lack of general rules, coordination might be better than the absence of coordination, but it would be better to be in a system in which coordination would not be necessary (for instance, the gold standard, floating rates or a regime of competing currencies).

At this point, we can summarise the reasons the EMS arrangement is not optimal:

1. The main target of any monetary system should be to avoid inflation. In the EMS there is no such explicit target and no instrument to reach it.
2. There are no precise rules for adjustment and the distribution of respective responsibilities between countries. Adjustments are made according to a discretionary system.

3. There is little or no coordination of monetary policies, contrary to what is necessary in a symmetrical fixed rate system.
4. Consequently the fixity of exchange rates is not perfect, which means that the European monetary system is a 'non-system': one cannot blend in a consistent way two principles which are opposed to each other.
5. In spite of the claim for monetary integration, exchange controls still exist or have existed for a long time, mainly in France or Italy.

It is therefore not surprising that monetary crises do occur. The negotiations which take place on such occasions do not favour the development of some common 'European spirit', but, on the contrary, exacerbate the conflicts between more or less illusory national interests.

The Delors Report mainly endorses the present arrangement and it merely proposes some modifications, among which are a more extensive pooling of reserves and an increased role for the ECU.

Pooling of reserves

The Delors Report proposes a pooling of official reserves in some sort of a European Reserve System during the second stage of monetary integration. However, such a pooling has little meaning other than to illustrate once more the desire to reinforce integration between European countries through centralisation, instead of diversification and competition.

In order to understand fully what is implied by the pooling of reserves, it is necessary to go back to the basic question: What is the role of official reserves? In a fixed rate system, where central banks exist and are in charge of maintaining this fixity, reserves have a regulatory role. If the reserves of one given central bank decrease, it is a signal that its currency is too abundant and that there is a risk that a fixed rate cannot be maintained between that currency and other ones. According to the normal rule of the game (which is inherent to a fixed rate system), a more restrictive monetary policy has to be adopted.

It is difficult to manage a fixed-rate system because there are several decision centres and fixity can be maintained only as long as the various monetary policies are not inconsistent. The 'rule of the game' we just recalled is the efficient way to make this coordinating work in a decentralised way.

With the pooling of reserves there is a risk that this regulatory mechanism be weakened. It can lead to a dilution of responsibilities, and therefore to a loosening of adjustment processes. If the monetary policy of a central bank is too lax, the alarm signal – the loss of reserves – is no longer 'individualised'. The proposed European central bank would have access to practically unlimited common reserves. Here we come across a specific illustration of the fact that moral hazard is inherent in a centralised system. One may argue that such a situation would not be allowed to develop and that 'coordination mechanisms' between central banks would have to be organised in order to 'share the burden of adjustment' whenever it should be necessary. However, there is little to be gained by replacing decentralised and efficient methods of coordination by others which are more nebulous and by their very nature less efficient.

Strictly speaking, a fixed-rate system should determine that the central bank be little more than a sort of conversion agent, transforming foreign currencies into national currencies, on a one-to-one basis. At present, the monetary system of Hong Kong is perhaps the only example of such an organisation. Other monetary systems suffer from the fact that foreign assets are often only a small part of total assets held by central banks. If European central banks were to abandon their foreign assets to a central institution, the essential adjustment tool – fluctuations of foreign reserves – would disappear. It is curious that the members of the Delors committee should recommend a measure which is so clearly inconsistent with the basic principles of the system they favour, namely fixed rates.

A system of reserve pooling makes discretionary cooperation between central banks more necessary in order to prevent the system from exploding, but this does not mean that the system is improved. A preferable system is one in which discretionary cooperation between decision centres is not necessary. Unhappily, politicians and public opinion look very positively upon 'cooperation' but as Harry Johnson used to say, 'Cooperation is not necessarily good: thus the members of the Mafia are cooperating'.

The ECU

Europeans do not need the ECU, a constructivist creation of technocrats. The ECU is not a currency, it is only a way to label some specific claims and debts such as those between European central banks.

The ECU is not yet a currency since only official institutions hold ECUs and ECUs can be exchanged only against European currencies. When a central bank obtains a credit for its interventions on the foreign exchange markets, it is obvious that it can only use its ECU credits by converting them into European currencies, because non-governmental entities do not hold ECUs and they cannot be traded on the market. In short, the ECU is only a mechanism for requiring the central banks to hold a portion of their reserves in European currencies, to diversify their portfolios. But there is no indication that this corresponds to what the central bank would spontaneously have chosen to do.

One can imagine the ECU evolving one day into a real currency, held in the private sector. In view of that possibility, one can consider all the current efforts on behalf of the ECU as aimed at promoting a 'brand of money' not via the usual advertising techniques but through political marketing. This viewpoint is defensible, but the fact remains that as it is presently defined, the ECU is not a true currency. Representing a basket of currencies, its value in terms of goods evolves in a less favourable manner than that of the less inflationary currencies, but more favourably than that of the more inflationary currencies. Why would anyone choose to hold ECUs if he felt certain that a European currency, such as the DM at the moment, represented a better reserve of purchasing power?

The relative success of the ECU is due to two factors:

1. In some countries – as is the case in France – the ECU is the only numeraire, beside the national currency, which can be used to denominate bonds and overcome some exchange control constraints.
2. The ECU has benefited from gigantic free advertising in all official statements, echoed in the mass media.

PROPOSALS FOR EUROPEAN MONETARY INTEGRATION

We should avoid any forced process towards 'monetary integration'. However, a more spontaneous process of selection would be desirable. When there is free competition, producers diversify to compete with other producers. Customers select the best products, which may possibly lead to the selection of a limited number of competing goods or, in some special cases, of a single product. However, this selection process does not come about through coercion, for it is the result of countless consumers making a free choice.

From our previous analysis we can give a rapid evaluation of possible schemes for monetary integration in Europe.

The Present EMS Arrangement and its Improvement

The present EMS arrangement is one of the worst solutions to the European monetary problem, since there are different decision centres which have neither the possibility nor the will to 'coordinate' their monetary policies, although such 'coordination' should be inherent to such an arrangement. It is true that some improvements could be introduced, particularly by substituting the 'rules of the game' for discretionary decision-making processes. Thus, it could be decided that whenever an exchange imbalance appeared, the responsibility for an adjustment should lie in the 'deficit country': on the monetary authorities which are issuing a currency which tends to depreciate. It would be assumed that the 'surplus countries' operating a less expansionary, less inflationary monetary policy, would have no obligation to 'share the burden of adjustment'. However, it remains true that the worst solution to European monetary problems is one where mixed systems are trying to reconcile fixed and flexible rates. It is hard to see any justification for transitory periods of fixed rates, interrupted by discretionary exchange rate changes.

Perfect Fixity of Exchange Rates

The traditional myth according to which 'money is an attribute of national sovereignty', although contrary to historical facts, induces many newly-independent developing countries to consider that the creation of a 'national currency' is a priority. We know from many recent examples that this policy reaction has been the most efficient way of destroying an economy and preventing economic development. Similarly, it is usually considered – without any further economic analysis – that the ultimate goal of European integration is to substitute present national and public currencies for a European 'supranational' public currency.

In principle, we should not be completely hostile to perfect fixity of exchange rates (which implies that parity changes are not possible and that there is no flexibility band). It could even be true that perfect fixity might be preferable to present loose arrangements. All the same, there are at least three reasons to consider this orientation with caution:

1. We do not know if Europe is an optimal monetary zone and if European citizens would gain anything from perfect fixity. Only free competition can give us the necessary information. The selection of a single currency in place of the present multiplicity of currencies might be the 'natural' outcome of a process of competition, but we do not know. Therefore, we should give priority to a process of market selection and not to a constructivist approach which pretends to decide from the outset what ought to be the outcome of a so-called process of monetary integration.

2. Fixity *per se* should not be considered a defensible policy target. What people need is not a monetary unit which is perfectly substitutable with other monetary units, but monetary units which, to put it simply, have a constant purchasing power.

   From this point of view, the definition of rules to ensure efficient monetary management is more important than deciding to fix exchange rates. 'European integration' would be a costly exercise for Europeans if, for instance, a European central bank could impose upon them a single and very inflationary currency whilst stopping them from using another (European or extra-European) currency.

3. This proposal is incompatible with an evolutionary approach to monetary integration. The problem is to replace the present decision centres with one central one. When firms are merging to create a cartel or monopoly, there is a once-and-

for-all change within a very limited period of time, which modifies the whole decision-process. It is pure fallacy to believe that, as far as money production is concerned, a gradual change in the relative powers of the 'deciders' would be possible. But it is also true that if ever this conception of monetary integration were to prevail, there would not be enormous difficulty in changing the system overnight.

Competitive Solutions

These consist in letting European money-holders and money-producers decide which monetary systems they prefer. From this point of view I would certainly favour free banking. I shall not discuss this proposal because it may not be practicable for the time being. However, thinking about free currency competition may suggest practical solutions to some specific problems of monetary organisation.

There remain two categories of solutions implying limited competition. The first one is an (improved) status quo and we should not be against such a 'solution'. Politicians are not naturally inclined to be conservative because they prefer to feel that they have an influence on society by deciding upon important reforms, whether they are good or bad. In fact, we have already stressed that real integration should mean a free choice for consumers and producers. Free production of money does not exist in Europe, since national monetary authorities have granted themselves a local monopoly (the EMS being a cartel of producers with a more or less explicit sharing of sub-markets). Even if one did not wish to suppress these public monopolies, any increase in the freedom of choice of money-holders would mean a reinforcement of monetary integration, which already exists to a large extent. Future measures aiming at the liberalisation of monetary and financial flows would thus contribute to monetary and financial integration far more than the EMS or plans for a European central bank and/or single currency.

But initiatives can also be conceived on the production side. In fact, modern banks and financial organisations are producing many differentiated and sophisticated monetary and financial services. There is no reason to suppose that the optimal size of production is the same for all these activities. Only the spontaneous working of the market can reveal optimal sizes.

European financial and monetary integration requires more freedom for banks and financial organisations to participate in various 'coordination systems'. Let us take an example. The production of confidence and security is essential for the good working of any monetary-financial system. In most present systems, the central bank plays an important role in that respect, because it acts as a lender of last resort or as an issuer of regulations. Would it not be possible for European banks to adhere freely to various safety systems, such as insurance companies, in order to insure deposits? From that point of view. European authorities would reinforce integration by exerting pressure in favour of deregulation in member countries.

Secondly, some European politicians may consider that a symbolic move is necessary in the monetary field. The creation of a parallel currency, competing with existing national currencies, could be more than a symbolic step.[2] In effect, the parallel currency approach presents big advantages in comparison with the usual approach (exchange rate fixity with the final target of a single currency and a single central bank). It leaves the choice of the most desirable currencies to the spontaneous working of the markets, which means that exchange rates have to be freely floating between national currencies, as well as between them and the parallel currency. Freedom of choice exists, though within a limited domain.

Presently, the main problem may be an intellectual one. For decades, politicians have constantly pushed at public opinion the idea that further improvements in economic integration were impossible without monetary integration, and that monetary integration meant fixed rates and a single European currency. A more diversified, more progressive approach may not be easy to propose. I do not believe that there is sufficient reason to postpone this effort until such a time when the traditional approach will have been proved a failure.

Europeans do not need a common currency, but what they do need is freedom in monetary and financial activities. The most promising way towards European monetary integration consists in definitively suppressing all exchange controls, implementing freedom of entry for monetary and financial activities, and pursuing financial deregulation. A valid programme for monetary integration is a 'common market for currencies'. The principle of mutual recognition, which has been – at least temporarily – accepted for norms, should be accepted for currencies as well.

There is not one *single* view about European integration, the one which apparently supported by the EC Commission and many governments, which implies centralisation, harmonisation and bureaucratisation. Nevertheless there is a consensus in public opinion around these ideas, particularly in France. But this does not mean that people are right, since truth cannot be reached by majority voting. The alternative approach we are supporting lies on sound economic analysis and as such should not be dismissed.

Consequently, at the end of this presentation, I should like to express my sincere desire that some governments – for instance the British – will firmly oppose any step towards enforced monetary integration. Refusing to join the EMS would be the best contribution the British government could make to real European integration.

NOTES

1.   The present statement draws partly on former papers of mine, especially: *European Monetary Unity: For Whose Benefit?* (Brussels: Institutum Europeaum, 1980); *Monetary Areas and Choice in Currencies* (report prepared for the Conference on the 'The European Monetary System: Its Consequences for the Unity of Europe and for the International Monetary System', organised by the Instituto de Economia de Mercado, Avila, 31 March and 1 April 1989).
2.   In the 'All Saints' Day Manifesto' – signed by nine European economists – a constant purchasing power was suggested for the parallel currency. See 'A Currency for Europe – The All Saints' Day Manifesto for European Monetary Union', *The Economist*, 1 November 1975.

Part Three
Competition, Employment and the World Economy

11 Europe's Position in a Changing World Economy

Christian Watrin

After the devastations of the Second World War, Western Europe quickly regained her prominent role as one of the main areas of economic progress in the world economy. Today her nations belong, with minor exceptions, to the first world and the per capita income of her core countries (Great Britain, France, Benelux, Italy, Germany) rank among the highest in international comparisons.

In the late 1970s and the early 1980s Europe underwent a severe stagflation. Economic analysis developed the thesis that during long periods of peace rich countries sooner or later enter a phase of sclerosis or 'Eurosclerosis' which not only brings economic expansion to a halt, but causes stagnation together with increasing inflation, resulting in economic decline.

The economic expansion which started in 1982, and has not come to an end in countries like Germany,[1] has refuted this theory. Major changes in economic policies became possible, such as Thatcherism, Mitterrand's revision of his early socialist experiments and Kohl's policy to deregulate at least some areas of the German economy. Many claim as well that the European Commission's programme for a 'Europe without frontiers' was another important factor. Its supporters argue that the date 1992 has captivated European industrialists, economists and politicians ever since, and that the idea of a Western Europe which matches the economic strength of American and Japan has fascinated national leaders and is applauded by the general public in many countries. Indeed, many initiatives have been taken to prepare businesses for the internal European market. The EC has started a programme to dismantle the obstacles which, after a not very successful thirty-year period of economic integration, still remained and severely inhibited the free flow of commodities and services as well as the free migration of labour and capital within the Common Market.

Since November 1989 the unforeseen revolution in what can now be called the ex-Communist countries (ECCs) of Eastern Europe has changed this situation totally. Germany has been unified politically and economically. Poland, Czechoslovakia and Hungary are demanding to become full members of the European Economic Community (EC). The European Commission, which in the mid-1980s decided that its policy would be oriented towards 'deepening' the Community at least until 1992, and which had excluded any enlargement ('widening') before that date, is now confronted with a totally new situation. There is little doubt that the East European countries cannot manage the transition to a market economy without receiving for at least an extended period of time unilateral access to the West European market. However, despite democratisation in the former Soviet bloc countries and their adoption of a market order, Brussels authorities are remaining by the policy of deepening the Community. Their first argument is that they want to keep a united Germany inside the Western world and prevent it from following a neutralist policy; their second argument is that the East Europeans have only just started their economic transformation and that their economies are at a level which would not allow them to become full members very soon.

This policy puts heavy strains upon the new Germany. In absorbing the former German Democratic Republic with its run-down economy, the Federal Republic of Germany is undergoing the most difficult phase in its recent economic history. The financial burden of the unification process is growing tremendously. The democratised Eastern European countries are asking for generous financial help from Germany. The Soviet Union has received a large subsidy for promising to pull out her troops from East German territory within the next four years, and Gorbachev has asked for further financial help in order to prevent the collapse of the Soviet economy, which, according to many observers, is imminent.

These developments must be viewed against the background of very optimistic forecasts for the early 1990s; for instance, OECD projections foresee a steady real GNP expansion of approximately 3 per cent for 1990 and 1991. However, the hope that a sustained, satisfactory economic performance will prevail during the years to come is not only threatened by the Gulf War, but also by the enormous economic problems which must be solved in Eastern Europe.

This raises the question whether the EC countries will be able to create a greater European community under the rules of a market economy, thereby laying the ground for the development of a new prosperous area in the world economy. Whether this will be the case depends on the success of the economic unification of Germany, on the future results of the internal market policy and on the ability of the EC to avoid a 'Fortress Europe'.

GERMANY'S ECONOMIC UNIFICATION

On 18 May 1990, the two Germanies agreed to form an economic, monetary and social union which came into effect on 1 July. Then on 3 October of the same year the political unification was officially consummated. On 1 July the GDR currency was replaced by the deutschmark, thus creating out of the two countries one national market. Since then the Germans have not only shared the same currency, but there are also no obstacles to the free movement of labour and capital. Plans to dissociate the two national markets through an East German import tax were scratched at the very last minute.

The economic unification of the two Germanies within one day was the most severe shock-therapy ever applied in recent economic history. When the small Saarland was integrated into West Germany from 1957 to 1959, there was a three-year transition period, with the monetary union with West Germany being the last step taken in the whole integration process. In the case of the GDR, however, the monetary union was the starting point. This was, without a doubt, unique.

One of the main advantages of this shock-policy was that neither political parties nor interest groups which opposed the economic unification process had a chance to become sufficiently organised in order to put much pressure on the negotiations between the two states. The two governments acted very quickly in working out two treaties (named 'Staatsvertrag' and 'Einigungsvertrag') within a short period. Furthermore, there were no nerve-racking debates similar to those which have accompanied the European integration process over many years. Finally the political and military grip of the Soviet Union, which is still able to shake Eastern European countries as in the case of the Baltic states, was loosened. In addition to these political aspects, what have been the economic results?

The shock-therapy led to a situation in which all the inefficiencies of the former centrally administered East German economy became visible immediately. The highly monopolised firms, the so-called combinates (Kombinate), and the people's owned factories (volkseigene Betriebe) which recently came under the control of a state-run trust agency (Treuhandanstalt) must compete now with the much more efficient companies in West Germany, the EC and the world. That was foreseeable. Therefore, many economists argued that it would have been better to begin with an economic union with flexible exchange rates between the two countries. This would have meant that the East German economy would have had an exchange rate different from the conversion rates chosen by the contracting parties.[2]

Among these rates the most important one was the 1:1 conversion rate for wages. It put the former GDR under heavy deflationary pressure. Companies previously competing under the protection of a foreign trade monopoly, where their export products were priced on average at 4.6 East German marks for one deutschmark, have been forced to compete under conditions of a sharp revaluation. They had to decrease their prices, which some did, to avoid going bankrupt. Most companies, however, did not follow this line. They accepted subsidies handed out by the trust agency, which then led to a situation in which incomes rose (according to public funds channelled from West to East Germany), and where at the same time East Germans substituted the poor and lower-quality goods they produced with the higher-quality Western goods. The result has been that the amount of dead stock in inventories is rapidly increasing, and that industrial production is rapidly decreasing.[3] This has already caused many lay-offs (approx. 600,000) and many workers are employed only temporarily (approx. 1.5 million), which in many cases means imminent unemployment.

The employment situation has been aggravated by wage increases during the last few months. West German labour unions, eager to recruit members in the East, have put heavy pressure on employers to increase wages without paying much attention to the lower productivity of East German workers and the economic situation of their companies. Unfortunately, employers in the East German context are not employers in a normal market sense, but in many cases former members of the old Communist party elite which ruined the country. Their opposition to wage increases is not very strong; many of them hope to keep their positions by not resisting wage demands. Finally, there are many obstacles to dismiss workers. According to German labour law, dismissed workers have the right to demand a compensation depending on the time they are with a company, and there is further a mandatory rule that any new owner of a firm must continue all existing labour contracts at least for one year.

Despite these serious obstacles to investment, there are many politicians and quite a few economists who claim that East Germany could become a prosperous market not only for West Germany, but also for the EC and the rest of the world. They point to the fact that there are a great number of entre-preneurially minded people who desire to create their own businesses. If they succeed, labour demand will rise. In addition, many West German companies which had subsidiaries or even headquarters in the Eastern parts of the country before 1945 hope to revive their previous connections and invest con-siderable amounts of money in order to achieve a new foothold in their old markets.

From this point of view, the main problem is whether – as Schumpeter pointed out – the process of 'destruction' will be surpassed by the process of 'creative restructuring', i.e. the inflow of new capital, machinery and production methods and an increasing demand for labour. With the help of a dynamic growth process, the difficulties arising out of the collapse of many parts of the East German economy could be overcome after an adjustment period.

Thinking along these lines the European Commission fore-casts that West Germany will gain one extra per cent of real GNP growth through the economic unification process in the years to come and that the Community as a whole will grow an extra 0.5 per cent from German–German integration. West German economic research institutes are making similar

forecasts. The prosperous West German economy with its annual 3 to 4 per cent real growth rate will gain more momentum.
Like a huge locomotive, the Western part of the economy
will provide the power to pull along the poor and economically small East German economy, which produces only one-
tenth of the West German GNP with a relatively much larger
workforce.[4]

There are several preconditions which must be fulfilled in
order for such a dynamic catch-up process to occur. First of all,
the East German labour cost situation must not worsen. Because
productivity is low (on average 25 to 40 per cent of West German productivity) wages must also be low, otherwise the Eastern parts of the country would suffer from real wage-induced
unemployment. Second, private investors outside the former
GDR must be convinced that East Germany is a favourable
place for their investments. Third, the costs of plant closures
and employment reduction in the overstaffed factories must
not be excessive,[5] otherwise capital investment and restructuring efforts might not be attractive.

It is unlikely that these conditions can be met in the near
future. Even if they could though, the most serious problem
would still not have been overcome: the unclarified issue of
property rights. The two German governments have agreed
that property confiscated from private owners by the Communist government should be given back to the former owners
(with the exception of the expropriation initiated by the Soviet
military government between 1945 and 1949). From the equity
point of view, this policy is laudable; from an economic point of
view, it is a serious obstacle in the whole restructuring process.
In 1990 more than one million Germans and foreigners raised
claims on property expropriated by the Communists. These
claims are difficult to settle because the Communist party tried
to conceal all former property rights to land, buildings and
companies. For instance, land registers simply disappeared or
were destroyed; in many cases, it is by no means clear what
belonged to whom.[6]

A restitution policy, regardless of its legal justification, has
the disadvantage that it seriously impedes capital investments
by private individuals or banks outside the territory of the
former GDR as long as property-right claims are not settled.
The confusion regarding property rights provides an incentive

for innumerable, long-lasting and costly lawsuits over owner-ship questions.

Further, the costs of reorganising the run-down companies could be high in many cases. The two treaties on unification between the two Germanies make it rather costly to lay off workers. Many are protected by labour legislation until the end of next year, and in the case of lay-offs, a social compensation plan (Sozialplan) must be agreed upon between the manage-ment and the works council of the companies concerned. If there is no agreement between the parties, arbitration must take place and the outcome may be expensive for the compa-nies. From an economic point of view, scarce resources which might otherwise be used for investment are channelled mainly into private consumption.

At present, it is not possible to forecast how the legal obsta-cles to new investments will be dismantled. The new all-German government which came into office in January 1991 will be faced with rapidly growing unemployment in the East. Part of the unemployment will be the unavoidable outcome of the liquidation of the old centrally planned economy. In the previous system factories were overstaffed, huge numbers were employed in the enormous bureaucracy typical of a command economy, and many more were involved as full-time functionaires in the SED party with its much hated and feared State Security Bureau (Staatssicherheitsdienst). Therefore, it is no wonder that up to one million or more of the 8.5 million workforce in East Ger-many have to be counted as workers whose services are either no longer needed, or who were already among the 'hidden unemployed' in the old system.

Against this background East Germany's economic future does not look very bright. Nevertheless, the problems German politicians have to handle are complicated but not insolvable. If the right policy measures are taken, the huge public funds to be channelled into East Germany in 1991 will benefit people in both parts of the country. The German government has an-nounced that 140 to 150 billion German marks (US$100 billion) will be raised to finance the budget deficits in the five new states in order to improve the ruined infrastructure (for instance, the crumbling transport network and the malfunctioning telephone system) and to clean up Eastern Germany's disastrous pollution. If great parts of the public money would be invested and only smaller parts consumed this would have a considerable positive impact on Western business to put money into the former GDR and to make use of skilled workers in the East. Whether this will initiate an investment boom already by the second half of 1991 as many officials claim or whether the depressionary tendency will go on, depends on the determination of the government to follow a strictly market-oriented policy.

THE EC'S INTERNAL MARKET POLICY – WILL IT BE SUCCESSFUL?

The outcome of the internal market policy is the second important aspect of Europe's future role in the world economy. The authors of the Cecchini report,[7] which was initiated by the Brussels Commission, claim (without mentioning a time-period!) that the completion of the internal market will strengthen economic growth in the Community by approximately 4.5 to 7 per cent, that consumer prices will decrease considerably and that total employment will increase by 1.8 million workers.[8] Therefore, it is important to ask whether or not it is possible to complete a single market in just two years from now.

The European Commission's report on the topic appears very impressive. More than half of the 279 measures mentioned in the 1985 Cockfield report (which later became known as the White Paper on the completion of the Single Market) have been agreed upon. The Single Market programme has already changed the behaviour of many large businesses. Companies are revising their strategies in anticipation of the post-1992 market. Restrictions on capital movements, among the main obstacles preventing the integration of markets, especially capital markets in Europe, were dismantled in 1990. However, in contrast to a fully integrated national market, some important elements might still be missing after 1992. There will be no common tax structure in Europe during the years to come. Instead of harmonising VAT rates, a task the European Community has not been able to solve for decades, the governments seem to have agreed upon a system which on the one hand will make border controls unnecessary, but on the other hand will transfer control to the companies themselves. Importers and exporters will have to report their VAT liabilities to their national tax authorities. This makes it possible to eliminate the customs houses, which are a convenient place to execute the destination principle, but this policy will also mean the introduction of a very complicated clearing system among the member countries.

The most discussed topic on the European agenda is whether a common currency should replace the national currencies in the near future. After the publication of the Delors Report on a European Central Bank System (ECBS) some steps were taken in this direction; there seems to be a far-reaching consensus among the member states to continue with the project of instituting a common currency.

The central question to be raised is: will European consumers be better off in a single market with one common currency, or with competing currencies? Those who favour a common currency in Europe argue that the costs of cross-border transactions will sink, that the risks of exchange rate fluctuations will disappear, and that there would no longer exist the possibility of distorting competition through discretionary exchange rate policies. More importantly, it is claimed by the supporters of a single currency that there will be an end to capital flights motivated by expected exchange rate changes. They argue that this will promote the movement of goods in the common market and have a positive influence on capital formation and innovations. Because a single currency area enables capital to circulate free from administrative hindrances and exchange risks, it could migrate to those places where it achieves the highest yields, thereby providing the greatest contribution to overall economic prosperity.

Those who raise objections point out that a common currency under today's monetary conditions would not necessarily guarantee that a future European central bank would be able to perform better than the existing national central banks. Inflation has not been eliminated during the last four decades, and even the most stable currency, the German mark, has lost two-thirds of its internal value since 1950. The prospect of a European central bank with an all-European management and board disconcerts many Germans, who are afraid that its monetary policy might be not as stability-oriented as the German Bundesbank's. They fear that a European central bank might try to promote economic growth through inflationary policies, an economic strategy which has failed repeatedly over the last few decades, or that countries with large budget deficits[9] will press for an easy-money policy.

As far as the monetary constitution of a European central bank is concerned, there is a growing consensus that it should resemble the legal rules and regulations of the German Bundesbank. In other words, the Eurofed would be politically independent, the objective of its monetary policy would be price stability, and there would be neither the guarantee of bail-out if a member state of the currency union went bankrupt, nor would there exist a direct link between the European central bank and the EC's regional funds.

This is indeed an impressive list of normative rules; however, there are some problems in the Delors committee proposals and the policies that would be built upon them. The first is that the European Finance Ministers (Ecofin) could set external exchange rates, which the European central bank would then be responsible for carrying out. However, it is impossible for a central bank to follow the two goals of guaranteeing both price stability as well as maintaining exchange rates set by politicians. Eventually the result would be an impairment of the European central bank's ability to secure monetary stability.

Moreover, objections can be raised to the Commission's proposal that monetary policy in Europe should gradually become the responsibility of the European Community. The Delors Report proposes a two-stage procedure, the second phase of which is characterised by the increasing influence of the European Board of Central Bank Governors and three sub-committees which must agree on monetary matters. At the same time, the Delors Report proposes that during that stage ultimate responsibility should be held by the national central banks. This is obviously contradictory. There cannot be a European and a national responsibility for monetary stability at the same time. Thus there remains the concern that in practice, actual responsibility would tend to fall to the European authorities and render the national banks' responsibilities to mere formalities.

Finally, there are major differences in the monetary constitutions of the individual national banks in Europe at present. Most central banks are not independent of political directives. Some of them are in constant danger of being undermined by the political process, either through a change in the relevant laws, by the election of central bank governors who do not rank monetary stability very high, or by direct political interventions. Therefore, expectations should not be too high that political pressure from individual nation states concerning monetary stability will be able to be disregarded when creating a future European bank. Even under favourable circumstances, the outcome could very well be the familiar discretionary policy with its inflationary ups and downs.

British and German economists have made the proposal that competing currencies are a favourable alternative to a single European currency. Whether this is the case depends on several factors. The first is whether or not convertibility and the free flow of capital will exist in the future single market. Free capital movements have been introduced by all member countries, but according to the EC directives on capital movements, they can be suspended temporarily by escape clauses. This makes the European capital market integration unstable. However, if no country resorts to capital movement controls, free capital movements inside Europe will have a decisive impact on monetary discipline of the member countries. If under such conditions a participating country's currency were to inflate at a rate higher than the rate of the more stable currencies, a 'capital flight' from the weak to the strong currency is likely to occur.[10]

In our present computer age this could happen very quickly, especially in big companies which can easily switch from one currency to another. Long before the respective currency could be depreciated, it would be voted out in favour of the more stable ones. This would put heavy political pressure upon national currencies not to be thrown out of the market. Therefore, currency competition is an attractive alternative to a single European currency for those who regard monetary stability as the primary objective of monetary policies. Unfortunately, the Treaty of Rome does not guarantee irrevocable freedom of capital movements and unhampered convertibility. There are several articles (Articles 76, 108, 109) which permit member countries to resort temporarily to protective measures in case of 'capital flights', or when confronted with the danger that they might occur. In reality this would lead to economic disintegration and to disruptions in the proper functioning of the single market. Therefore, those in favour of monetary competition must strongly insist on the elimination of all escape clauses from the Treaty of Rome.

Whether this is politically feasible remains debatable. However, if the goal of economic integration in Europe is to be attained, all escape clauses must be deleted. If this course is followed, the proponents of a monetary union would also make an important step forward. Monetary policies would then be harmonised by market forces and exchange rates would fluctuate only within the very narrow band set by transaction costs.

Under such circumstances, proponents of a monetary union might call for an irrevocable fixing of exchange rates, i.e. the establishment of an exchange rate union. The economic conditions for a monetary union would then be fulfilled and monetary competition would work as if a common currency had been established. However, it might be better not to establish a monetary union under these conditions, because a much higher degree of monetary stability could be preserved under monetary competition rather than under the rules of a single European central bank, which cannot rule out the danger of at some point following a politically influenced monetary policy.[11]

The political question to be raised is which route the Community will take. In recent debates it has seemed that a single currency would be the final outcome; however, the debate has changed since the British proposal to introduce the ECU as a parallel currency has gained ground.

In addition to the details of the very technical discussion, some simple economic facts should be kept in mind by those who favour a single monetary unit in Europe. A common currency in an area with great regional and structural differences between the participating countries makes it politically necessary to raise huge amounts of public funds in order to be channelled into the respective depressed areas, otherwise the regional imbalances would become unsustainable and large-scale labour migration could cause serious problems. Equalisation payments among regions of a single nation are, however, already politicised, and wealthier regions are normally not willing to make payments to poorer regions. It is therefore likely that equalisation payments among European nations might create even more severe political version between member states than among regions inside individual nations.

Furthermore, a common currency requires a unified economic policy and restrictions on national fiscal policies. The printing press would no longer be available to finance budget deficits. However, it is still an open question whether the countries with high inflation rates and large budget deficits would be willing to change their fiscal policies in favour of a more stable currency.

As long as the EC is not a homogeneous economic area where differences in prosperity levels, especially between the Southern periphery and the wealthy Northern states, are greatly reduced, the economic preconditions for a successful common money are not fulfilled. A 'Union monétaire à deux vitesses' initiated by two or three central banks (for instance by France, the Netherlands and Germany) which would form a stability bloc might be a first step towards a single European currency. This would bring an element of monetary competition into the EC. However, this might also facilitate the growing risk that the other countries which pursue less stability-oriented monetary policies might resort back to capital movement controls if their respective currencies were put under pressure by the stability bloc. In the end this would lead to economic disintegration and not, as the 1986 Single European Act expresses in a paragraph heading, to an 'economic and monetary union'.

THE DANGER OF A 'FORTRESS EUROPE'

One of the reservations of countries outside the Community is that the EC authorities might follow a market-oriented policy among member countries but opt for a highly protectionist policy concerning outside countries. Indeed, the Community has played a poor role in the Uruguay Round, which in 1990 unsuccessfully tried to liberate international trade in goods and services. Protectionist tendencies are, however, also observable in other major countries. For example, the 1988 US Trade Act provides for a comprehensive set of protectionist measures, allowing industries to demand additional bilateral trade agreements and antidumping measures whenever they complain to have been hurt by so-called unfair trading practices. In addition, criticism of Japan is justified because of its barriers against import competition and government support for its business. Finally, Taiwan lowered its trade barriers only after much political pressure from the United States.

Despite these facts, however, the Community's own record concerning liberal trade measures with foreign countries is not convincing. The European Commission's agricultural protectionism with its inefficiencies and distorting results has made it especially vulnerable to the accusation of having destabilised world agricultural markets. Indeed, the Community's agricultural price policy produces huge surpluses which either have to be destroyed or sold on the world market supported by massive subsidies. Furthermore, the new forms of protectionism, the so-called voluntary export-restraint arrangements, non-tariff barriers and 'grey-area measures' in order to protect some industries against foreign competition, are increasing the worries and fears in non-EC countries about a 'Fortress Europe'.

The Community is not only confronted with its economic relations to countries outside Europe, but also with its European neighbours, the European Free Trade Association (EFTA) and the former Eastern bloc countries. The negotiations between the EC and EFTA aim at establishing a common market not only with free trade for manufactured goods, but also with fewer obstacles to labour and capital migration between the two trading blocks. From the EFTA point of view it is important that in contrast to the EC, which aims at a full economic and political union according to the Single European Act of 1986, the political and economic sovereignty of its members should remain untouched. One might question whether this will be the case in practice. Most Eurocrats agree that even in the case of a European Economic Area, some powers would have to be transferred to a supranational body, whereas those in favour of world-wide free trade claim that stable and enforced international treaties would be sufficient.

The European Economic Area has been under discussion for years. This is, however, not the case concerning the most recent development, namely the wish of the new democracies in Eastern Europe not merely to become associated members of the EC, but rather to gain full membership in the EC as soon as possible. Their argument is that the process of restructuring their badly ruined economies can only succeed if they gain full access to the Single Market. From the EC's point of view, these countries (which are economically much weaker than the members in the Southern periphery) will demand access not only to its markets but also to its regional funds. Either huge transfers of public funds will be necessary in order to balance the regional and structural differences, or large migrations of workers from East to West will result.

At present, the Community has not developed a policy to solve this problem. If the Eastern countries only become associated members of the EC, their economic situation would not improve significantly. The ailing Soviet Union is no longer a country to be regarded as a potential market, which further increases the economic importance of the EC market. If Poland and Hungary, for instance, were only to have the status of associated members they would not gain much from trade with the EC. As exporters of agricultural products they would only receive small export quotas due to the EC's fear that the European agricultural system might otherwise be undermined.

However, any postponement of economic expansion in the former Eastern bloc countries and a failure to increase their living standards would have serious repercussions in the debate between the proponents of a market order and the defenders of socialism. The Eastern European countries are transforming their economic systems from socialist command-economics to market economies with the expectation that they will gain in personal freedom and economic wealth. They cannot reach these aims solely by deregulating and liberalising their national markets, but they must also enter the European and world market, and participate in the world-wide division of labour. In other words, Europe, which according to the legendary General Charles de Gaulle stretches from the Atlantic to the Urals, cannot be confined any longer to the twelve countries which now constitute the EC. Europe as a historical, political and economic unit must be redefined from a larger perspective, embracing all the democratic countries which base their economics on a market order. Whether or not certain republics of the Soviet Union will belong to a democratic Europe in the future, though, is very doubtful.

EUROPE IN A GLOBAL CONTEXT

It is crucial for Europe now to redefine its political and economic position in the world. The 'iron curtain' between East and West Europe has been torn down. The Gulf crisis demonstrates that the previous bipolarity between the two superpowers has become obsolete. The United States is clearly the strongest military power currently, but as an economic power it will never be able to regain its role as the *économie dominante* which it played in the 1950s and 1960s. As the world's largest debtor with a huge current account deficit, a depreciating dollar and a very serious budget deficit crisis, the US can still be the *primus inter pares*, the first among equals, but no longer the country which sets the pace for the world economy.

Europe is not the tightly knit unit which many imagine it to be. The Single Market will stiffen internal competition, intra-European trade will still grow further, but there will be neither a full-fledged economic nor a monetary union by the end of 1992. There will continue to be, in one form or another, restrictions on trade under different national technical, health and safety standards. The introduction of temporary capital movement controls, which in practice might last quite a long time, is still possible. Finally, desirable or not, it will not be possible to instal a monetary union in the near future.

The question with which Europe's citizens are now confronted is whether they prefer to live under the auspices of a politically unified Europe, or whether they think that a loose confederation of sovereign states bound together by common values and a common cultural heritage is a preferable option. The former argument that Europe must achieve full political as well as economic unity has lost its strength because of the upheavals in the Eastern countries, but on the other hand it is once again gaining strength in face of the Gulf War.

Some political developments have strengthened the arguments in favour of a 'community of independent states'. Ten years ago, the now-famous Australian economic historian E.C. Jones wrote a book entitled *The European Miracle*.[12] He points out that the success of Europe and the Western World has not depended on her political unity and on her forming a great empire; on the contrary, Europe has been always the part of the world where rivalry among states prevailed and where countless wars were fought. Rivalry also means competition though. The kings, dukes and other rulers were always forced to take account of the fact that migration into neighbouring countries was an option for their citizens. Migration, or as Hirschman puts it 'exit', was also the lever which tore down the Iron Curtain in Europe. When the Hungarian government decided to let the East German refugees migrate to West Germany and when approximately a quarter of a million people took that chance within the space of a few weeks, the collapse of the communist governments was inevitable.

This demonstrates the long-run benefits of rivalry and competition between political and economic entities. Hence, a 'concert of independent states' where citizens live under the rule of law will protect not only individuals, but also create economic prosperity better than a highly centralised system could do. Europe's economic history in the second half of the nineteenth century and in the years before the First World War is an example of how the economic problems arising in a world of independent states can be successfully overcome.

During this period the flow of commodities and services as well as the movement of labour and capital were not impeded. The Europeans relied on a common currency, the old gold standard, and Europeans could even travel within Europe without a passport. Obviously this was not an ideal world, but at the same time it is in essence the goal aimed at by a great majority of Europeans today. A Europe of independent states tied together by international treaties, such as the Treaty of Rome, which establish freedom of goods, services and capital and free migration would also be a much better solution for the Eastern European states, which at present need not only help, but open markets to re-enter Western civilisation.

NOTES

1. At the beginning of 1991 there is a debate whether Great Britain and France have entered a recession. Since the outbreak of the second phase of the Gulf War which started with the Iraqi occupation of Kuwait on 2 August 1990, there are some doubts to be raised whether recessionary or inflationary tendencies will prevail during 1991.

2. Three conversion rates were created. For wages it was 1:1, for savings 2:1 (except for an amount of 2,000 marks per person which was con-

verted at a rate of 1:1), and for those who were selling Western goods on GDR markets before 1 July it was 3:1.

3. Industrial production fell in the second half of 1990 by approximately 50 per cent and also labour productivity which should have increased under the rules of a market economy decreased heavily.

4. The West German GNP in 1990 was 2.4 trillion German marks, whereas the GNP of the former GDR was only 272 billion marks. Total employment measures 28.2 million in the West and 8.5 in the East of the country. See Deutsches Institut für Wirtschaftsforschung, Wochenbericht 26/90 (28 June 1990).

5. Overstaffing was typical for the central command economy in the former GDR. It was one of the so-called achievements of the socialist system that there was a job guarantee for everyone – except political dissidents. This policy caused tremendous 'over-employment' in East German factories. Many West German employers point to the fact that approximately half of the Eastern workforce is redundant according to Western standards.

6. One good example of the prevailing chaos is the Swiss government's claim that the huge television tower, with which the Communist party wanted to demonstrate its technological superiority, was built on Swiss-owned land in East Berlin.

7. *Europe '92 Der Vorteil des Binnenmarktes*, 1988.

8. Cecchini Report, op. cit., p. 134.

9. For example, Greece, which had a deficit equivalent to 18 per cent of its GDP in 1989, or Italy with a deficit of approximately 12 per cent of its GDP in the same year.

10. In some respects the much used term 'capital flight' is misleading. A more correct description would be that the citizens of the country concerned vote with their money against their national currency in favour of a more stable one. In other words, freedom of capital movement creates competition among the currencies of the participating countries.

11. The above argument holds only under the assumption that the production of money is not a natural monopoly. If it were, the strongest currency would drive all the weaker currencies out of the market. But even then the history of a future Europe would be a history of the creation of a stable money and its social benefits.

12. Cambridge University Press, 1981.

12 European Competition Law
Daniel Oliver

INTRODUCTION

The American View

As you all can imagine, watching the development of the Single Market is particularly fascinating for an American – especially for one who believes in limited government. But right away that raises the question, how limited should government be?

And anyway, how *do* you limit the power of the state, and provide good government? At the Mont Pelerin Society meeting in Munich in September of this year, Nobel Prize Winner James Buchanan suggested that a central provision of any newly formed European community should be the freedom to secede. Is there a better way to encourage the observance of other contractual guarantees of freedom than to provide the right to pick up your bat and ball and go home if you don't like the way the game is being played?

Now that is an arresting suggestion, especially coming from an American. The history of our racial problems has tended to inhibit Americans from making too much of the right to secede, and that, I think, is too bad. Too bad, because we Americans, like other people, should keep freedom as our paramount concern, however much our forebears may have misused it. Certainly the threat of secession is one way to limit Leviathan and protect freedom.

US History: Commerce Clause

Limiting the lesser Leviathans was the goal of the US Constitutional Convention. It is widely believed, I suspect, that the driving force behind the formation of the US Constitution was a concern, not for economic freedom, but for what are known today as 'political rights' (which are mistakenly thought to be separate from economic rights). That in fact was not the case.

The problem the Constitutional Convention was called to solve was domestic trade protectionism – barriers to trade, erected by the several states, to protect their own citizens' special interests. The goal of the Convention was to promote freer trade.

The solution to the problem was the Commerce Clause in Section 8 of Article I of the Constitution, and the provision of Section 10 of Article I prohibiting the states from laying imposts or duties.

Now to some, calling a convention to provide economic freedom may not seem as noble as founding a new government to institutionalise, say, the Equality of Man. But I suspect people who think that way have not studied economic history, or simply have not bothered to recognise – or perhaps have steadfastly refused to recognise – the benefits, the political benefits, a free market provides to its participants. After the recent collapses of the socialist paradises, however, the benefits of a free market should be more apparent.

Part of the landscape of a modern free market is competition law. In theory, we – or as we often say in the US, We the People – want to encourage competition so that all people will reap the benefits a free market offers. We think competition will maximise consumer welfare ('consumer welfare' is another way of describing the general interest), and so we seek to thwart those who, whether in commerce or in government and at whatever level of government, would spoil the system and deprive others of the magic of the market.

The State has Goals Other than Competition

Straight off, however, we run into problems – at least those of us in the US run into problems, and I have no doubt those of you in Europe run into the same problems.

One problem is that it turns out to be the state that is the primary source of anti-competitive activity. We find, everywhere, the apparatus of the state captured by particular groups to promote their own special interest at the expense of the general interest.

The dirty little secret is we really don't believe in competition after all. (Why are we continually surprised the emperor has no clothes?) We pay lip service to the idea of competition through antitrust laws or competition laws. But those antitrust or competition laws are really just a kind of civic religion. If you look at the activities of the state, at least of the federal, state and local legislatures in the US, with regard to antitrust and other areas, you will see that the state is often – the cynic would say 'primarily' – engaged in granting exceptions and exemptions from the competition laws to firms and groups that have the necessary clout to influence policy-makers.

Examples of state-sponsored impediments to competition number in the hundreds or thousands and include: licensure laws, which erect barriers to trades and professions; minimum wages laws which, in the US, were designed to keep jobs from going to the South where labour was cheaper, i.e. more competitive; barriers to international trade; education policies, which require parents to send their children to state schools, which, not facing competition, are generally inferior to what in the US we call private schools; and, perhaps the most egregious of all, farm legislation – which costs the average European family of four almost £1,000 a year.[1] Can it be said that a legislator who votes for the typical farm programme *really* believes in competition?

Another problem is that the state tends to use the actual competition laws themselves for purposes other than promoting competition. In the US, the antitrust laws were used for years to protect small businesses, partly as pure protectionism for owners of small businesses, but partly as a social policy to protect a class of people who were thought to be, in some not well-defined way, particularly, well, virtuous, and whose survival in a competitive world, therefore, it was thought the state should make an extra effort to ensure. That policy may have been good for small businessmen (. . . except when it was they who wanted to sell out to large companies) but it was surely bad for consumers in general.

It is a constant challenge, in administering competition laws as well as other laws, to make them serve the general interest. It is the challenge that faces the competition authorities in Brussels.

EUROPEAN MERGER LAW

On September 21 of this year, as many of you know, a new merger regulation became effective in the European Community. The Regulation is sufficiently new that I will refrain from commenting on it in detail – because there aren't many details yet. Let me instead make some general observations on merger law, drawing on the US experience with administering merger laws in a federal system, and let me make some observations on other aspects of competition law.

Postwar Europe was, in some respects, like early America: barriers erected by the several European states prevented the development of a single, common market. Europe has spent years trying to solve that problem, but there is still considerable disagreement over how much power the central government should have.

To Americans, that looks like a debate over federalism – the doctrine that some powers are appropriate to the national, central government, some to the local governments. Federalism is refined by the principal of subsidiarity – the idea the government shouldn't perform a function that can be performed by the private sector, and a higher level of government shouldn't perform a task that can be performed by a lower level of government.

Defining the terms is easy. The problem is, people can't agree on what functions are properly performed by government, and they can't agree on what level of government should perform the functions they can agree are proper government functions.

Advocates of greater freedom tend to prefer a limited central government, but a paradox vexes those who advocate less central government as the means to more freedom. The paradox is that a limited central government may not be able to protect the people's freedom against encroachment by powerful local government.

US Antitrust Policy

In the US, during the 1980s the Reagan Administration had considerable success in deregulating – freeing up the market –

at the federal level, especially in antitrust. The Justice Department and the Federal Trade Commission substantially lowered the level of government interference in the market-place.

The problem was, and remains, however, that deregulation of antitrust seemed to some to create a power vacuum in antitrust enforcement. Politicians abhor power vacuums. State attorneys general are politicians. So ... in a number of merger cases, state attorneys-general blocked mergers that the federal authorities, after careful consideration, had concluded were not likely to harm competition.

The interference by the state attorneys-general impeded interstate commerce – and violated the principles of federalism and subsidiarity. The mergers the attorneys-general interfered with were national in effect, although, obviously, all companies (managers, employees) as well as people and firms connected to companies in the economic chain are located in particular states. Because some people may lose their jobs following a merger, the attorneys-general of the states where those people live have an incentive to ride to their protection and attempt to block the merger – and on the way, to ride roughshod over the principles of federalism and subsidiarity.

New EC Merger Regulation

The new merger regulation the European Community has just adopted will govern mergers in Europe – but it will not govern many of them. Only the biggest deals will be subject to scrutiny at the Community level, deals involving companies with a combined turnover of approximately ECU5bn ($4 billion). Current estimates are that only forty to fifty mergers a year will go to the Competition Commission, as against some 2,500 mergers that are vetted by the US federal authorities each year.

Some people in Britain don't want the European Community interfering in any but the largest mergers. That means, however, that most transactions will be examined by the individual countries who will then approve or disapprove them. Do those people really want, say, the France of Jacques Delors making the rules governing, and perhaps forbidding, a merger between two firms that are not British but that have a substantial number of customers in Britain? Or preventing a British buyout of a French company that would not be prevented by British rules?

That is what is about to happen – except in those few cases where the mergers are big enough to be governed by the European Community regulation.

The American Experience

The American experience suggests that a *limited* interventionist policy – a free market policy – enforced by the highest level of government, will provide the best climate for corporate restructuring and economic growth.

NON-MERGER EUROPEAN COMPETITION LAW

Mergers and acquisitions have been front-page news, and so all eyes have tended to focus on the European Community's new Merger Control Regulation. But there's more to competition than mergers. In fact, much of European competition law relates to other business practices – especially vertical distribution arrangements (arrangements between businesses on different levels of the production/distribution chain, e.g. manufacturers, wholesalers and retailers). A glance at this other part of competition law reveals that the hearts and minds of the Brussels bureaucrats don't yet give pre-eminence to freedom.

The goal of modern antitrust law in the US is consumer welfare. That means business practices – mergers, distributions, arrangements, whatever – are judged by whether they pose a threat to consumer welfare in terms of higher prices, reduced output, less innovation, and the like. Other considerations are for the most part ignored. The importance of consumer welfare as a standard is that it's the standard most conducive to freedom (what's good government for?).

In addition to focusing on consumer welfare, we use economic analysis to make objective judgments, and that tends to keep bureaucrats honest. Focusing on the general interest and using objective standards tends to limit the power of the state, and that promotes freedom – the freedom of consumers to get the best possible deal in the market-place, and the freedom of businessmen to do business *their* way. It's as important – more important? – to focus on the aspect of freedom as it is on the efficiency a market system provides.

But in the European Community, freedom and consumer welfare take a back seat in competition law enforcement. A different goal, the goal of 'integrating' the European Community, takes precedence over consumer welfare. As a result, not only do consumers lose some of the benefits a free market provides, but – the other side of the coin – businessmen are less free as well.

The European Community's basic competition law text is the Treaty of Rome. Article 85(1) of the Treaty prohibits ' . . . all agreements . . . which may affect trade between Member States and which have as their object or effect the prevention, restriction or distortion of competition within the Common Market . . . '

In a 1966 case involving the Grundig corporation, a manufacturer of consumer electronic goods, the Commission and the European Court of Justice made it perfectly plain they could find 'distortion of competition' without finding any threat to consumer welfare.

Grundig had entered into exclusive dealing contracts that contained territorial restrictions with dealers in various countries (dealers in each country were allowed to sell in only that country) – classical vertical distribution arrangements. It's tempting to conclude that the Commission simply didn't understand the economics: didn't understand that Grundig was limiting competition *between its* dealers in order to encourage them to compete more energetically with sellers of non-Grundig products. Surely Grundig thought its contracts would have an effect on the number of sales to consumers – and surely the effect they hoped for was not fewer sales (would they want to sell *less*?) but more sales . . . to happy consumers – a consumer welfare standard.

There are, it is true, some people (often demagogic politicians and musty pre-Chicago School economics professors) who argue that such vertical arrangements harm consumers. But the Brussels regulators understood (and understand) the economics, and in the Grundig case (where there was no suggestion of monopoly power) they conceded that Grundig's contracts could increase competition between Grundig dealers and non-Grundig dealers – and that that could benefit consumers. The problem was – the problem *is* – they didn't care. They held that Grundig's contracts violated the

Treaty because they 'distorted the interplay of competition', and impeded integration.

Both Grundig's freedom – its freedom to conduct its business in ways it thought was efficient – and the welfare of consumers were sacrificed to the standard of 'integrating the Community'.

But that's not all. In some cases the Commission's pro-integration standard may actually impede integration, and the sacrifice of freedom and consumer welfare will be for naught. If, for example, a manufacturer in one country of the Common Market wanted to sell its product in another country where consumers were not yet familiar with the product, it might lower the price there as an inducement to new consumers.

The manufacturer, of course, would want to prevent its dealers in that new market from 'transhipping' the products to other markets (other Common Market countries) where, because there was no 'introductory special', the retail price was higher. If the manufacturer didn't limit its dealers, they would be the ones to profit from the manufacturer's lower prices, and the 'introductory offer' programme would be less successful – hurting the cause of integration. Under European competition rules, however, both the lower price in the new market and restriction on transshipping would be illegal.

Although 1966 is a long time ago, *Grundig* is still valid law. Since then there have been enough decisions involving vertical business arrangements to leave no doubt that the businessman is not free to substitute his business judgment for the Commission's judgment. The substance of the law affects hundreds, if not thousands, of contractual arrangements. It promotes neither consumer welfare nor freedom.

The European Commissioners do, of course, grant exceptions and exemptions and 'negative clearances' by the hundreds – decisions that to some extent modify the effect of the *Grundig* decision. And sometimes the *Grundig* rule may be useful to consumers – the market doesn't always work perfectly. But the basic rule of European competition law is that consumer welfare and freedom will not be allowed to stand in the way of integration.

Perhaps back in 1966 when the Grundig case was decided (or back in 1957 when the Treaty of Rome was signed), persuading reluctant businessmen to be less parochial was the single most important policy objective. But today, when businessmen see Europe as already largely integrated – except for annoying government restrictions – freedom and consumer welfare should take precedence over integration. European competition policy needs to be rethought.

The European Commissioners can't hit – but they can't field either. Their procedure also needs to be rethought.

As we've seen, Article 85(1) prohibits ' . . . all agreements . . . which may affect trade between Member States . . .' In the judgment of the Commission, that covers just about every agreement, which would make them all illegal . . . except that the Commission has devised a system of granting exemptions, both to individual petitioners, and to 'blocks', or categories, of contractual arrangements. But the procedure is clear: parties are guilty until proven innocent, and that gives the Commissioners (politicians, with the powers of prosecutor and judge, making *ex parte* decisions) enormous discretionary power.

Enormous discretionary government power is not the stuff of political liberty. And presumably increased liberty is one of the goals of the new Europe – can the Europeans be uniting for reasons that don't include increased liberty and prosperity?

CONCLUSION

In the end, as at the beginning, the question is, what is good government for? Is there an answer other than: to promote liberty (and justice), which includes most especially promoting a free market – including a competition policy that protects people *from government* as well as from their fellow citizens.

Surely it is an act of Providence that liberty and prosperity go hand in hand. It might have been different. It might have been that to be rich required living in a socialist paradise. Or that to be free meant being poor. But Providence decreed otherwise, and we know now, most of us, that it is only liberty that can bring prosperity. And for that we should be thankful – and vigilant against encroachments on our liberty.

The collapse of the socialist systems may give us free market enthusiasts hope, but the continued bickering in the GATT over farm policies and elsewhere over school policies should give us pause – and remind us that as long as power tends to corrupt and a legislature is in session, competition policy is subject to being commandeered to push programmes that have little or nothing to do with promoting liberty and prosperity for all.

NOTE

1.   Richard Howarth, *The Common Agricultural Policy*, Occasional Paper No. 7, The Bruges Group, March 1990.

13 Industrial Relations in Europe

B.C. Roberts

It has long been an objective of the Directorate of Employment, Industrial Relations and Social Affairs of the European Commission to promote the harmonisation of the different national systems of industrial relations in order to bring about a unified European model. The inspiration for this objective is the belief of the Directorate that the unification of Europe's industrial relations systems – based on the Commission's notion of the best practices in the Community – would significantly benefit the trade unions, improve productive efficiency of all forms of enterprise, bring tangible economic and social benefits to employees, employers and the general public, and make a major contribution to the achievement of a European political union.

This paper will seek to show that the harmonisation of industrial relations in the Community will not easily be achieved, that its effects would not necessarily satisfy the assumptions behind them and that strengthening the unions is likely to have consequences which are likely to conflict with other goals the Commission wishes to achieve. It will be argued that the social action programme of the Commission associated with its harmonisation objectives is not a necessary condition for improving social conditions of employees, nor for bringing about an effective single market and a more integrated political union.

According to the Treaty of Rome, industrial relations are an area of economic activity in which the Commission should be mainly concerned to encourage cooperation between member states, to 'make studies and arrange consultations'. The type of European industrial system which the Commission is seeking to establish goes far beyond these limits and – will have significant disadvantages. It is likely to create an imbalance in the relations between employers and unions and cause distortions which will damage the efficiency and social benefits that the single market should bring. Furthermore, as a means of protecting the interests of workers (which is a primary aim of the Commission), it will duplicate what has already been achieved through other international institutions. The costs will include the creation of unnecessary uniformity and the entrenchment of bureaucratic intervention in employment relations.

THE COMMISSION'S CHANGING INTERPRETATION OF THE TREATY

The Commission's interpretation of its priorities under the Treaty of Rome has altered under the influence of changes in the economic and political climate, and the growth and consolidation of the Community. In the first decade after 1957 it was mainly concerned with establishing the Common Agricultural Policy. In the second decade, under the influence of much more turbulent economic and political conditions, it began to respond to the unrest in European labour markets by seeking to give the Community a more positive social role. This development was significantly influenced by problems of unemployment, a growth of immigration from Third World countries and serious social unrest in France and Italy at the end of the 1960s, followed a few years later by the effects of the recession caused by the first oil crisis. The resulting swing to the left across Europe led the Commission to propose a radical programme of social action.

In 1972, the principal recommendations made to a meeting of the heads of state were that the Community should adopt a wide range of social reforms designed to strengthen the role of the unions and give more power to the workers as well as protection to those in a weak bargaining position. This was to be achieved, *inter alia*, by directives that would increase employee participation, extend minimum wage legislation, give protection against sex discrimination, improve health and safety at work, provide help for younger workers and elderly employees and better housing for the low paid.

In 1974 the Council of Ministers' response to this programme for radical action was cautious. It accepted that the Community had a responsibility under the Treaty of Rome to take action 'with a view to realising the social aims of the European Union, in order to attain the following broad objectives: full and better employment, at Community, national and regional levels, which is an essential condition for an effective social policy; improvement of living and working conditions so as to make possible their harmonisation while improvement is being attained; increased involvement of management and labour in the economic and social decision of the Community and of workers in the life of undertakings'. The Council stated that these objectives might be achieved either by Community measures or by encouraging national social goals. This should be done, it emphasised, 'without seeking a standard solution to all social problems or attempting to transfer to the Community level any responsibilities which are assumed more effectively at other levels'.

The Council thus made a clear statement of what has come to be known as the principle of 'subsidiarity', thereby serving notice on the Commission that it would resist proposals that violated this principle. But since the principle was subject to the balance of power within the Community's decision-making institutions and ultimately to judicial interpretation, the Commission was able to choose to interpret the Council's words as approval for the general thrust of its social action programme and licence to seek its particular objectives.

The determination of the Commission to press forward reflected the strong commitment of the Commissioner who was generally a former trade unionist or close sympathiser, and within the staff of the Directorate of Employment, Industrial Relations and Social Affairs (known as DG5), who were supported by the pressures of the trade unions and the strong political support for socialist measures in most of the member states of the Community. Although the Treaty had said relatively little specifically about issues of central importance to industrial relations and the role of trade unions, it had said enough for the Commission to continue to press its social programme on the Council.

The Treaty of Rome (Article 117, para. 1), states that 'Member states agree upon the need to promote improved working conditions and an improved standard of living for workers so as to make possible their harmonisation while the improvement is being maintained.' This suggests that the authors of the Treaty believed that harmonisation would be an outcome of improvements in working and living conditions, rather than a specific means of achieving them. However, in the second paragraph of this Article the Treaty states, 'such a development will ensue not only from the functioning of the common market which will favour harmonisation of social systems, but also from procedures provided for in this Treaty and from the approximation provisions laid down by law, regulation or administrative action.'

The Treaty also lists (Article 118) seven areas in which the Commission shall have the task of promoting 'close cooperation between member states in the social field, particularly in matters relating to: employment; labour law and working conditions; basic and advanced vocational training; social security; prevention of occupational accidents and diseases; occupational hygiene; the right of association and collective bargaining between employers and workers.'

INTRODUCTION OF QUALIFIED MAJORITY VOTING

In 1986, during the negotiations for the amendment of the Treaty to bring about the single market in 1993, Article 118 was amended in one significant respect by calling on member states 'to pay particular attention to encouraging improvements especially in the working environment as regards the health and safety of workers, and to set as their objective the harmonisation of conditions in this area, while maintaining the improvements made'. In order to help achieve this objective 'the Council, acting by a qualified majority on a proposal from the Commission, in cooperation with the European Parliament and after consulting the Economic and Social Committee, shall adopt by means of directives, minimum requirements for gradual implementation having regard to the conditions and technical rules obtaining in each of the Member States.' This requirement was modified in the next paragraph by specifying that 'such directives shall avoid imposing administrative, financial and legal constraints in a way which would hold back the creation and development of the small and medium sized undertakings.'

The extension of qualified majority voting in place of unanimity which had been limited in the original Treaty to deal with specific distortions of competition by provisions within member states, put a potentially powerful weapon into the hands of the Commission to achieve its objectives. Although the use of the qualified majority was limited to issues of health and safety and was further limited by a new clause 100a – which specifically excluded provisions relating to the free movement of people and those relating to the rights and interests of employed people – a bold Commissioner can argue that virtually any aspect of employment has health and safety implications, or alternatively has implications for competition which entitles the Commission to seek approval by a qualified majority. The Commission has already exploited this deviously engineered and constitutionally dubious procedure in a number of proposed directives relating to pregnant women workers, part-time workers, temporary workers, and workers doing night-work and shift-work. More ominous is a reported statement by the Commissioner concerned that every opportunity to use this questionable device will be taken and many other directives are expected to follow in the wake of the adoption of the Social Charter, which was the culmination of a campaign vigorously pursued by the President of the Commission, Jacques Delors – a former trade union leader and socialist minister of finance in France – following the amendment of the Treaty in 1986. This campaign, enthusiastically supported by the trade unions and member states with socialist governments, was strongly resisted by employers' organisations throughout the Community who believed it would burden business with a mass of prescriptive social legislation which would reduce their competitiveness. The Charter was also opposed by the British government which feared it would greatly extend the role of the Community into areas it believed were the prerogative of the member states. Faced by a threat of veto by the British government, M. Delors tried to get round the unanimity rule by persuading a Council of heads of state to adopt a solemn declaration of support for the Charter, thus committing them in advance to supporting unseen directives necessary to give effect to the specific items it covered. Britain (which was the only country not to vote in favour of the Charter) made it clear that it would exercise its veto against any attempts to secure passage of directives which it thought undesirable and, in its opinion, were covered by the unanimity rule. There is no guarantee that this opposition will be successful.

CONVERGENCE, COERCION OR COMPETITION?

There is a strong case on both theoretical and pragmatic grounds against the Commission's desire to unify the differing systems of industrial relations and social benefits in the twelve member states. Implicit in the Commission's determination to harmonise national systems is the belief that this is a necessary condition for fair competition, and that this is best achieved by directives which would impose a uniform model of industrial relations procedures and substantive levels of wages and social benefits. This notion that social systems – the result of differing historical circumstances that have produced differing economic and political structures – can and ought to be unified by the imposition of a theoretical model, is somewhat akin to the fallacy of the Russian revolution which has been exposed with devastating effect in the last few years.

There has recently been much debate among academics about whether, under the influence of technological and economic change, industrial relations systems are converging. A case has been made out by some scholars that this is happening.[1] They have argued that as countries have industrialised they have developed institutions such as trade unions, which had their origins in the industrial revolution and the emergence of the market economy, leading to methods of pay determination and conflict resolution which have followed similar patterns in industrially advanced societies. Countries do borrow social institutions from each other, and this is to be welcomed, but there is much evidence that this element of convergence is not producing uniformity. Systems of industrial relations which have been exported abroad (such as the British model) have been greatly modified as they were adopted in the United States, Canada and Australia, and in African and Asian countries. Whilst there are similarities, such as the existence of trade unions, diversity in institutions and procedures is as evident as uniformity. There is no good reason for believing that diversity (which clearly exists in Europe) will inevitably be replaced by a uniform model simply because of a common market. Even with a federal Europe, it would take a long time for a uniform model to develop. The degree of convergence which has taken place is not a ground for believing uniformity can be safely imposed, or that it is an essential condition for economic efficiency or social justice.

A unified system based upon some theoretical concept, or what is believed to be *best* practice in member states, is likely to have damaging consequences. The evidence suggests that the larger the scale of an industrial relations system the more there are regional variations. Differences in local practices that reflect differences in local economic and social factors should be welcome as a dynamic response to the freedom to adjust in a market economy. Differences in structures and procedures ought not to be treated as 'market rigging' devices so long as they are open to other employers and workers and their collective organisations freely to adopt, and providing they impose no restrictions on movement of people, goods and capital. Indeed, it is the essence of an efficient market economy that it allows comparative advantages to be exploited. They should not be frustrated by spurious notions of egalitarianism.

GERMANY VERSUS BRITAIN

Despite such theoretical and practical objections, the Commission has since the early 1970s made resolute efforts to bring about harmonisation of industrial relations though it has been compelled to allow for some flexibility. It has sought to persuade the Council of Ministers to adopt directives which would impose common procedures of corporate management on the larger enterprises, including the establishment of European companies, worker participation, and procedures for informing and consulting employees. These directives were first introduced more than a decade ago modelled on procedures in Germany, thought then by the Commission to be the best in Europe; they have now been significantly changed so that they can be adapted to the differing systems in the European states. In short, for tactical political reasons, the Commission has considerably modified its concern to bring about harmonisation in order to accommodate the realities of diversity. In the light of this concession it must be asked why are these modified directives necessary? The answer is that DG5 has not abandoned its basic belief that a uniform model of industrial relations would produce better results in terms of corporate efficiency and social justice. If these directives do not go as far as the Commission would like, they add to the corpus of Community regulation of the industrial relations systems of the member states and are steps towards the Commission's long-term objective of imposing a uniform European model on differing national systems.

It is typical of a body driven by a desire to achieve a political goal by bureaucratic means that it cannot easily accept that the effects of its measures may be very different from those intended. This problem has long been recognised in industrial relations as exemplified by the process of collective bargaining. It may be inferred from various studies and documents published by the Commission that the staff of DG5 would favour a system which encompassed collective bargaining agreements at three levels: the enterprise, sectoral (i.e. industry-wide) and Community-wide.

In Germany the system of sectoral bargaining agreements has worked relatively well. That is to say it has resulted in wage levels not unduly inflationary and agreements reached without significant costs from industrial conflict. In Britain by contrast, where there used to be a two-tier system of sectoral and enterprise bargaining, sectoral bargaining has virtually disappeared in the private sector and bargaining primarily takes place at the level of the enterprise or undertaking. Days lost from strikes in Britain, though low in many enterprises, are much more numerous than in Germany, and really substantial losses occur at the sectoral level, especially in the public sector. The main reason for this difference arises from bargaining in Britain being largely dominated by a concept of adversarial employment relations activated by shop stewards who have the power and legal right to call strikes subject to approval by a ballot of employees. In Germany sectoral agreements with union officials are administered at the enterprise level by Works Councils which are autonomous bodies required by law to represent all employees, whether union members or not, and have no legal right to strike. Enterprise bargaining thus has quite a different significance in the two countries. Similarly there are important differences in the public sector where the right to strike has been legally and institutionally constrained in Germany to quite a different extent than in Britain.

Marked differences also apply to employee representation on boards of directors. In Britain, where workplace industrial relations are usually conducted as a bargaining process, there is a general distrust by workers of employee directors, as shown by the experiments in the post office and the steel industry. The German model of co-determination, through supervisory boards on which employees have minority representation, would work quite differently in the British context, since its principal effect would be to strengthen union bargaining power. The fact that there are many effective models of participative industrial relations, including the highly successful models introduced into Britain by Japanese companies, proves that changes can be made in the classic British pattern, but bitter union opposition has limited this development to a tiny fraction of companies. Participational systems of this kind are to be welcomed, but they must be tailored to British circumstances and call for highly skilful management and supportive union representatives. It would be of great benefit to Britain if all British employers and employees would discard their adversarial attitudes in favour of the German and Japanese preference for solutions to employment and problems through peaceful processes based upon trust and cooperation, but there is certainly no guarantee that such would result from employee participation models imposed by directives from Brussels.

TRADE UNION INFLUENCE

Trends in Europe suggest that the policies on which the Commission seeks to base its system of industrial relations may in certain aspects be out of date. The Treaty of Rome does not mention the role of trade unions and employers' organisations other than to endorse the right of association and collective bargaining between employers and workers. Nevertheless, from its early stages the Commission has regarded the unions as a highly significant 'social partner', perhaps even more so than employers' organisations. The influence of both organisations on the Commission and the European Parliament, as well as on the Council of Ministers through their weight with national governments, is considerable, but varies according to the colour of the ruling parties in the member states. Provision is not made in the Treaty for the representation of unions and employers' organisations on the Economic and Social Committee which has an important constitutional role. The treaty states 'The Committee shall consist of representatives of the various categories of economic and social activity, in particular representatives of producers, farmers, carriers, dealers, craftsmen, professional occupations and representatives of the general public.' Despite lack of specific reference to unions and employers' organisations, both are strongly represented and exert a considerable influence.

There are many other influential advisory and consultative committees on which the unions and employers' organisations have membership or access. One of the most important channels of influence is through the Social Partners Bureau attached to the office of President of the Commission. Through this office, with the aid of the European Trade Union Confederation (ETUC) and the Union of Industries of the European Community (UNICE), direct access to the President, Commissioners and senior officials can be arranged.

It has often been claimed that the unions have shown a much greater aptitude than the employers in exploiting the opportunities to lobby the Commission and Parliament, although officials of UNICE vigorously deny it. The truth is that under pressure from the unions the Commission has shown an increased readiness to shift the balance of Community law in favour of the workers' organisations, and has thereby forced the employers to react more positively. A crucial question for the future is whether the influence of the unions will become less effective as a result of their decline in membership and influence, visible in most member states.

The most dramatic fall in union membership has taken place in France where in the private sector it is probably not more than 5 per cent of the labour force. In Britain membership has tumbled by more than four million in the past decade, falling from 58 per cent to below 40 per cent of the labour force. In the Netherlands membership has come down from about 40 per cent to not more than 25 per cent. Significant falls have also occurred in Germany, Spain, Portugal and Greece. Only in

Belgium and Denmark have numbers held at substantially higher levels and this has been mainly due to the support the unions have enjoyed from the corporatist wage fixing system in the former and from the union linked social insurance system in the latter.

The evidence points to falling interest in union membership, not only in the European Community, but across the world. Similar declines have occurred in the USA, Japan, Canada and Australia. There is much discussion of the cause of these declines and opinions differ, but the most important factors seem to be the effects of rising prosperity, decline in state corporatism and a desire of workers for greater freedom to move occupationally and geographically and more liberal policies of employers in the private sector. The growth in the philosophy of human resource management is of increasing importance. This philosophy has been fostered by changes in the technological and market environment, which call for a flexible and cooperative response which can only be effectively achieved if managers and workers accept a mutual responsibility for the success of the enterprise for which they work. It requires a shift from collective bargaining to industrial contracts which provide job security, career development, pay and other conditions of employment that recognise the contribution of workers to corporate performance as individual employees rather than as members of a union which seeks to impose standardised conditions of employment, disciplined support of restrictive work rules and inflationary tolls on essential change.

As union membership has declined in the private sector, in most countries it has become more concentrated in the public sector. There can be little doubt that this is due to the absence of commercial pressures and the influence of bureaucratic factors related to the scale of operation and rigidity of the rules surrounding the contract of employment, which is a feature of the work process in the public sector. In addition, employment relations are sensitive to political influences and public pressures which encourage, to a far greater extent than in the private sector, the desire of employees to belong to trade unions. This growth of public sector unionism has been accompanied by a rising level of militancy and strike action in many countries. The withdrawal of labour in essential public services as a means of securing improvements in pay and working conditions has raised fundamental questions of its legitimacy and the need for reforms which would protect the public interest.

FROM NATIONAL TO LOCAL BARGAINING

In spite of these trends the Commission seems mainly concerned with an increasingly outdated concept of two sides and is determined to give the unions as much support as it can muster. It funds a European trade union research centre and gives great emphasis to what it calls 'social dialogue' with the unions and employers' organisation. It displays no awareness of the adverse effects its policies might have on the great majority of the European public who are not members of unions. In this respect the efforts of the Commission to promote European-wide collective bargaining is of especial concern. Jack Peel, a former British trade union leader and Director of Industrial Relations of the Commission, has set out clearly the way in which the Commission has tried to do this. In his book *The Real Power*,[2] he suggested that it would be naive or foolish to believe that industrial relations can be kept permanently in a national context when new international dimensions are being created for industry by the Community. He points to the whole new code of labour legislation which is being created by the Commission at the European level. He revealed that a register of collective agreements was being kept by the Commission to facilitate international comparisons of industrial activities. A network of joint committees serviced by the European Commission had been brought into existence. 'They are bipartite, sectoral and voluntary and currently cover eight industrial sectors: coal, steel, sea-fishing, agriculture, road transport, rail transport, footwear and inland waterways.'

In spite of its encouragement by the Commission, Euro-bargaining at the sectoral level has been strongly opposed by European enterprises and their employers' organisations. The trend in all the European countries, to a greater or lesser degree, is away from sectoral bargaining to bargaining at the enterprise and undertaking levels. Bargaining everywhere in the Community takes place within the boundaries of each member state. Every attempt which has been made by the unions to persuade employers to enter into transnational bar-

gaining arrangements has been rejected and has failed to mate-
rialise, yet this perverse move against the tide remains a prime
objective of DG5.

The trend away from centralised forms of collective bargaining was clearly shown in a survey by the OECD in 1986.[3] Declining
inflation, increased competitiveness, the need for improved
company performance, the advent of new technology and the
need for greater flexibility all contributed to this development.
A more recent study made for the European Commission con-
firms that this trend is likely to continue; it concluded 'company wage negotiations, the break-up of wage structures and
new sectoral discussion topics seem likely to be the main features of future wage bargaining in the Community.'[4] In spite of
this finding the report stubbornly insists that the aim of a
European wage policy should be to maintain sectoral bargaining as a means of protecting the social role of the unions.

Sectoral bargaining will probably continue in the public sector
in most countries, but in spite of the support it may receive
from the Commission Community-wide sectoral bargaining is
unlikely to be easily established without the Europeanising of
the unions. Tentative ideas in this direction have recently been
mooted by some British trade union leaders who, faced by
declining memberships and serious financial deficits, have initiated exploratory talks with their European counterparts. They
might ponder that transnational mergers of companies have
proved extremely difficult, compared with the success of outright
takeovers of foreign companies and the establishment of off-
shoots by direct investment overseas. If unions try to match this
development, they will find that by comparison the problems of
joint mergers of unions will be horrendous, while any attempts
to take over foreign unions would almost certainly give rise to
bitter opposition. The less ambitious notion of joint bargaining
arrangements transnationally have been sought by the unions
in the past, but have had no success in the face of employer
hostility.[5] Had they succeeded they would have brought higher
labour costs, inhibited labour, mobility and efficiency.

EFFICIENCY AND EMPLOYMENT AT RISK

The European Commission's aim to strengthen the unions

supported by socialist majorities in the European Parliament and the Economic and Social Committee, and to promote collective bargaining, risks conflicting with the primary objective of the Treaty of Rome to achieve a competitive free market economy, by giving them power to impose restrictions on the free movement of labour, capital and goods. It was for this reason that when the United States passed antitrust legislation against cartels to fix prices, the courts held that this law also covered fixing the price of labour collectively. Although the Clayton Act was subsequently passed to protect collective agreements between individual employers and unions, there has been a reluctance on the part of employers' organisations to negotiate sectoral agreements, especially across state boundaries. Although probably not unlawful there have been relatively few such agreements for fear of possible legal actions.

The wide-ranging restrictions which the Commission proposes to impose on employers, through the many directives it would like to see passed, together with the help it is giving to the unions to increase their bargaining power, will inevitably be to the advantage of union members at the expense of the majority of employees in the Community who are not union members who will be left behind as costs rise and inflation is encouraged. The industrial relations and social policies pursued by the Commission to equalise wages and social benefits are neither necessary for promoting a single market, nor for achieving social justice for employees. The effect will be to raise costs in the less efficient firms and in the less efficient countries. If unit labour costs are raised relatively the unemployment rate will rise where this occurs. This result would be the very opposite of what the Commission wishes to achieve. The danger is that the Commission would seek to avert this consequence by increasing subsidies from the social and regional funds which must exacerbate the danger of misuse already existing with the programmes of social assistance such as the notorious Common Agricultural Policy. What is to be feared above all is that the Commission's ambitious programme of social action will sacrifice the very benefits of competitiveness which is the prime promise of the single market. The real objective of many who support the Charter was confirmed by the leader of the Labour Party's MEPs at the 1990 Labour Party Annual conference. He declared that the Social Charter was the first step to the achievement of a 'Socialist Europe'.

As a means of increasing social justice the social action programme is otiose. All members of the community are already covered by the international labour code of the International Labour Organisation which establishes minimum standards in the social policies. All members of the Community are also members of the Council of Europe and with the exception of two have ratified the Social Charter which was first adopted by the Council in 1961, which covers all the issues itemised in the proposals of the Commission for a Community Social Charter.

The Council of Europe's Social Charter has an advantage over the Commission's Charter by allowing member states an opportunity to accept those parts of the Code that would reinforce the member states' own social legislation and so avoid the distortions and disruptive effects of an arbitrarily imposed social code. The proposal has already been made by the Council of Europe to the European Commission that it should adopt the Social Charter of the Council. This would entail the Community accepting the voluntary procedures of the Council instead of the more legalistic methods of the Community. It is of significance that in the regulation of transnational standards of radio and television broadcasts where the Council has a voluntary code the Commission adopted the Council's code after failing to obtain the agreement of member states to compulsory standards enforced through directives. This precedent is one that the Community would do well to follow in the case of the Social Charter.

The prime reason the Commission wishes to regulate industrial relations and social rights in the Community is the influence of powerful elements in the Commission, the European Parliament, the Council of Ministers and the Economic and Social Committee who wish to create a centralised state committed to a social market economy in which trade union collectivism has a dominant role. Such a development is likely to be at the expense of economic efficiency, individual rights, competitiveness, and valued national sovereignty as well as a discouragement to the EFTA and Eastern European countries which we should all be ready to welcome as members of the Community. The industrial relations systems which have evolved over more than a century, and are rooted deeply in national cultures, are more likely to perform effectively if they are free to evolve as they are doing, to meet the challenges of European integration and the single market and not forced into a common mould based upon concepts of corporatism and collectivism that have been outdated by the evolution of open market economies across Europe, from the Atlantic to the Pacific rim.

NOTES

1. Kerr, Clark, Dunlop, John T., Harbison, Frederick and Myers, Charles A., *Industrialism and Industrial Man* (Harvard University Press, 1960).
2. Maidenhead: McGraw-Hill, 1979.
3. OECD Report, *Flexibility in the Labour Market* (1986).
4. Commission of the European Communities, *Wage Bargaining in Europe*, Social Europe Supplement 2/90.
5. Northrup, Herbert R. and Rowan, Richard L., *Multinational Collective Bargaining Attempts: The Record, Cases and the Prospects* (Philadelphia: The Wharton School, University of Pennsylvania, 1979).

14 EC Employment Law
Tim Johnson

INTRODUCTION

It is in the area of employment law that EC law has affected most directly the lives of individual citizens in the United Kingdom. Nowhere has the influence been more marked than in the areas of equal pay and sex discrimination. In a series of landmark judgments the European Court of Justice and the House of Lords have recognised the shortcomings of our own law on sex discrimination and have established new rights in areas such as retirement and discrimination on grounds of pregnancy. It has been necessary to amend our own Equal Pay Act of 1970 and to pass new legislation, notably the Sex Discrimination Act 1986 and the Employment Act 1989, to bring law in the United Kingdom into line with the requirements of Article 119.

To appreciate fully the impact which EC laws have had on our own law in these areas, it is necessary to put more recent developments into their historical context. Only by doing so is it possible to distinguish the rights which UK governments have intended to confer and those which have been created, unwittingly, by the Treaty of Rome.

HISTORICAL BACKGROUND

The TUC passed a resolution calling for equal pay for women as long ago as 1888, but it was not until after the Second World War that the idea that women should receive the same rates of pay as men gained widespread support. This change in attitude may have been related to the increase in the number of women working outside the home during the war and subsequently.

The Labour government which came to power in 1964 committed itself to introducing equal pay. The main issue of principle was whether the law should provide for equal pay for 'work of equal value' or for equal pay for 'the same work'. The former, equal pay for 'work of equal value', was a principle advocated by the International Labour Organisation. The Government took the view that if Britain was to become a member of the EEC, it would be sufficient to comply with the requirements of the Treaty of Rome. At the time, Article 119 was understood to require only that women be paid equally for the same work. It was not thought to be necessary to provide a right to equal pay for work of equal value. This was not to be the last time that a UK government underestimated the implications of Article 119.

So it was that Barbara Castle introduced the Equal Pay Bill in the House of Commons and the Equal Pay Act 1970 subsequently became law. The implementation of the Act was delayed until 1975 to give employers a chance to bring the pay of women into line with that of men. It provided a right to equal pay in two different situations:

1. where men and women are doing the same 'or broadly similar' work; and
2. where men and women are doing work which is different, but which has been found to be equivalent under a job evaluation scheme.

(In addition there were provisions in relation to discriminatory collective agreements, which were subsequently repealed.) The basis of the Act was, and still is, that every contract of employment contains an equality clause which is triggered in the situations described above. The equality clause modifies any terms in the woman's contract which are less favourable than those of the man. Thus if a woman is paid less than a man doing the same work she is entitled to the same rate of pay.

To enforce this right an employee applies to an industrial tribunal. The issue for the tribunal is essentially one of fact – is the work done by the woman and the man either broadly similar or has it been rated equivalent under a job evaluation scheme?

During the five year period before the Act took effect, many employers introduced job evaluation schemes and the average female weekly wage increased significantly as a proportion of average male earnings. Since that period female earnings as a proportion of male earnings have not changed significantly.

EC INFRINGEMENT PROCEEDINGS

Because the UK government believed that the Treaty of Rome required only that the people doing the *same* work receive equal pay, it saw the UK legislation as going beyond the requirements of the Treaty. In 1972, the year in which the UK joined the EEC the European Commission was asked to draw up a Social Action Plan providing for, among other things, the approximation of the legislation of member states concerning the application of the principle of equal pay for men and women. The Commission initially proposed that a directive should define equal pay in terms of equal pay for work of equal value. The UK government objected to the principle of equal pay being formulated in these terms and, as a result, the Equal Pay Directive was drafted ambiguously. It states:

> The 'principle of equal pay' means for the same work or for work to which equal value is attributed, the elimination of all discrimination on grounds of sex with regard to all aspects and conditions of remuneration.
>
> (Article 1 of Directive 75/117)

Member states were required by Article 2 to introduce into their national legal systems measures to enable *all* employees to pursue a claim to enforce the principle of equal pay.

The UK government believed that the Equal Pay Act 1970 complied with the requirements of the Directive. At the final Council of Ministers meeting they placed on record their view that 'the circumstances in which work is considered to have had equal value attributed to it' for the purposes of Article 1 'are where the work is broadly similar, or where pay is based on the results of job evaluation', i.e. the circumstances covered by the Act.

The Commission, when it reviewed the application of the Directive in 1979, did not agree. It therefore started infringement proceedings against the UK which were eventually heard by the European Court of Justice in 1982. The Commission argued that the UK had failed to implement fully the Directive because the Equal Pay Act only enabled a woman to obtain equal pay for work of equal value where her employer had implemented a job evaluation scheme. The UK government, on the other hand, argued that the Directive required that there be a remedy only where equal value has been 'attributed' to the work.

The European Court of Justice held that the Directive required member states to enable employees to claim equal pay regardless of the employer's wishes. Thus any statute which did not achieve that result prevented the aims of the Directive being achieved. The Court therefore held that the UK government has not fully complied with the Directive.

As a result the UK was obliged to amend its equal pay law to give effect to the EC principle of equal pay for equal work. As the government had resisted the infringement proceedings, it was not surprising that they chose to describe the difference between the Act and the EC requirements as 'a small gap'. They therefore decided not to start again with a new Act of Parliament, but rather to make minimal amendments by Ministerial Order.

THE HAYWARD CASE

Hayward v. *Cammell Laird Shipbuilders Limited* (No. 2) [1987] 1 All ER 503

Julie Hayward was one of the first to rely on the Equal Pay (Amendment) Regulations 1983. Her case caused much controversy. As it involved novel issues it was not until the House of Lords gave judgment in 1987 that it was finally decided. The most controversial aspect of the decision was the leap-frogging effect which the employers anticipated might result. Julie Hayward, unlike the men to whom she compared herself, was entitled to a lunchbreak, free lunches and additional holidays. As a result of the Lords' decision she was entitled to retain these benefits and have the same rate of pay as the men. The logical consequence seemed to be that the men were entitled to the benefits Julie Hayward enjoyed. The consequences of the Hayward case did not, however, stop there.

Statutory Construction

The Hayward case was followed by several further important cases on equal pay. Perhaps the most important was *Pickstone* v.

Freemans plc [1986] IRLR 335. The House of Lords held in that case that the fact that a man was employed on the same terms as a woman claiming equal pay for work of equal value did not prevent her claim from proceeding. The decision is important because it acknowledges as a principle of statutory construction that the words of a statute passed to implement EC obligations are to be construed, provided that they are capable of bearing that meaning, as being intended to give effect to that obligation. Since *Pickstone* any ambiguities in Acts passed to implement EC obligations, have to be construed having regard to those obligations. As a result of *Pickstone* the Equality Act 1970 has to be construed in the light of the Equal Pay Directive. This process has been taken a step further by the decision of the House of Lords in *Litster* v. *Forth Dry Dock and Engineering Co Ltd* [1989] IRLR 161 where the House of Lords held that the Transfer of Undertakings Regulations 1981, which were also passed to implement an EC Directive, are to be construed so as to conform with the UK's obligations under the Directive and the rulings of the European Court of Justice which have interpreted it 'even though, perhaps, it may involve some departure from the strict and literal application of the words which the legislature has elected to use'.

THE ROLE OF THE EUROPEAN COURT OF JUSTICE

One of the most surprising aspects of the development of EC law has been the role played by the European Court of Justice. As the history set out above in relation to equal pay shows, the European Commission were given the role of developing the principles of equal pay set out in Article 119 and promoting directives obliging member states to implement national laws to implement these EC obligations. The ECJ has in several instances reached decisions which are in advance of proposals made by the Commission, showing that directives and proposed directives have been unnecessary. The effect of these decisions of the ECJ is to recognise that rights already exist under Article 119 and that they are directly enforceable by citizens and member states without the need for national legislation in conformity with EC directives. A good example is the *Barber* case (see below).

THE MARSHALL CASE

One case which cannot be omitted from this account of the impact of EC law on employment law is *Marshall* v. *Southampton and South West Hampshire Health Authority (Teaching)* [1986] 2 All ER 584. Mrs Marshall was obliged to retire at the age of 60 when, if she had been a man, she would have been allowed to continue until she was 65. Although the Health Authority's policy reflected the state pension age, and despite the fact that issues relating to retirement are expressly excluded from the scope of United Kingdom equal opportunities legislation, Mrs Marshall argued that her compulsory retirement was contrary to the EC equal treatment directive.

Directives take effect in a different way from Articles of the Treaty of Rome. Some Articles, for instance Article 119, have been held to be directly enforceable between individuals in member states. Those Articles are described as having 'horizontal' direct effect. Directives are binding on member states as to the result to be achieved. Individuals can therefore enforce a directive against the State but not against other individuals. This means that employees of the state can, in certain circumstances, directly enforce rights conferred by a directive, but employees of companies in the private sector cannot.

The European Court of Justice held that Mrs Marshall, who was employed by an Area Health Authority, has been discriminated against. As a direct consequence Parliament passed the Sex Discrimination Act 1986 which made it unlawful under UK law for employees compulsorily to retire men and women at different ages.

THE BARBER CASE

Barber v. *Guardian Royal Exchange Assurance* [1990] IRLR

Guardian Royal Exchange made Mr Barber redundant in 1980 at the age of 52. The company's contractual severance package provided that members of the pension fund were entitled to an immediate pension provided they had attained the age of 55 in the case of a man or 50 in the case of a woman. Accordingly, Mr Barber was not entitled to an immediate pension. Instead he received a contractual redundancy payment, a statutory payment and an ex-gratia payment. It was not disputed that if he had been a woman he would have been entitled to an immediate pension and that the value of that pension would have been greater than the package he received.

Mr Barber claimed that he had been unlawfully discriminated against in breach of Article 119 of the Treaty of Rome. His claim was rejected by both an industrial tribunal and the EAT. The Court of Appeal took the view that his case raised five questions of EC law, and referred these questions to the European Court of Justice for a preliminary ruling.

The European Court of Justice ruled as follows:

1. The benefits paid by an employer to a worker in connection with the latter's compulsory redundancy fall within the scope of the second paragraph of Article 119 of the Treaty, whether they are paid under a contract of employment, by virtue of legislative provisions or on a voluntary basis.
2. A pension paid under a contracted-out private occupational scheme falls within the scope of Article 119 of the Treaty.
3. It is contrary to Article 119 of the Treaty for a man who has been made compulsorily redundant to be entitled to claim only a deferred pension payable at the normal retirement age when a woman in the same position is entitled to an immediate retirement payment as a result of the application of an age condition that varies according to sex in the same way as is provided for by the national statutory pension scheme. The application of the principle of equal pay must be ensured in respect of each element of remuneration and not only on the basis of a comprehensive assessment of the consideration paid to workers.
4. Article 119 of the Treaty may be relied upon before the national courts. It is for those courts to safeguard the rights which that provision confers on individuals, in particular where a contracted-out pension scheme does not pay a man on a redundancy an immediate pension such as would be granted in a similar case to a woman.
5. The direct effect of Article 119 of the Treaty may not be relied upon in order to claim entitlement to a pension, with effect from a date prior to that of this judgment, except in the case of workers or those claiming under them who have

before that date initiated legal proceedings or raised an equivalent claim under the applicable national law.

The Guardian Royal scheme was a contracted-out contributory scheme. The judgment makes it plain that as a result of the decision of the ECJ in *Bilka-Kaufhaus* v. *Weber von Hartz* [1986] IRLR 317, benefits under contracted-in schemes also count as 'pay' for the purpose of Article 119. It would appear that the decision also applies to non-contributory schemes.

The decision of the European Court of Justice in *Barber* v. *Guardian Royal Exchange Assurance Company* is likely to prove to be one of the most important employment law decisions ever made. It has fundamentally changed the pension entitlement of male and female members of occupational pension schemes throughout the European Community by outlawing discrimination in the benefits such schemes provide.

Many people have accepted it as a fact of life that women are entitled to retire on a full pension at an earlier age than men. With effect from 17 May, the date of the judgment, this is no longer the case, at least so far as private occupational pension schemes are concerned. Men in occupational pension schemes are now entitled to retire with a full pension at the same age as women, and to disregard rules relating to early retirement which are less advantageous to them. Equally, women are now entitled to death-in-service benefits as widows. These general principles are clear. It is less clear what retrospective effect the decision will have. The judgment states that Article 119 may not be relied on to claim entitlement to a pension with effect from a date prior to that of the judgment, unless proceedings had already been initiated on that date. This suggests that men who have already retired cannot use Article 119 to recover pension benefits for a period prior to 17 May 1990. It is not clear, however, whether it also means that rights under Article 119 can only be enforced with effect from 17 May, i.e. that men and women who retire after 17 May 1990 will only be entitled to equal benefits with effect from that date, or whether equal benefits will only accrue in respect of service after that date.

Despite the obvious importance of the decision and the need to bring UK national law into line with European law, the government has, as yet said nothing about its implications.

There are strong parallels between the present situation and the situation after the European Court of Justice decided *Marshall*. In both cases the ECJ found that Article 119 conferred rights on individuals which had not previously been recognised in UK national law. The *Marshall* case recognised that discriminatory compulsory retirements ages were unlawful. Initially, there was some confusion in the UK as it was not clear whether the rights recognised in *Marshall* would be directly enforceable by bringing a claim in an industrial tribunal. Subsequent events showed that in practice tribunals are prepared to accept that they have jurisdiction and they have been prepared directly to enforce rights under Article 119. The position is still not entirely free from doubt, but cases brought relying on the *Marshall* decision have beaten a path for applicants relying on the *Barber* case to follow.

There are some important differences between *Barber* and *Marshall*. First, given that European law requires that benefits are levelled up rather than down, the adjustment to equal pension ages is likely to be much more costly. Secondly, the *Marshall* case arose from a directive and was therefore enforceable only by employees of the state. Not only was the number of employees affected smaller, but in many cases the government had, to a large extent, control of the remedy: it could in many cases allow the relevant women to stay at work. Thirdly, the number of men wishing to retire at 60, given the chance to do so on a full pension, is likely to be greater than the number of women wishing to work until 65.

In the UK the benefit received under an occupational pension scheme is generally linked to the state scheme. Although this decision does not directly affect the state pension age, it is difficult to see how the government can legislate for occupational pension schemes without also indicating how it proposes to deal with the equalisation of the state pension ages. The costs of equalising the state benefit upwards would be enormous and the government is in a very difficult position.

It was some time before Parliament passed the Sex Discrimination Act 1986 to bring UK law into line with the *Marshall* case and a further period elapsed before it subsequently came into force. There are good reasons to believe that it will have to act more quickly to bring UK legislation into line with the *Barber* decision.

15 Economic Disarmament: Prosperity, Interdependence and Stability

The Hon. Francis Maude

The end of the 1980s was a period of change in international affairs unprecedented since the 1940s. The postwar order was transformed. In 1989, the year of revolutions, Communist hegemony was swept away in Central and Eastern Europe. In 1990, international relations were further transformed with the near-unanimous rejection of Iraq's aggression against Kuwait by the United Nations, and its determination to reverse it. Meanwhile in Western Europe we have been making our own revolution, as the European Community's unique model of cooperation has rapidly evolved.

The 2+4, the EC twelve, the NATO sixteen, the Council of Europe 23, the CSCE 35 – the arithmetic can be bewildering, but in each organisation the last two years have seen fervour, ferment, debate and construction. In each, new structures have been built, as well as new roles and new relationships. The petrification of the Eastern bloc, which for 45 years permitted stability in Europe at a dreadful price for its participants, has given place to flux and plasticity. And we all revel in the chance that comes so seldom to exploit this plasticity, to help mould the new international order. We are all architects now.

I possess a globe puzzle, a spherical Rubik's cube, in which the world is divided into segments which can be rotated round the surface of the globe in three axes. The aim is to return each segment to its proper position, the right way round and the right way up. It is fiendishly hard, even for those for whom the geography presents no difficulties. The real world in the past two years has seemed not dissimilar, with blocs breaking up, and countries, even whole continents, being realigned.

It is perhaps inevitable that the world's attention should have been captured by this glamorous, high-profile, fast-moving activity, whose dramas are so entrancing for the participants. It is, after all, the red meat of diplomacy.

But away from the limelight, in dark corners in Geneva, have been proceeding discussions less dramatic, much less glamorous, frequently mundane, but which ultimately matter more. These are the arms reduction talks of economics, whose substance is no less than the dismantling of the protectionist arsenals of the world.

Less sexy than START and SALT, than CFE and CSCE, than NATO, than EC or UN, this is the GATT, the General Agreement on Tariffs and Trade. On these talks has been hanging the future of the open world trading system, the source of Adam Smith's 'Wealth of Nations', which is the key to world prosperity and hence to peace and stability.

The trading impulse is as old as human history itself. Traders, as much as statesmen, generals, scientists and philosophers have shaped the course of history. Columbus was originally looking for a trade route to the Orient, and the trading impulse in various guises helped to establish the British Empire in India, Africa and the Far East, and led to the opening up of China and Japan in the last century. In our own century the breakdown of the world trading system in the 1930s and the subsequent exacerbation of the Great Depression was at least one of the factors responsible for the destabilisation of the Weimar Republic in Germany.

General examples like this can be multiplied, but the point is clear: trade is important in political as well as in economic terms. It has mattered more than ever since the Second World War. Within the broadly stable and liberal multilateral framework of the GATT, burgeoning trade has been essential to the growth and wealth of the world economy. It has brought increasing economic interdependence and cooperation and, by mobilising common interest through self-interest, greater international stability.

It is this key connection between prosperity, interdependence and stability that I want to examine.

The purpose of this paper is to put the case for making trade as free as it can be made, as the underpinning foundation of peace and order in the world.

THE CASE FOR FREE TRADE

John Bright, that outstanding partisan for free trade, spoke of 'that commerce which is everywhere the handmaid of freedom and civilisation'. The classical theory shows that free trade is a positive-sum game. It permits countries to exploit their comparative advantage in certain goods and thereby to optimise output, consumption and efficiency. Producers can more fully exploit economies of scale and consumers can enjoy wider choice. The competitive spur of open markets encourages entrepreneurship and innovation in each domestic economy.

By contrast, protection almost always entails loss to the economy. Sheltered behind protective barriers, an economy uses resources less efficiently, costs are higher and choice is reduced. Overall competitiveness suffers. Arguments for protection are sometimes advanced in terms of correcting 'market distortions': for example, to allow an industry time to develop its long-term comparative advantage. But governments are always worse judges than the market of where the advantage lies, and intervention to promote adjustment generally ends up perpetuating inefficiency. Temporary restrictions become permanent. Where studies have sought to quantify the costs of protection their conclusions suggest it is high: 7 per cent of annual GDP in Brazil, 6 per cent in Pakistan, $10 billion annually in the US textile sector alone.

Moreover, protection risks retaliation by injured competitors. Protection lobbies in one country provoke retaliation lobbies in others. The disastrous consequences of 'beggar-my-neighbour' protection were evident in the 1929–32 depression. A trade recession was compounded by the destruction of the liberal trading order.

The US Smoot-Hawley tariffs of 1929–30 set off a retaliatory wave which abrogated the multilateral principle. Britain, France, Japan and the Netherlands introduced imperial preference. Germany, France, Italy, Japan, Eastern Europe, Latin America and others introduced quantitative controls on trade. World trade in manufactures collapsed by 40 per cent. World manufacturing output fell by 35 per cent. GDP in the countries now part of the OECD fell by 18 per cent (28 per cent in the US). By contrast, in the recession of the early 1980s there were no very significant increases in protection, world trade in manufactures held up, and manufacturing output and OECD GDP fell in 1982 by only 3 per cent and 0.6 per cent respectively.

The theoretical case against protectionism and its first cousin, retaliation, is thus confirmed by empirical experience. But the argument is not new. Sir T.H. Farrer summarised the consequences of protection neatly in a splendid Board of Trade publication of 1881:

> ... as all experience shows, protection breeds protection, and, once established, is most difficult to get rid of ... Retaliation is not calculated to effect its object; it is calculated to effect the very opposite. It grows upon itself. It provokes additional retaliation, until the nations are hopelessly alienated.

THE POSTWAR EXPERIENCE

A look at the development of the postwar economy underlines the benefits – and increased interdependence – which freer trade has delivered.

The GATT emerged from the common international effort, beginning at Bretton Woods in 1944, to lay the foundations of an international economic system which would avoid the strains and mistakes of the 1930s. Tariff reduction was also stimulated by Marshall Aid, which was made conditional on mutual removal of barriers to trade and payments.

Seven rounds of GATT negotiations in the period to 1979 succeeded in reducing tariff levels very substantially – to averages of under 6 per cent in Canada, Japan, the US and Western Europe. In the period 1950–88, world output increased more than threefold, while world trade increased at least tenfold. Average real GDP growth in the OECD countries was 4.0 per cent a year in the period 1950–73, and a slower but still respectable 2.4 per cent in the period 1973–87. As one would expect, the importance of trade to the major economies increased sharply. The OECD ratio of trade to GDP rose from 16 per cent in 1950 to 28 per cent in 1986. The facts speak for themselves: lower tariffs have accompanied increased trade, output and wealth.

There is nothing exclusive about the benefits of free trade. The World Bank's *World Development Report* in 1987 found that, among 41 developing countries, the highest growth in real income per head, GDP and manufacturing output value added was recorded by those countries pursuing strongly outward-looking trade and economic policies. The most inward-looking economies fared worst.

Hong Kong is a classic example. It is a textbook free-trader. It plays by the GATT rules and has been a separate party to the agreement since 1986. It imposes no tariffs or other import restrictions, and no foreign exchange controls. Ninety per cent of its domestic production is for export. Its commitment to free trade has delivered substantial growth and prosperity. Growth has averaged 7.4 per cent annually over the past decade, and GDP per capita, at US$11,000 in 1989, was second only to Japan in Asia.

Contrast that with the performance of what were the 'State Trading Nations'. The Communist economies were insulated from the open world trading system (despite some being parties to the GATT) by their non-market structures and artificial exchange rates. They have thus failed to share in the sustained trade-driven growth of the West and newly-industralised economies. Their trading arrangements with each other were conducted on a bilateral barter basis through COMECON. Lacking the stimulus of competition, or a price mechanism for effective resource allocation, growth was generally achieved only at the cost of highly inefficient volumes of investment, storing up problems of performance and productivity for the future. In the Soviet Union, for example, average annual GDP growth rates were an impressive-looking 5 per cent in the period 1950–73, but total factor productivity grew at only 0.5 per cent and became substantially negative thereafter. And behind these figures were hidden the constant hardships and frustrations suffered by the average Soviet consumer.

THE WIDER CONTEXT

The success of the West owes much to the open world trading system. And it has contributed significantly to our stability.

Within that trading system, we have needed to cooperate more closely to increase our prosperity. All experience shows that trade can both *energise* and *stabilise* relationships between states. Of course trade disputes can be bitter, and damage political relations. The United States and Japan, to take the prime example, have sometimes been in dispute. But neither country should have an interest in pursuing a quarrel so that it seriously damages the substantial overall level of trade between them (amounting to $131 billion in 1988), on which both depend. Today, more than ever, the family of nations that trades together stays together.

Trade is a catalyst which can forge common interest from enlightened self-interest. It can make nations readier to cooperate, assisting stability. It has a role extending beyond the economic sphere to political and security relationships between states.

The founders of the European Coal and Steel and European Economic Communities, for example, regarded trade and economic cooperation as a means to a more explicitly political end. In the words of the preamble to the Treaty which established the former, the states party were:

> Resolved to substitute for age-old rivalries the merging of their essential interest; to create, by establishing an economic community, the basis for a broader and deeper community among peoples long divided by bloody conflicts; and to lay the foundations for institutions which will give direction to a destiny henceforward shared.

Bright and Cobden would have approved. In 1877, Bright spoke of: 'the effect which extended commercial intercourse between countries has in rendering war between them almost impossible . . . ', and he suggested 'the formation of an international committee, which should endeavour to bring about the reduction of tariffs all over Europe, until the various countries should be so bound together by their commercial interests that the maintenance of large armaments would be an act of absolute and obvious lunacy.' In the EC/EFTA negotiations, and the proposals for closer association with the countries of Eastern and Central Europe, we have been moving towards that goal.

The imperative of economic reform in the Eastern bloc, and the political change inevitably accompanying it, have made possible relationships between East and West undreamed of a few years ago.

These processes form the basis of an emerging new international order, which has yet to find its final shape. But its main features are increasingly clear: a decline in East–West tension, and the progressive removal of ideological confrontation from international affairs, an end to the division of Germany and Europe, and a growing willingness to look at the future of the Continent's security and stability, not just in terms of military forces, but also in terms of pan-European cooperation on the basis of common values and interests. The 1990 Paris Summit set out how the CSCE would embody this, giving substance to Margaret Thatcher's vision.

Concepts such as 'cooperative' and 'political' security have been invented. As a result of the transformation in East–West relations, the third World has been cut adrift: what future now for non-alignment? In the past the imperatives of superpower competition assisted the survival of governments whose political and economic policies were repressive and misguided. To-day, with a developing East–West consensus on the importance of democratic, free-market values, the pressure on other countries to move towards these values are likely to increase.

The nature of power itself may also be changing. Military power – in the hands of nations dedicated to peace – remains an essential guardian of world stability and the rights of nations. Political power – the power of persuasion or influence – remains important; it depends most heavily on the nature of relationships, interests and perceptions. But economic power will grow in importance.

On the whole economic power works in benevolent ways, through successful example, cooperation and trade. Its coercive possibilities are limited: sanctions are rarely effective and retaliatory protection, even if it achieves an immediate objective, is usually counter-productive, as I have argued earlier. And economic power, especially in a free-enterprise world, is less and less the exclusive province of governments and politicians. Successful 'People's Capitalism' diffuses power right through society. It increases the public's stake in peace and stability, and reinforces the commitment of governments to these goals.

Finally, there is already a growing trend towards economic interdependence. The spread of multinational companies and the globalisation of markets through the influence of technology are aspects of this interdependence. But trade dependency lies at its heart. Economic interdependence and trade dependency are likely to increase further, and faster, in a world where more and more nations pursue market-based economic growth.

These wider global trends underline the importance of free trade in the international system. It is not just a stepping stone to prosperity. It mobilises self-interest to bind nations more closely together, in a world where opportunities for cooperation, and interdependence, are growing, and where no country can hope to preserve its status while neglecting the sources of economic strength. So the reinforcement of the open world trading system can make a substantial contribution to global stability as well as to prosperity.

THE GATT SYSTEM

The essential basis of trade growth throughout the free world over the past forty or so years has been the GATT system. The GATT is a curious creation, and in some respects its success has been surprising. But for several decades self-interest and a solid record of achievement have kept it going. At the time of writing, however, it is under attack as never before.

The classical free traders might not have approved of the GATT's *modus operandi*. Classical theorists advocate *unilateral* action to remove barriers to trade, regardless of the barriers maintained by others. They argue that a higher standard of living would invariably accrue from specialisation and the more efficient use of resources. Robert Peel, a unilateralist free trader, referred dismissively to 'haggling with foreign countries about reciprocal concessions' – but this, in effect, has been the way in which the GATT has worked. It has had to codify and to limit the ways in which governments intervene in the processes of trade, to provide mechanisms for progressive market opening and a framework for the resolution of disputes on an agreed, multilateral basis. It has therefore worked through 'reciprocal and mutually advantageous arrangements'.

So to the purist, the GATT has been far from perfect. But so is the world in which it has had to operate. Broad, 'balanced' concessions may be the best that can be achieved given the very different interests of the 101 GATT parties. The GATT's principles have been at heart sound ones in the climate of what has been realistically attainable – and they have brought results.

The GATT system's success to date has relied on a non-discriminatory, flexible, fair and transparent approach to trade concessions and tariff restrictions. It has used an arbitration procedure with expert 'panels' to rule in cases of dispute, though their effectiveness has been limited by a requirement that there must be a consensus before their findings can be accepted. It is open to a party to a dispute to block consensus in a case which it has lost.

The GATT has suffered from other weaknesses. Its scope has been confined to merchandise, but world exports of financial and commercial *services* now account for over 20 per cent of total world trade. Agriculture and textiles have been notable exclusions from GATT's mainstream coverage. The GATT's rules and disciplines have also been increasingly subject to evasion through the use of Voluntary Restraint Agreements and other administrative devices. Such non-tariff measures may have shorn world trade by as much as $330 billion in 1987. Its state trading members have hitherto stood apart from the main elements of the system.

THE URUGUAY ROUND

The continued expansion of world trade depends on the reversal of a growing trend to protectionism, especially in agriculture. The best way to meet that challenge would be by improving the scope and effectiveness of GATT's procedures. The aim of the Uruguay Round of negotiations, which began in 1986, has been to correct the GATT's deficiencies and shortcomings, and so to equip it for its vital role in facilitating the expansion of trade in the 1990s.

The round has aimed at both widening and deepening the GATT system by:

1. improving and strengthening dispute settlement procedures;

2. extending GATT's coverage to include services, intellectual property and inward investment;
3. tightening the application of GATT rules in the problem areas of agriculture and textiles;
4. strengthening GATT rules and discipline on safeguards, dumping subsidies and non-tariff measures;
5. achieving greater compliance with the rules by *all* GATT parties, so as to improve the coherence and interdependence of the world trading system as a whole.

This has been an ambitious, difficult, but essential agenda. Four years of negotiations were due to end in December 1990. Negotiations did end, temporarily – but without reaching agreement. A dispute between the US, EC and other countries – mainly about agriculture – prevented agreement at that stage on the Round as a whole. At the time of writing, we are still waiting for negotiations to resume. We cannot say what the consequences of failure would be, but there must be a risk that the GATT system will progressively unravel. That would in turn threaten a disorderly retreat into unilateral and bilateral disputes and deals.

The costs to the world of abandoning free trade would be huge. I turn once again to Bright for a vision of the apocalypse: 'I see before me a vast commerce collapsed, a mighty industry paralysed, people impoverished and exhausted with ever-increasing burdens, and a gathering discontent.'

It need not happen. The best way to *ensure* that it does not would be the success of the Uruguay Round. This requires a common commitment of political will. The different parties have different interests at stake, and are exercised by differing interests and priorities.

Compromises will be necessary, and will not always be easy for politicians to contemplate. Producer interest groups are often not persuaded of the benefits of free trade. As Macaulay put it: 'Free Trade, one of the greatest blessings which a Government can confer on a people, is almost in every country unpopular.'

But unpopular with whom? Of course producer interests are readier to lobby for protection – and make themselves heard – than consumers are for freer trade. Where are the deputations of consumers at my constituency surgery urging the abrogation of the Multi-Fibre Arrangement because it increases the price of their clothes by 5 per cent? But I have deputations from producers complaining of 'unfair' competition by cheaper producers abroad. The advantage to the consumer is broadly spread: it may be only a few pounds or even pence off the price of a single item. Yet the cumulative cost of such protection can be very high. A report by the National Consumer Council, for example, found that the annual cost to the consumer of EC anti-dumping restrictions on consumer electronic imports was almost £1.7 billion across the Community, and £270 million in the UK alone.

The Uruguay Round must escape from these constraints. There will need to be compromises. But it is essential that compromises should in every case be made in a *liberal* rather than a protectionist direction. Slow liberalisation is a poor second best to free trade, but better than protection. Liberalisation may exact a short-term adjustment cost, but as all experience shows, there are huge longer-term gains.

The leading industrialised powers – the US, Japan and the EC – have a particular responsibility to use their weight constructively.

The US needs, in its own interest, to suppress its tendency towards protection and the unilateral retaliation envisaged in the amended Section 301 of the 1988 Trade Act. Japan must continue with its programme of structural economic reform, to benefit its consumers and reduce tensions with its trading partners.

The EC is setting an example of market opening in the 1992 programme. Many of the Single Market measures will improve, unilaterally, access to EC markets for third countries, as an incidental benefit of liberalisation. We hear arguments for making this access conditional on reciprocity, to provide negotiating leverage in the GATT and combat clear cases of discrimination.

We should tread with great care. The EC should lead by example rather than seek to compel virtue in others. For this reason we believe the EC can best strengthen the GATT system by ensuring that any reciprocity provisions are of a reserve and non-binding nature. In the Uruguay Round itself, the EC needs to move substantially further on agriculture.

CONCLUSION

The greatest hope for the 1990s must be that the world-wide rejection of Marxism, with the tyrannies that accompany it, should continue; and that the enthusiastic embracing of democracy and free enterprise that we have seen in Central and Eastern Europe spreads ever further. One can now envisage that by 2000 Marxist junk and those who purvey it might have been discarded right across the globe. By that time there could be another twenty, thirty, even fifty countries that have chosen the path of democracy and free enterprise.

This will release huge economic energy, leading to dramatic growth. Generally these will be countries without large domestic markets; many of them will not be part of a trading bloc. They will need to be free to trade with the developed nations, and vice versa. If they cannot, dangerous frictions will emerge.

This exploding economic energy could be a force for instability across the whole world. But it could equally be mobilised to entrench stability across the whole world in a way that has never been achieved before. The key to this is trade. Free trade will mean that growth will be even faster. But it will also mean that the new prosperity is built on interdependence. It will mean that the continuation of each nation's prosperity depends on peace. At the moment there are still too many countries which have no stake in peace.

At the very least, the preservation of free trade offers those countries which participate in it the rich prize of enhanced growth. But we have a historic opportunity, unlikely to recur, to create a new world peace order, where, by building on each nation's enlightened self-interest, there emerges a common interest in peace and stability that can endure.

Part Four
Security and Defence in a New World Order

16 A Defence Role for the European Community

Peter Schmidt

A big package awaits discussion at the EC intergovernmental conference which began in December 1990: the Political Union of Europe. It will be a delicate process. The lack of Margaret Thatcher's vibrant anti-Delors voice in the future will probably bring the more silent voices of opposition elements to the forefront. Differences in the way the representatives of the twelve states interpret the term 'political union' will become clearer than ever before. The German Chancellor has recently presented his vision of this impending Western Europe: a federal state comparable and similar to the recently extended Federal Republic of Germany. There is much resistance to that idea, thus the model will not be accepted immediately.

Nevertheless, the conference which started in December might pave the way either for a Western Europe based mostly on intergovernmental cooperation, as preferred by the British and many French, or for a new one based on the ideas of a Federal State. Is there, in the long run, a superpower in the making? The managing of European defence will be crucial. After the failure of a 'defence first' approach in the 1950s experiencing the flop of the European Defence Community (EDC), the European integrationists have discovered defence again. They want to use it even as a 'federator' for a new Western Europe. They claim to charge the Community with all the defence duties at present within the competence of member states and/or NATO. The European Council emphasised in its Presidency Conclusions of the December 1990 summit, that 'the prospect of a role for the Union in *defence matters* should be considered'.[1]

It seems that the traditional 'functional or horizontal approach' examining on a step-by-step basis which tasks could or should be taken over by the EC has been replaced by a 'top-down or deductive' approach, which regards political union as an end in itself. Which way will be chosen? The decision will

211

deeply influence the political environment. Not too many ask what is at stake? Are there really good reasons for the EC to capture a defence role? Is it sensible to include a defence role for the twelve in the redrafting of the European and world order?

There is, in general, no analytical tool to decide the political problem at stake in an objective way: there are too many uncertainties, as well as both unknown and hidden effects of political actions which will influence the outcome of certain steps with regard to the given question.

Given this limitation, the objective of this article is, nevertheless, to give an answer to the question by arguing from the point of view of the 'international system'[2] by discussing a number of points often made to give reasons for the soundness and logic of a defence role for the EC.

In analysing the vast literature, political statements and proposed models with regard to the given question, a distinction has to be made between the two basic approaches to the problem already mentioned above: first, the top-down or deductive approach and, second, the functional or horizontal approach.

The *first* way of thinking regards the political union of Western Europe within the framework of the EC as an end in itself, whilst the *second* asks in a practical way which defence functions can and should be handled within a Western European framework, which ones can remain attached to the existing defence arrangements – that means NATO above all – and which ones can stay at the disposal of the nation states.

The *top-down approach* seems to be the dominant one today. The finality of the political union of Western Europe is even emphasised in important political declarations of EC summits, like the Dublin and Rome summits of last year (1990). From an analytical point of view, this is quite a simple concept, attracting many politicians today. In case you are in favour of this guiding idea, all pieces fall quite easily into place: you need an institutional framework under EC auspices to handle defence questions, including a general staff. Currently, the idea is to organise a possible defence role for the EC in an intergovernmental way,[3] but nevertheless there is some integrative undertow in relation to this approach.

This is due to three facts:

1. From the point of view of the philosophical concept of the European top–down approach, all arguments for not communalising basic defence functions are merely remaining obstacles or even parochial hindrances which have to be overcome in the longer run in order to reach the great goal of political union. Political forces opposing this end get quite negative scores, whereas the factors working for the great goal get positive ones. This works in favour of communalising defence functions.

2. Given the dominance of the top-down approach, the EC Commission gets probably quite an influence even on defence questions in the longer run. This results from the high probability that Europeans will not easily find a common denominator which gives the potential for political initiatives to the Commission.

3. There will certainly be some spill-over effect from the envisaged economic and monetary union to the defence sector. How should such a union work without some far-reaching ideas about the amount and structure of the defence expenditures of the member states?

This gives even more reasons for gauging the seriousness of the defence integrationists' arguments.

In the first instance, it is argued that the melting down of Communism and the turmoils in the East have to be responded to by a deepening of Western European integration, including defence. The fact is that, although the East–West antagonism seems to belong to the past and there are already – at least in Hungary and Poland – serious debates about joining the formerly hostile NATO, there remains a rather gigantic potential on the Soviet or Russian side which we have to take into consideration in structuring our future defence. However, a specific argument to undertake the remaining defence efforts within the framework of the twelve cannot be drawn from this argument. NATO did a good job in balancing the Soviet Union in the past – why should it be incapable of handling the remaining residual threats in the future?

The supporting reason, that we need a West European institution to compensate for the departure of US troops from Europe as the next consequence of the changes, is not a convincing point either. Europe seems to remain a decisive spot in

US strategic thinking for the foreseeable future. And even if the US army were to leave Europe totally, nothing spectacular would occur. NATO's political and military structure would still be there – only minus the Americans. The situation would not be worse were it the case that the EC developed a defence role. There is no basic need for the restructuring of institutions from this point of view.

In the second instance, a particularly French view regards NATO as an institution which has too much of a US bias or represents even an instrument for American hegemony over Europe. This political current conceives a potential defence role of the EC as a counterpoise to US guidance or dominance over Europe. Without discussing the question whether the US has ever been this hegemonic power in Europe by means of NATO, the main point against this view is the following: everybody knows that there will be a much lower US troop level on European soil in the future. The reductions of US forces will even exceed Western European troop cuts.

Adding the fact that the US nuclear capacity will not remain a decisive element determining future Atlantic relations, US influence on European defence policy as well as on other issues will decrease even further, with the result that European impact on Atlantic relations will increase automatically. Under these circumstances, any scenario that a US president could or would ignore a common European standpoint on certain important issues lacks credibility.

With regard to the third instance, many see a potential renationalisation of defence policies in Western Europe as a daunting danger. This points at two risks: the first is the re-emergence of traditional inter-nation-state struggles among the Western Europeans and, second, the danger of a race for the peace divided among the Western Europeans leading possibly once again to an imbalance between the Soviet Union or Russia and Western Europe. This tendency could be reinforced by the probable consequence that America will not be ready to keep some of its forces in Europe under these conditions.

It seems to me that there is a lot of pseudo-historical analysis behind the first subpoint. Sometimes people try to unearth the danger of the 'Balkanisation' of Western Europe or a fall back into the European nation-state system in the nineteenth century. This sounds very strange against the background of the many hymns honouring the high level of integration in Western Europe already achieved. And indeed, much has been done to entangle and integrate the countries of Western Europe. This does not only apply to the fields of economic exchange and social interaction. Beyond the high standard of economic relations and exchanges, we have created a political system in Western Europe characterised by intergovernmental coordination on various levels and different subjects and an assembly of still viable nation-states. This system doubtlessly is unique and delivers no incentives for a fall-back to the world of 1914 or even for the Balkanisation of Western Europe. We even stress the Western European system as an outstanding model for the overcoming of rivalries or even hostilities among states and wait to sell this model to the East Europeans.

It is a specificum of the German discussion – based on the experience of how devastating the consequences of an exaggerated nationalism can be – that the legitimisation of the nation-state *per se* is put into question. However, is it logical to fight for a defence role for the EC as a counterpoise to this perceived danger?

Certainly not! There may be good reasons for adding more competencies to the Brussels authorities, but in this context it does not make great sense.

Broadening the scope of the EC and adding to its competencies in the field of defence means that the EC will evolve to a new and much bigger state on a Western European level. Fighting against an international structure based on nation-states by working for a bigger one only means transferring the problem to a higher level. The historical singularity of the Western European model is not that there is a new superpower in the making, but the fact that the still viable states are imbedded in an intergovernmental cooperative structure.

The *second subpoint*, emphasising the danger of an uncoordinated rush for the peace dividend, has to be taken more seriously. And indeed, recent developments on the French, the British and the German side – see the announcement for unilateral troop withdrawals or the German self-restriction to 370,000 troops – give some evidence of that.

There is no doubt that we need a certain cohesion in our defence structure in Western Europe and a rather high level of common understanding about our future capabilities in order to defend our common interests and to avoid a rush for the peace dividend. The question here is rather a practical one: in which framework can you do it best?

There are three structures available,[4] the first being NATO, the second WEU, and the third the EC.

NATO has established its working procedures on an inter-governmental basis and demonstrated a lot of flexibility.[5] The decision to prefer the EC as the framework for defence policy seems to me mostly motivated by the demand for an integrated political system in Western Europe rather than by searching for practical solutions for the identified problems. The preference for the EC is much more based on a certain idea of how the future Western European system should look like rather than on the specific challenge to preserve a certain cohesion in Western European defence efforts. You certainly can work for this goal outside the EC too.

A fourth argument looks at the current Gulf crisis – the high profile the United States is showing in this episode, and the rather low level of Western European activity in the military field. The different characteristics of this crisis are regarded as supporting points for a defence role of the EC. The following two arguments address the problems from two different angles.

The *first* looks quite Atlantic-minded in saying that we need a political infrastructure from our response to this crisis which delivers a coherent and overall politico-military answer and gives a bit more satisfaction to the Americans who suffer from bearing too great a burden. It is argued that this supports the old American objection that the Europeans are interested everywhere but engaged nowhere, thus damaging our Atlantic ties. From my point of view this argument supports a more substantial military contribution to the Gulf forces, but I would like to argue down these people, because it is not at all an argument in favour of a certain framework within which this European action should take place.

The US asked for a WEU action, and even substantial *ad hoc* actions of key European countries based on an experienced NATO *ad hoc* staff would have satisfied Washington.

Let us assume for some seconds that the EC already had a defence role. Given the current interests in Europe, would an EC defence council have produced different – more positive – results?

Given the general German reluctance to do anything with a military touch, the French hesitation to do anything alongside the Americans, and the British eagerness to support the Americans, one can assume that an EC defence structure would be unable to find a common platform.[6] This argument remains valid as long as the principle of unanimity was applied to those decisions – and would not be replaced by majority vote, at least for the medium term. And, one must add, that the current Western security system has a build-in flexibility which is a high-ranking criterion for evaluating any EC defence set-up.

The *second* line of argument pleads for a defence role for the EC in exploiting the Gulf crisis, saying that events give evidence of our dependence on the United States in important regional conflicts. However, I would like to ask: will this really change in case we incorporate defence questions in an EC setting? I doubt it. It is not the time in Europe for rearmament in order to replace the US out-of-area. It is much more a period for the avoidance of over-sized disarmament holding the sheep in the flock together.

A fifth point refers to the idea of taming the Germans with the help of an EC defence role. However, it seems reasonable not to overemphasise the difficulty of integrating a greater Germany in a political framework as a problem for the European continent. The unification of Germany will not lead to an economic or political 'superpower'. The nervousness sometimes dominating the debate is mainly a reflection of past experience with the Third Reich. It is, however, out of proportion given recent German conduct and the actual weight of a united Germany in relation to its international environment. Germany has unilaterally limited its military forces and re-emphasised its renouncement of nuclear, biological and chemical weapons. Furthermore, it remains embedded in NATO, WEU, the EC and the CSCE framework and many other international institutions like the United Nations, the World Bank and the IMF. Overdoing the German question in this regard could divert attention from problems of much more urgency, such as arms reductions or support for Eastern European reform policies.

This leads us to the question of whether we need a defence role for the twelve because of the inabilities and turmoils in the formerly hostile Eastern parts of Europe.

It is often argued that NATO is not needed any more because the Soviet threat has gone and nobody in NATO would favour the idea of intervening in Eastern Europe in case of military conflicts among those states. That is, however, true for both the existing NATO and a possible EC defence body. We can only imagine peace-keeping actions which are based on a broader international consensus under United Nations auspices, or perhaps based on a CSCE decision. The remaining task is to prevent that crisis and/or military actions spill over to the territory of Western Europe. This task can be handled by either NATO or the WEU. An EC defence setting is not a must for that.

In conclusion, it seems suitable also to add a few more positive points for an EC defence role to the checklist of arguments.

There are definitely some convincing elements in the argument for coordinating the main political functions with a single political framework. We might expect more effectiveness and less waste of time. And indeed, the competencies already concentrated in Brussels cover some security-related matters which have to be seen in more or less close connection with the defence sector in a narrow sense. There is no doubt that the possible next steps towards an economic and monetary union would add to the interrelationship between the EC and the defence sector. There will be quite a lot of spill-over from an economic and monetary union to the national defence decision-making processes. In case of a fully-fledged economic and monetary union, there must be a common policy concerning the amount of money given to the defence sector. Given the presumed lack of money for defence in the future, much pressure might be put on defence establishments to save money by some division of labour or even an overall European defence plan in order to avoid the doubling of military research and expensive competition in the field of armament production.

Finally, we should stress again the two capital points. First, the main support for an EC defence role comes from the general idea that Western European integration is a high-ranking goal. From this point of view, adding defence to the EC authorities is just a measure to complete the political union of Western Europe. Second, even in case the states decide not to add defence to the EC framework, there will nevertheless be a substantial spill-over effect on the Community, *if* the EC members actually establish a real monetary and economic union.

Thus it might be hard – if not quite impossible – to avoid any defence role for the EC.

In this regard, we are at the crossroads of important decisions. The next steps within the EC will probably free the way for a Western European superstate. Is the grand tool which could prise open the Pandora's box of a Western European defence union about to be found despite the actual lack of convincing arguments?

NOTES

1. European Council, Rome, 14 and 15 December 1990, Presidency Conclusions (Part 1), in *Europe*, No. 5393, 16 December 1990, p. 7. Edited extracts from the summit can be found *The Times*, 17 December 1990, p. 2.
2. There are other 'internal' arguments in favour of a defence union, such as cost-effectiveness, which are discussed here in greater detail.
3. The European Council of December 1990 established a broad framework for the negotiations on political union. According to the conclusions of the Council, the Council itself should basically serve as the decision-making centre (p. 6).
4. For the reasons why I don't see that the CSCE can replace these structures see the argumentation in Krause, J. and Schmidt, P., 'Europe's Evolving Architecture', *Washington Quarterly*, No. 4, Autumn 1990, pp. 79–92.
5. NATO will complete its strategic review before summer 1991. For a recent state of affairs see the Final Communiqué of the Defence Planning Committee and the Nuclear Planning Group of NATO in *Atlantic News*, No. 2280 (Annex), 8 December 1990.
6. For a general overview of basic differences in the Franco-German case in security matters see Schmidt, P., 'West Germany and France: Convergent or Divergent Perspectives on European Security Cooperation?', in *The Evolution of an International Actor: Western Europe's New Assertiveness* (Boulder, Col.: Westview Press, 1990), pp. 161–78.

17 Out-of-Area Challenges and Western Security

Miguel Herrero de Miñón

Among the consequences of the Gulf crisis, one of the most important for Western security is the renewed interest in out-of-area challenges.

Out-of-area challenges are a concept of Atlantic strategy, meaning any conflict outside the limits of the Atlantic Alliance which threatens, not only the Alliance as a whole, but the vital interests of any of its members in such a way that it should affect the global strategic status quo of those values to which the Alliance is committed.

For historical reasons, NATO's area is well defined in Article VI of the Washington Treaty; but because developments since its inception, the meaning of these limits has changed somewhat since 1949.

When NATO was created in 1949, the USA refused to extend its guarantees further than the North Atlantic and the Mediterranean, because its liberal-minded foreign policy refused to be involved in the colonial conflicts of European allies. Years later, when those same allies wrongly believed in the divisibility of security and the possibility of replacing global responsibilities with regional interests, they invoked the limits established in Article VI to avoid sharing USA's world-wide responsibilities while maintaining its benefits.

After a long period of consultation over out-of-area challenges, (1952–79), and a phase of more cooperative strategy through logistic support and compensation of forces among allies – a more relevant example being the South West Asia Impact Study prepared in 1983 by NATO's International General Staff – the situation began to change after the first Gulf crisis in the 1980s.

During the Cold War, any out-of-area challenge to Western security, whether autochthonous or not, was interpreted by Western analysts as an expression of Soviet indirect strategy.

And, once the crisis had broken out, for example as a result of ethnic conflicts or social injustice, the Soviets tried to capitalise on it to harm the West.

Now the Soviet threat to Europe and elsewhere is less than in the past, and if it should increase in the future, it would be a quite different threat; from aggression to migration, from imperialism to contagious internal conflicts.

But at the same time, there are economic, military and political powers all over the world. The most threatening dangers for the West, therefore, come from areas out of NATO's responsibilities and capacities.

The first reaction to this has been the naive proposal to extend the NATO area by modifying Article VI of its founding treaty, something as easy to imagine as difficult to carry out. The reasons for this difficulty are clear: rightly or wrongly, NATO has now placed political interests above military interests; all its continental European members are reluctant to accept such a modification; neither France – which has a main role to play in out-of-area deployments – nor Spain, are part of NATO's integrated military structure; and finally, nothing would be so difficult and unpopular as to have a revised 1949 Washington Treaty ratified by sixteen parliaments.

Because of these political and legal difficulties, a powerful school of thought supports the *de facto* extension of NATO into new areas of conflict through special contingency planning.

In my opinion, Atlanticism means promotion of common values which exceed any institution, even NATO. Atlanticism means defending the interests and capabilities of the Atlantic powers, which hold the main reponsibility for international security, but it does not mean believing in the general usefulness of NATO; and, of course, Atlanticism means maintaining NATO as a cornerstone of Western security, but without forgetting that the West already has a trilateral structure and the Pacific is its eastern flank.

As with any organisation, NATO is very useful in its own area and its own specific activity. Because it was conceived as just a regional and military alliance, it could be the most integrated and permanent alliance in modern history. And the extension of its goals from military security to political cooperation, and of its limits from its present borders to new areas of potential conflicts, would no doubt erode its current restricted but highly efficient capacities. Extension and intensity are, in political efficiency as in peripatetic logic, inverse options.

A more elaborate solution, which was used back in 1987 and again last August, consists in using the 'sleeping beauty', the WEU, as an excuse for out-of-area military deployment – just an excuse, as at the start of the Gulf crisis deployment had already been put into practice by Great Britain before the WEU could intervene. France, which backed WEU revival, actually prevented its operative coordination. Moreover, interests threatened are not only in NATO's European area, and Japanese financing of the military force deployment is a good example of the trilateralisation of the Western security structure.

However, there is a clear need to establish mechanisms which will enable the West to face challenges and threats originating outside the NATO area.

In my view, the conceptual *indivisibility of security* as well as its *territorial fragmentation* are the dialectical terms of the new architecture of world-wide security.

Security should be *global,* that is deep enough to be comprehensive of the economical and social requirements of stability, as emphasised by the 1980 Bonn Atlantic Summit, and *indivisible,* for the erosion of security anywhere could affect the equilibrium of an interdependent world. Aggression in the Gulf threatens Western security, not only because it disturbs energy supplies with disastrous effects to industrial democracies – and even more so to developing countries – but because it creates instability in the Moslem world, from the Far East to the Atlantic, and introduces to the whole international community new aggressive patterns of behaviour.

But if security is indivisible, it can be better achieved through *different regional systems.* Even in the new undivided Europe, there are very diverse strategic priorities. The interests of Atlantic or Mediterranean powers in out-of-area challenges cannot be equal to those of other Continental powers. The problems of building an EC security policy are mainly the consequence of the asymmetry between economic integration and strategic requirements, between the implementation of the unified European market in the first case, and defence cooperation in the second.

What has really worked, both politically and militarily, has been the Anglo-American relationship to which France, as an

Atlantic power, adhered after her first ambiguities over the Gulf crisis. The logistic support plans for out-of-area actions contained in the bilateral treaties of the US with Portugal, Spain, Italy, Greece and Turkey, have also proved their worth.

And what was the EC's reaction to the Gulf crisis? The US line of action received political back-up and the economic embargo was actively followed. But that was all and, as I said before, the European cover of the WEU was just an alibi for reluctant allies.

As regards Germany's participation in the security operation, this was limited to some naval contributions in the Mediterranean accompanied by grudging financial support, coinciding with the reunification summit and enthusiastic glances to the East. It is a mere exposure of the difference in strategic outlooks: the continent or the sea.

Outside the European and North Atlantic area, regional arrangements are as important as the Western presence. The lack of those arrangements would be a breeding ground for local conflicts and at the same time would turn the Western powers into alien policemen.

To this effect,the first and most coherent attempts took place in the 1950s, namely in the Far East and Middle East. But these initiatives failed after the British retreat from East of Suez and America's ambiguity towards CENTO. Current projects to create a Middle East regional security system are only a newer version of what should have been the Baghdad Pact.

In my view, the cornerstones of the new security architecture could be as follows:

1. Regionalisation of security through different organisations for arms control and defensive solidarity.
2. Reinforcement of the above-mentioned regional systems through the commitment of those principally involved Western nations with specific interests and capacities in the area. This is a better option than the hegemony of any local power as dramatically shown by the perverse effects of Western support to Imperial Iran or to anti-fundamentalist Iraq. The massive rearmament of Arabic by Western powers as a balance to Iraq's strength could become another important threat in the future, in spite of the pro-Western goodwill shown by the current Arab rulers.

3. The connection of such various regional systems through the common membership of a core of states with global experience, interests and influence and, if needed, military deployment, amongst which there would be the USA, Britain and France.

The age of unilateralism is over, and in order for security to be effective, it should be a collective task. But the naive approach of universalism is not yet operative.

Western powers should organise this very complex and difficult task, *sharing responsibilities and distribution missions*, according to their different interests and capacities.

Part Five
Concluding Reflections

18 How Not To Oppose Political Union

J. Enoch Powell

The question how and by whom this country is to be governed is at the heart of politics. What is more, in the last ten days the men of Bruges – perhaps I had better define that expression: by the men of Bruges I mean the people who had hoped, and hope still, to see their country again an independent self-governing nation – have had one hell of a political lesson. It is that political lesson which I want to underline and comment upon this morning. It consists in the association of two facts which might be identified, as it were, as the minor and major premises of a syllogism and in the drawing of a conclusion from the juxtaposition of those two facts.

The first of those facts was something we knew already before the events of the last few days, and that is that the declaration of Bruges, made by the Prime Minister on 20 September 1988, is totally incompatible with the European Communities Act 1972. The European Communities Act of 1972 renounced on behalf of the United Kingdom the overriding authority in legislation and the overriding authority in taxation, and it transferred to an external court the power to decide the ultimate questions in interpretation of the law and to decide them upon the basis of laws and principles which are not the laws and principles of the United Kingdom.

The declaration of Bruges was deliberately and could not have been more deliberately incompatible with the terms of the 1972 Act which paved the way for our entry into the European Economic Community in 1973. It was in direct antithesis therefore to what had necessarily been accepted by all who sought to play a part in the public life of this country since 1972. Since 1972 there has been no place in that public life for those whose language was not Euro-speak and who did not acknowledge and accept as the basis of all their political actions the terms of renunciation embodied in the European Communities Act of 1972.

By what she said and did in September 1988 the Prime Minister of this country called for the performance by politicians on a gargantuan scale of that skill in which they are past masters, the eating of words and the changing of minds. It is the mark of a professional politician that he is expert in eating past words. It is the profession to which those belong who one week can declare they have no intention of opposing the Prime Minister and next week can discover good reasons why they can do so without embarrassment and without apology. It is an activity in which long years of practice bring extraordinary aptitude. It is an activity therefore in which the layman should be reluctant to interfere. A layman offering politicians methods of swallowing their past words is rather like a child which has found its way into the workshop of a craftsman and goes around picking up and putting down the tools, saying what this or that tool would be good for.

To propose to politicians the methods by which they should crawl out from under what they have done in the past is time wasted and an insult to the intelligence of those who do it. (I did when I framed that phrase take a glance at the title of this conference, in case anybody asked me for an example of such a formula.) There is no good to be done by laymen and ordinary citizens advising politicians how to compromise and wheedle their way out of a position which they have decided to abandon. When once they have decided it is in their interest to abandon that position, then, as professionals in the art, they will find a way to do it.

So the first fact to get straight is that the declaration of Bruges in 1988 was flatly in opposition to what was legislated in 1972, legislation incidentally supported and voted for as a member of government by the very person who made the Bruges declaration, and legislation which had been amended and reinforced under guillotine imposed upon the House of Commons by her own administration only two years before. It was a startling as well as a gargantuan operation involving self-humiliation which was announced by the Prime Minister in that remarkable utterance.

The second fact, which we have to associate with that first fact – the minor premise of the syllogism – is a fact that we did not know until yesterday. We did not know that she did not have the collective assent of her ministers and her cabinet to the world-swallowing which was implicit in and essential to the Bruges declaration of 1988. We were entitled in the absence of that evidence, and the rest of the world was under an obligation in the absence of that evidence, to assume that when the Prime Minister of the United Kingdom spoke as such not in an *obiter dictum*, or an ill-considered fashion, but in a carefully prepared and officially distributed declaration, she was speaking for Her Majesty's Government in the United Kingdom. We now know that she was not. We now know that the Government of the United Kingdom was not associated, as the Government of the United Kingdom required to be associated, with the terms of that declaration. In fact it is the declaration of Bruges which broke up this present administration and has precipitated this country into the present political turmoil.

It was of course a severe demand which she placed upon her colleagues. I don't want to be personal, but insufficient attention has been drawn to the role in all of this of Sir Geoffrey Howe. Sir Geoffrey Howe was the Solicitor General who drafted the Bill of 1972 and was in charge of forcing it through the House of Commons by majorities which dropped as low as four. He has ever since continued to declare his pride and satisfaction in that work and regarded it as one of the principal achievements of his life in Parliament. If he remained silent after the Bruges declaration and continued to withhold his assent to it only by biting his lips and maintaining a straight face, that lasted only as long as his interest in maintaining that stance lasted. As soon as he judged that interest had come to an end, he declared himself and thus precipitated the course of events which we have witnessed in the last few days. But the Government as a whole – we must remember, and it is charitable to remember – is composed of people who gained their position by paying a lip service which we are entitled to regard as heartfelt to the renunciation which was made in 1972. To demand of them that they should take part in the repudiation of what was done in 1972 and in the recovery of the parliamentary self-government of the United Kingdom was a severe requirement. It was a requirement which the Prime Minister did not succeed, we now know, in enforcing.

That is the second fact. The old refrain 'U turn, if you want to; the lady is not for turning' had been replaced by a new refrain: 'U turn if you can, the lady has turned already'. They were not yet ready or prepared to make that shift in their position. That was not due to any lack of skill in self-adjustment to the necessities of political circumstances. It was not due to loss or failure of the ability to propose weasel-worded compromises or contradictions. It was due to causes which were deep seated in the past eighteen years during which the public of this country remained relatively supine in the presence of the deprivation of everything which made this a self-governing country.

So the second fact, therefore, is that the Bruges declaration did not have the assent of Her Majesty's Government as a whole. It was the Bruges declaration which destroyed the Thatcher administration, or rather it was the fact that the Bruges declaration did not represent the collective will and opinion of the Government of the United Kingdom. These are the political facts which the men of Bruges have now got to recognise. The men of Bruges have to face the fact that a battle has been lost; and the rest of what I have to say to you is an adjuration to perceive that, although a battle has been lost, the campaign has not been lost. The war is not over. It may indeed be that the war is still in its earlier stages. If that were so, it would be a familiar and congenial situation for the people of this country, who have always been distinguished by their unwillingness to be warned of dangers before they incurred them. They have always been allergic to those who come before them to argue upon theoretical grounds that they are about to be robbed of their gold watch. They are a people who have always waited until the last minute before they defended what they valued most and regained what had been most precious to them. So there would be nothing unusual, nothing out of the ordinary for the people of this country, if it were the case that the war to recover what was lost in 1972 is in a relatively early stage.

There are other considerations which the men of Bruges ought to be taking to heart in an otherwise dismal scene. First, nothing will ever be the same since 20 September 1988. It remains a fact, a historic fact, made more historic by having come from one of the most astute politicians this country has known in the years since the war, somebody apt at intuitively appraising the mood of the people of this country. That person at that time said those things. That person at that time announced the intention that we should again be a self-governing

sovereign nation in a relationship of cooperation, not subordination, with the inhabitants of the adjacent continent. That is
an event which can no more be taken out of history than the
abasement of 1972, and its consequences which continue to
reverberate and will continue to reverberate.

The speech at Bruges was not made under the assumption
that it would run contrary to the wishes and the aspirations and
sentiments of the bulk of the electorate. I do not rate the
altruism of any fellow politician so high as to suppose that they
would deliberately, in the supreme office, choose to enunciate
intentions and opinions which they regard as contrary to the
prejudices and wishes of the bulk of the electorate.

Somebody may be muttering 'Poll tax'; but then you have
forgotten if you are muttering 'poll tax' how unpopular was
that rating system for which providence has decreed that no
alternative is known to man had become when the poll tax and
the intention to introduce it were first announced. Politicians,
particularly politicians of the status and intuition of Margaret
Thatcher, do not make announcements which they calculate to
be repugnant to the bulk of their fellow citizens. What happened
in 1988 is that she had recognised that changes in Europe,
changes in the outside world, had begun to render 1972 and
our adherence to that European Economic Community obsolete: the world had moved on beyond 1972. The people of this
country also knew that it had moved on. Looking across Europe,
they saw other nations emerging and claiming to govern
themselves and not be subordinated to a new empire, a new
imperial bureaucracy. She noticed too that at last – you may say
belatedly, but then we do these things belatedly – the people of
this country were becoming irritated and even mildly alarmed
when they learned that an external authority was laying down
what Parliament might and might not enact and was interpreting
the law in this country over the heads of Her Majesty's judges.
So it was a speech made on an assumption about the people of
this country. The assumption was that the people of this country
were becoming ripe for a reversal of the surrender made in
1972.

You would be unfair – and I exhort you not to be unfair – to
her former colleagues if you imagined that they too were un-
aware of this changed atmosphere to which the Prime Minister
was responding. My personal observation of public opinion

upon this subject is under suspicion. After all, since 1974 I have been living by myself in a tent on Hill 60 with nothing to keep me company but the Union Jack. Those who in such a situation find themselves ageing, are apt to be subject to hallucinations and may even mistake the mood and opinion of their fellow citizens. They might even mistake – as I did mistake – the prospects of success the female warrior figure observes one day at the head of the host approaching to their relief. So I have been disposed to discount my own prejudices and my own judgment upon the state of opinion in this country on the subject of the European Economic Community; but I have been greatly surprised, since I permitted myself after 1988 to begin to talk again to audiences upon this subject and accept invitations from Conservative Associations from one end of the country to the other, to discover how widespread in the Conservative Party and in its organisations were what I supposed was the mood of the people of this country. It even began to percolate to me that on the back benches of the Conservative Party in the House of Commons and not least, so they told me themselves, amongst members sitting for marginal seats, similar intimations and sensations were noted.

That is something not unknown to those who announce that they expect to win the next general election. Winning the next general election is of course the business of all politicians, to which they should earnestly attend. In doing so, there are two considerations which they are likely to bear heavily in mind: what is the public mood? and what is the mood of those on whose votes we rely?

Perhaps in addition too: what should we be saying in order to win the next general election? When the aspirants address themselves to these questions, they appear no more ignorant than I am of the change which has come over public opinion on this subject and which was crystallised by the declaration of 1988. They know that there is in the electorate a disposition at any rate to listen to those who promise to recover for them their rights of national self-government and to liberate them from the indignity of having their laws made, their taxes imposed and their policies framed outside the United Kingdom. They also are disposed to use their votes at a general election in order to declare their position upon that question. It is, after all, the most fundamental question possible: there is no point in general elections if the matters which are put before the electorate are matters no longer to be decided by those who seek election, and if the electors of this country still want to decide these matters themselves through those whom they elect to the House of Commons in their traditional and time honoured fashion, what better opportunity than a general election itself for saying so? They are getting ripe to decide at a general election by whom they intend to be governed, and for what they intend those whom they elect to acknowledge responsibility to them the electorate. Since 1988 – I might even say, since 1990 – that disposition of the electorate is not unknown to those who will be enjoying office in the Conservative Party and in Her Majesty's Government in the coming months. Their business, remember, their ultimate concern, the ultimate concern of all politicians, namely, to obtain the chance to go on with the same jobs, or if possible better jobs, depends upon winning the next election, upon having a majority at the next election despite all that has transpired, dare I say, despite the poll tax?

After all, what cheek it is to argue about the poll tax while at the same time telling the people of this country that they ought to surrender the right to set their own levels and forms of taxation in a monetary union with their neighbours on the adjacent continent. The politicians know that here is one of the winning cards in the political game. They salivate when they imagine the predicament of a candidate who can confront his electorate at a general election and say: 'My friends, here is my election address; here is the manifesto of my party. These are the things which we think *you* ought to decide. It will be *your* vote on Thursday week which decides whether the matters set out therein are put into effect so far as humanly possible. But, my friends, across the way is my honourable opponent. He has not concealed from you the fact that you can tear his manifesto and his election address up. His overriding policy is that you shall not be the authority which decides the laws, the taxes and the policies of the United Kingdom.' As one who fought thirteen Parliamentary elections, I can hardly speak for salivating when I envisage the advantage enjoyed by such a candidate.

These are not matters which are being ventilated, at any rate in those vivid terms, by those who seek to maintain an appearance of self-consistency and who seek support from those who hold contradictory opinions on the central question. You will not hear them at this stage; but these are the thoughts which they are thinking and will be thinking furiously during the coming six or eighteen months. The people of this country who derive the right to govern themselves from their history and from their past endeavours, bear a deep grudge against those who would deprive them of it. It is near to their hearts. They are not in the mood, however long it takes, to relinquish an objective once they have formed it. That objective was vocalised for them in the speech which was made as Prime Minister by their Prime Minister on 20 September 1988. On the record it remains. Alive it still remains with all the vigour of an idea whose time has not yet come but 'is comin' yet for a' that and for a' that.'

19 Dangers and Opportunities
Norman Tebbit

Sometimes there is some form of interregnum to bridge the cocktail hour and the main meal. This evening I think I am the interregnum which bridges the gap between the main meal of intellectual delight you have savoured and the cocktail hour which you are shortly to enjoy.

It occurs to me to comment, of course, that this group was brought into being as a consequence of that speech which was made at Bruges by Mrs Thatcher. She is now all but gone as the Prime Minister. Nothing will be quite the same again. Love her, like her, loathe her, you cannot be indifferent to her – many people have both loved and loathed her. She has been a political colossus, not just in Britain, nor just in Europe, but across the whole world. For me it has been a very sad week. It has been gladdened and illuminated by one or two things. One is the extent to which people across the political divide, including some of those who have loathed her, have come to me quietly and said this is a tragedy which should not have happened.

The other is that my career really began with hers, as I was one of those who together with our dear late friend Airey Neave brought her to the leadership of the Conservative Party in what I always called the corporals' coup, because none of us were senior enough to be colonels. I was one of those and I have fought alongside her ever since. We have had our differences of course; we are both strong minded characters. But I was immensely proud and happy on the day that she was finally defeated – not in the country, not by a vote in the House of Commons, but by a callous coup – that I was beside her fighting to the very end with her. If she went down, then I went down, and I could not have known a better way in which my political career should be ended.

I could become emotional about it; I must not, because when the history of this period is written she will be remembered undefeated in any election, whilst those who brought her down

will have been forgotten for many years, except for the standard of their conduct. Perhaps someone will coin a new word to
describe it in the English language, this conduct of a kind
which I have not experienced before. It will make a great
difference of course in Europe, particularly in one respect. As
I remember her saying: 'When I'm not there Mitterrand will
not be able to hide behind my skirts.'

Let me say at once that I am profoundly convinced that we
should have joined the European Community and that we
should remain in the European Community. I am also profoundly convinced that it would have been a better Community
if it had been governed by the Treaty of London rather than
the Treaty of Rome. I operated in that Community for many
years as a minister. Time and time again at the Council of
Ministers, especially when the Commissioner for Social and
Labour Affairs was Mr Ivor Richards, manifest absurdities would
be proposed by the Commission to the Council. Most of my
colleagues would say that they were very good, that even if
slightly impractical we should make a political declaration about
them. And I would simply say, no, and sometimes quite often I
was alone in saying no. Until lunch time, when one after another
my colleagues would come to me and say, 'You won't give in will
you?' 'Of course not,' I would say, 'but I thought you wanted it?'
'No,' they would say, 'we don't want it, but, you see, we have a
coalition government and the teeny weeny little weedy party is
crucial to us. We could be precipitated into a general election
next week, and *they* like it, so *we* must say we like it, but *you* must
save us from it.'

Now, *I* think there may be quite a lot of that which has gone
on at the recent Council, between the Heads of Government,
and I think it will be very interesting indeed to see what now
happens when the defender of the national interest is off the
stage and national leaders may have to defend their national
interest for themselves instead of relying upon Mrs Thatcher to
do it for all of them.

I thought I would end this conference for you by looking at
some of the dangers and opportunities which are now in front
of us in the European Community. I think the greatest danger
to the European Community has always been that it should fall
somewhere off that marvellous platform of idealism and into
the trap of unrealistic aspirations. I think we have to remind

ourselves time and time again that we Europeans are not in the
same position as our American friends. We are not likely to
become a United States of Europe, simply on the basis that the
Americans have done it and why should not we? Our history has
not only bound us together, it has divided us. Perhaps most of
all, however, it is our language which has divided us and the
English language which has united the United States of America.

Language is enormously important. Language shapes
thoughts and it represents somehow the growth over centuries
of the way in which a community of people think. One can
scarcely think at all without words, words being the material for
our thinking and shaping our thoughts as surely as the materi-
als which are on hand shape the buildings which architects
design and in which we live. We have a long time yet to run
together before we are all adept in understanding and using
each other's language. And of course we English have the
advantages and disadvantages – for there are always two sides to
these things – of the most powerful language in the world,
which carries with it one of the most powerful and widespread
cultures in the world. At times it is resented, even in Wales and
Scotland.

Of course America had a single government even when it was
a British colony. The Americans simply rebelled and took it
over for themselves. In retrospect, perhaps we made a dreadful
mistake. Perhaps there was a moment when we should have
taken the seat of government from this city to New York – lovely
thought, America not as the United States, but still under the
British Monarchy. But that is all in the past. We are now in
Europe.

Above all because of our island history, we are perhaps most
divided from our continental neighbours by our law and of
course by much of our culture. We are twelve, so they tell me,
within the European Community. I don't believe that, for we
are more than twelve. Even within this Kingdom we have our
Scots and our Welsh and our Irish, let alone wider afield, the
Corsicans, the Basques, and so on. It is not least due to this fact
that there can be no such thing as a European public opinion.
Although there may be a European public opinion amongst an
intellectual elite, it is not one which extends to the great mass
of European people. Hence, democracy in that sense is impossible. We can very often reach a consensus amongst that intel-

lectual elite. But if that intellectual elite has not got laid upon
it clear limitations from the parliamentary and democratic
process, it will not speak for the masses, but itself, and thereby
I think is part of the problem which we face. The European
Commission, and to a considerable extent, the Parliament, see
themselves as part of that European intellectual super-class
which should govern in the interests of those people who are
unable at the moment to come together to form a common
impact.

There is also another danger, which is that because we have
to live together in the Community, because we have to come to
conclusions together, and because we often start from positions
which are wide apart, then we compromise and compromise
about everything until eventually the conclusion we reach is
often scarcely worth the effort of compromise, or indeed the
twelve sheets of paper on which it is written.

One could look most recently, for example, at the European
Community's attitude towards the crisis in the Gulf. Our American friends are realising at last that perhaps it is a very good
thing that Europe has not achieved political union, because if
it were so, perhaps the British troops – if they had ever been
sent at all – would have been on the French aircraft carrier
which had to turn back again. So I think our American friends
are perhaps beginning to see some of the disadvantages of a
single decision-making process within Europe.

Of course, the single most important difficulty and danger
which is facing us at the moment, is that of the single currency,
although that is a problem of a different kind. I take great
encouragement from the fact that the man who I think is most
likely to succeed the present prime minister, John Major, understands very clearly indeed that there can only be one
Chancellor of the Exchequer for one currency. There is no
recorded case of one currency with two finance ministers – it is
an absurdity – and we have seen that demonstrated in recent
times when as soon as the German deutshmark became the
legal currency of the two Germanies, the East German Finance
Minister closed the door of his office, threw away the key and
became unemployed. There are some consequences which run
from that.

I was deeply appalled when Leon Brittan, a man of considerable intellectual ability, suggested that this little problem could

be overcome by printing the world Sterling on the back of an ecu bank note. My good friend George Younger is Chairman of the Royal Bank of Scotland, which of course has the right to produce bank notes marked with thistles. It does not make him the Chancellor of Scotland, any more than matters would be changed if we were to have pound notes with thistles on some, leeks on others, and roses on the rest – perhaps some red and some white to satisfy the Lancastrians, the Yorkists and the members of the Labour Party. Some perhaps could have both the Shamrock and the Red Hand of Ulster to satisfy everybody in that unhappy province. Would we have five Chancellors of the Exchequer, and five independent budgetary and monetary policies? Would we hell! Nor would we do so if we had a series of a dozen or twenty variously decorated ecus.

I must say I understand more about Scottish nationalism since we have got involved in this European context, and why it exists and what are the difficulties for many Scots, than I ever did before. And I remember why we never could arrive at a satisfactory formula for devolved government in Scotland. Either the devolved government would have no power to tax, or it would have power to tax. The former was incompatible with a single currency unit because if there were real taxation powers in Scotland and a real divergence of monetary policy, one would have to break the currency union and Scotland would become an independent state. On the other, if the assembly had no powers to tax, sooner or later it would result in a call for those powers to be given and that would end in the same problem.

We can all see the absurdities of the suggestion that there might be an independent economic policy for Britain if we had a single European currency. After all we could not allow the Chancellor of this country nor the Finance Minister of Greece to have a budgetary policy which was grossly inflationary, let alone allow that inflationary consequence being spread not solely within Greece or within the United Kingdom, but across the whole of Europe. But that would be the consequence. Now the Germans have become quite tolerant in postwar years, but I fancy they would not tolerate that. So we would have to have a single policy and yet we are beginning to see the consequences of that in Germany. Because of the economic divergence between East and West Germany the imposition of a single currency means that to avoid a new revolution West Germany is having to subsidise East Germany heavily in order to achieve economic convergence.

I think that if we expected the Germans to pay the bill on a European scale to achieve convergence between Portugal, Greece,the Republic of Ireland and themselves, they would simply not be prepared to do so. Of course they could defend themselves against those consequences and they indeed have trifled with trying, but it would only make the matter worse. The Social Charter, for example, is a way of preventing economic convergence. After all, what has Portugal got to offer, and to some extent Spain too, and Britain, against the economic might of Germany? Perhaps lower labour costs amongst other things. Impose the social costs of German wage levels – not the wage levels themselves but the social costs associated with it, which are only possible to be borne in a highly productive, heavily invested economy – on a poorly productive economy, with low levels of investment, then you cripple that economy. I think the Germans became interested in the Social Charter at the stage when Volkswagen began to talk of building motor car factories in Spain. How could that be prevented? said our Bavarian friends. Why, by imposing our costs on them before the infrastructure of investment and culture change has been achieved. So that would make matters not better, but worse, and as Peter Shore has said, there would be no escape for any of us by adjusting to this through devaluation. We would be locked in. It is a recipe for the reawakening of the very worst aspects of nationalism which we had hopefully seen pushed out of the scene in Europe.

Bruce Anderson was interesting because he touched on these matters and also on the inevitable rivalry of competing parliaments. Wherever there are two democratically elected bodies whose powers overlap there will be a struggle for supremacy between the two. That is why in the United States they have a very carefully written constitution to govern the powers of the two chambers, and that is why here only one of our chambers is elected, so we know inevitably who is the master in any given situation. If ever we were foolish enough to have an elected second chamber, we would be on the road to a constitutional crisis every week.

There is another danger too, and a number of people have

spoken about this – the question of Eastern Europe. I hope those of you who are not from these islands will not think me unduly arrogant in these matters, but I have to say the concept of Jacques Delors' train is a peculiarly continental one. Why does it have to be a train? Why do we all have to get on at the same time, wait until somebody has blown the whistle, and watch the train then go along lines which have been built beforehand, remorselessly, to a direction which has been decided? And remember that on the train not even the man in the driver's cab decides where it will go. That is the prerogative of the signalman, not the drivers. Why do we have to have this collectivist approach? What's wrong with a road, or several roads? What is wrong with us choosing our own time to get into our cars – or on our bicycles – or even to stand at the side of the road? The right way forward for Europe is not Jacques Delors' train, which would leave once and once only, and leave behind the Eastern Europeans. The right approach is Mrs Thatcher's approach, of the road along which we can all travel, perhaps to a common destination, but at a speed which suits us.

A real danger of course is that of creating Fortress Europe. That is we might become inward looking and so concerned with our own affairs, and of course so trapped by that vile Common Agricultural Policy, that we will seek to defend ourselves against those outside with the inevitable outcome being trade wars and the creation of the fortresses of the three great super trading blocks, America, Japan and Europe. That is again the way to a sadly poorer world than it need be, and particularly to a sadly poorer Third World. For we see already that we grow sugar beet here at enormous cost in order to keep out the sugar which might have been grown by poorer countries in the Third World. And having done so, and ruined their economy, and paid more for sugar than we need, we then put upon ourselves the extra tax which is needed for overseas aid to help the poor devils we have ruined, to feed themselves. So there is every reason for the benefit not only of Europe, the United States, and Japan, but of the poorest countries in the world, to avoid that Fortress Europe.

There is yet another danger. I will forbear to use the American vulgar expression for it, but they have a good one to express the view that the bigger the decision, the more likely it will be to go wrong. If we take all our decisions centrally, sooner or later one

of them will go wrong, monumentally wrong. Yet if we dissemi-
nate our decision-making process, of course we will often get
decisions wrong, but none of them will be vital, likely to cause
us serious harm. The days of the IBM super-super-great computer
in the middle, sending instructions out to the video screens all
round, is gone. The day of the network of lots of computers
contributing together is here. Why should we take our political
institutions in the opposite direction?

We are all in favour of the single market, this great wide
European market. We have begun to create it but we are still
not there entirely. I beg you all to believe that for a British
company within this European Community it is still in general
easier to do business in the United States than it is on the
Continent of Europe. If you want to take over another company,
to establish your marketing and your products somewhere, oh
boy, try doing it on the continent and then try doing it in the
United States. That should not be. Why can British Telecom
own 20 per cent of an American telephone company, but not
scent the merest sniff of a look-in in Germany or France or our
other partners in this single market? I won't go on, for there are
some wounding things that might be said.

Of course we also have the opportunity within this Community
for the better control and elimination of both state subsidies
and monopolies, but we are not making terribly good progress
with either. I was proud to have taken part in the negotiations
which have led almost to the elimination of subsidy in the steel
industry. In consequence the British steel industry which was
probably the worst, most inefficient and backward steel industry in Europe is today probably the best, the most advanced, the
most profitable and the most competitive in Europe. These are
the advantages which can come if we eliminate subsidies across
the whole of Europe. Not only is British Steel better, but every
steel company in Europe is better, not at producing commodities
which people don't want to buy even at a loss, but at producing
commodities they do want to buy at a profit.

Of course protectionism, as I have said, is a danger, but
equally free trade is an opportunity. If we can make Europe a
Community devoted to free trade, if we can have the liberal
voice in GATT which we should have, then it can be an even
more powerful voice than that of any one of us twelve. If we can
include the states of Central and Eastern Europe within our

whole Community, then we shall be on the way to returning to what I regard as man's natural state. That is that he should have the liberty to go where he pleases without being required to produce evidence of his rights to do so. That he should be able to trade wherever he pleases, without having to apply for permission, other than the normal processes of safety and regulation against cheating and crime. We could be on the way to that. I believe we can achieve it, not by centralising, but by being a Europe of nations as De Gaulle proposed, as Ted Heath claimed that he believed, as I still believe. A Europe of nations binding itself together closer and closer in terms of economy, agreeing to consult, at least, on foreign affairs and indeed on defence too. A family of nations willing to cede sovereignty. Do not let us talk about pooling sovereignty, or sharing sovereignty. Sovereignty can't be shared, any more than wives can, not in any satisfactory long-term manner at least. Sovereignty is either here, there, or somewhere else. It can't be in all three places at once. If we give away sovereignty we are creating between us a new sovereignty which is different. I think we have to be realistic about that. I have no objection to delegating sovereignty where it is necessary for our best interest, but, that sovereignty should never be ceded freehold, but only leasehold. We must remain nations capable, if we wish, even though it might be expensive, of regaining our sovereignty. That of course is why I can accept a common currency, but I could never accept a single currency, because once that Rubicon is crossed, once one has no central bank of one's own, once one has given up the right to issue one's own currency, it cannot be regained short of revolution.

Our future and our opportunity lies as a family of nations drawing others into the family, some more closely attached, some loosely attached, outward looking, essentially liberal in the true nineteenth-century use of that word. Anti-bureaucratic, anti-corporatist, open, free, liberal. That is the concept which I believe lay behind what Mrs Thatcher said at Bruges, and it is what lies at the heart of this Group.

20 New Ideas for Europe
Peter Lilley

THE IMPORTANCE OF IDEAS

Interests – personal, commercial and national – play a part in the development of Europe. But, in my view, some people exaggerate the dangers to Britain of a Europe dominated either by continental business, farming and bureaucratic interests or by German, French or other national interests. My concern is not about the hegemony of other nations but the hegemony of ideas.

Practical people are inclined to dismiss the importance of ideas. But, as Keynes pointed out: 'Practical men, who believe themselves to be quite exempt from any intellectual influences, are usually the slaves of some defunct economist.' I fear that in European matters many of us are slaves to the ideas of defunct political theorists – ideas worked out in the aftermath of the Second World War and the shadow of the Cold War; ideas which are not only out of date and out of touch with a changing world but, what is more dangerous, out of line with the underlying realities of human nature.

The set of ideas which form the prevailing conventional wisdom are variously called the 'European ideal' or 'federalism'. Briefly it is based on the thesis that:

1. the nation state is out of date;
2. nation states are the cause of wars;
3. national feelings are vulgar, aggressive and uncivilised;
4. so nation states must give way to a supranational European state;
5. only a European state can stand up to the US and USSR;
6. only a state on a continental scale can enjoy the economies of size;
7. the process of creating a European state involves the gradual but systematic transfer of the attributes of statehood from the nation to the European level;
8. and that this process is inevitable, irreversible.

These ideas contain a number of inconsistencies:

1. Above all, what will a European state be if not a large nation-state?
2. If the difference is that its citizens would have no feelings of national allegiance, what would hold it together or justify its exercise of power over them?
3. If the citizens of Europe did transfer their national allegiance to the new superstate would not those feelings be the same vulgar, aggressive and uncivilised sentiments which were so distasteful at the existing national level?
4. If war is caused by the existence of states, would not bigger states lead to bigger wars?
5. If the process of agglomeration into superstates is inevitable, irreversible and desirable why, as soon as the people have got a chance to express their will, is the USSR fragmenting like so many multinational conglomerates before it?
6. If size is so essential to achieve economies of scale why have Switzerland, Korea, Hong Kong, Sweden, Singapore and many other small states achieved such rapid growth rates or high living standards?

However, in practice, these ideas are *not* subjected to critical analysis precisely because they have become the conventional wisdom. And they have become the conventional wisdom largely because they have rarely been subjected to criticism faced with a coherent alternative. As a result, even those who find federalist ideas uncongenial or unconvincing have tended to let them set the agenda and the values.

So any proposals tend to be judged by whether or not they contribute to the European ideal. Recently they gained a new injection of support as a result of the collapse of socialism. The demise of socialism as an intellectually credible and electorally potent creed left ex-socialists with a political vacuum. Federalism has filled that vacuum.

The idea of creating a bigger and better state is naturally congenial to those whose intellectual roots are on the Left. It also appeals to those in the Centre and Centre Right parties whose minds are predisposed to pursue a 'project', especially one involving the exercise of state power. The development of the corporate state, to which they were often attracted, has been discredited along with socialism. And federalism also fills the mental gap that leaves.

Is federalism therefore now irresistible? I believe it is not. It became the conventional wisdom by default and gained its recent impetus by the demise of socialism.

The answer to one set of ideas is another (better) set of ideas, more in tune with reality, more cogently argued and more persistently propagated.

The process of defining a coherent alternative to federalism began with the Bruges speech and the battle of ideas has been carried forward by the Bruges Group in a remarkable series of pamphlets of the highest calibre. Meanwhile the government has been pressing our views within the Council of Ministers and will continue vigorously to do so.

CONTRA-PESSIMISM

Many people are sceptical about the effectiveness of argument. May I counsel against undue pessimism? There is a widespread view that Britain never wins the argument in Europe. And that consequently Britain's proposals will be comprehensively rejected in the two Intergovernmental Conferences.

In fact, the record of recent years shows our ideas often do prevail. The most important success has been the Single European Market itself. Britain has been its most enthusiastic and consistent supporter. It was the natural development of our domestic strategy of extending choice and competition. Indeed the 1992 programme was largely the brainchild of the British Commissioner, Lord Cockfield.

Others saw the creation of a single market as primarily an opportunity for harmonising and centralising regulation. But in general we have been pretty successful in keeping the emphasis on deregulation and the removal of unnecessary restrictions.

We have also fought successfully to keep the Single Market open to the rest of the world, rather than building a Fortress Europe. We have seen off a proposal that foreign banks be refused a licence in Europe until their home country offered all European banks reciprocal freedoms. We have argued successfully against special favours to certain firms as 'Eurochampions'. We convinced our partners that exchange controls should be abolished, not just between member states but with the rest of the world.

Even where we start in a minority of one we can sometimes shift the consensus towards our ground. Take the case of indirect taxation. Originally the Commission proposed that tax rates had to be controlled centrally, through new and cumbersome machinery, before any liberalisation of border tax controls could start.

At first, all member states except the UK agreed with them. We argued for a market forces approach: get rid of fiscal controls at frontiers, allow travellers to take more goods across frontiers, and leave the rest to the market. If any state thereafter retains VAT rates so out of line with its neighbours that its citizens choose to shop over the border, the high tax country would either have to forego the tax revenue or reduce its taxes.

Choice for consumers, basic decisions on tax rates taken at *national* level, and abolition of unnecessary controls at frontiers – happily, after much debate, this argument is beginning to go our way. On the key issues, all twelve lined up behind our ideas. We have made good progress on the *structure* of indirect taxation, and the Commission have moved away from their more extreme ambitions on tax *rates*. There are long and difficult discussions ahead, but the technical arrangements to get rid of fiscal controls at frontiers were agreed at the end of last year – though, unfortunately, some member states have been blocking the raising of travellers' allowances for duty-paid goods. And while most attention has been on indirect taxation, we have also seen off a potentially damaging proposal for a compulsory Withholding Tax on savings.

These are not isolated examples. We have only been outvoted on a tiny handful of directives. Germany, by contrast, seems to be outvoted several times at each Council. Over the last year (July 1988 to June 1989) Germany was outvoted about four times as often as the UK.

EMU

I am far less pessimistic than some about the Intergovernmental Conference on economic and monetary union. We now find that our hard ECU proposal has already been taken up by the Spanish, and the French Finance Minister has expressed interest. As time goes by the Delors proposal for rapid imposition of a single currency by a single central bank looks increasingly unrealistic and divisive. It gives rise to at least three serious problems.

First, though he is clear enough where he would like Europe to get to eventually, M. Delors makes no credible detailed proposals on how to get there from where we are now. His Stage Two remains without substance, and does nothing to promote the economic convergence that is needed.

Second, it is hard to believe that the Germans, who are rightly proud of their anti-inflation record, will hand over monetary control to any central bank with less proven commitment to monetary discipline. But, whatever the statutes may say and wherever the central bank is located, who can be sure that governors will not reflect their differing national attitudes and circumstances, especially since the invention of the telephone?

Thirdly, the imposition of a single currency on economies which have converged to an inadequate degree will impose serious problems of adjustment, especially on those with more entrenched inflation and inflexible markets. The countries likely to be affected may be unwilling to accept such a prospect, except in return for major resource transfers. Taxpayers in the other countries are likely to be reluctant to foot this bill – especially in Germany, which is finding the massive cost of similar transfers to East Germany following currency union a heavy burden.

Of course, if and when economic performance and policies converge towards a common non-inflationary norm, the difficulties of introducing a single currency would be much diminished. So would many of its claimed benefits.

The great merit of our proposals for a hard ECU and European Monetary Fund is that they would reinforce pressures towards convergence without pre-empting any decisions on a single currency. Our proposals provide a powerful force for convergence of member states' economies focusing on the *best* anti-inflation performance, rather than the *average*. They maintain a clear distinction between the role of the EMF and that of national monetary authorities, with responsibility for national monetary policy firmly in the latter's hands. They capture the main advantages of a European currency – the establishment of a common European means of exchange and store of value – without the disadvantages of a premature move to a single currency. And they allow all member states to move forward together.

As yet the UK's proposals are the only fully worked up plans for making progress from where the Community stands now. They provide a practical way forward, not a Euro-starry-eyed one.

POLITICAL UNION

The other IGC will consider a whole variety of proposals for so-called political union. The UK has submitted a positive package of proposals for improving the working of the Community whilst preserving the present balance of power between institutions.

A number of commentators have suggested that the Community ought to shift from decision-making by the Council of Ministers responsible to their national legislatures towards decision-making by the Commission made responsible to the European Parliament. This is based on a simplistic equation of the Community with a unitary state which ignores what the Community actually does.

A large part of Community legislation is to implement the Single Market. The key issues in virtually every case involve the reconciliation of differing national institutions, interests and procedures. Each country's government, responsible to its national legislature, can decide how best to reconcile its national interest with the need for an open market. The party complexion of a government is often irrelevant in determining its position. Consequently, the best forum for developing legislation is the Council of Ministers.

By contrast, the European Parliament is organised on the presumption that national differences can be ignored. Issues are debated on transnational party lines. By their very nature, national interests and idiosyncrasies, which are often the central issues, cannot be adequately represented within such a body.

Let me illustrate this thesis by example. In drawing up the Capital Adequacy Directive, the key issue was how it should apply to the very diverse institutions in different states. The UK was determined that it should be amended to avoid crippling discount houses, gilt-edged market-makers and other institutions which do not exist in other countries, and which represent no competitive threat to them. I have no doubt a British Labour government would have taken much the same position as we did.

Likewise Germany was anxious to protect the position of its mortgage lending institutions (Hypothekenbanken) which have no counterpart in most other countries. Again I have little doubt a German Social Democratic government would have taken much the same position as did this CDU one.

Such national particularities would scarcely be properly reflected if decision-making powers were transferred from the Council of Ministers to a non-national Commission and Parliament.

POWER TO THE PEOPLE

It is vitally important to define, develop and propagate a new set ideas to counter federalism. It is important not just to reject federalism, but to put forward a positive vision of Europe which is both more attractive and more in tune with reality. The clear alternative to the process of transferring more and more power *up* from national governments to a European superstate is to transfer more and more power from national governments *down* to individual citizens.

Power springs from choice. The more freedom of choice that citizens in Europe have about where to trade, where to set up business, to invest, save, study, work – and even to live – the less power governments will have over them. And the more power individuals will have to ensure that governments are responsive to what their citizens want.

If we were to have a single European government pursuing one set of policies through one set of institutions, this would inevitably narrow the freedom of choice of European citizens. It would also increase the power of governments over those citizens. We all understand the importance of competition in the business world – about how the existence of vigorous and open competition spurs on each producer to improve its performance, to sharpen its product and to pay closer attention to what the customers want. If this is true for business, why not for governments?

Some might argue that freedom of choice between governments is more apparent than real, given that most people have no wish actually to leave home and more to another country, even if they do feel that the other country's policies and institutions are more attractive than their own. But choice at the margin is crucial. In the market-place it only takes a few customers to change their allegiance from one product to another to spur the unfavoured producer to improve his product to win back market share.

In just the same way it only requires a few citizens actually to exercise their choice to move their businesses or their homes from one jurisdiction to another to spur the unfavoured government to adjust its policies and priorities. And after all, the principle of mutual recognition established by the single market programme makes it possible for different national systems of regulations to compete alongside each other throughout the Community.

FREE COMPETITION

The Community has rightly agreed that member states should not compete with each other by bidding up subsidies to industry. Nevertheless, significant potential does and should remain for substantial differences:

1. in the business environment;
2. in efficiency and openness of regulation;
3. in the quality of infrastructure; and
4. in the responsiveness of individual governments to the needs of industry and commerce.

This leaves scope for national governments to 'compete' with their counterparts in other parts of Europe, not in the invidious self-defeating game of state aids, but in the overall climate.

The principle of mutual recognition established by the single market programme takes it further, because it makes it possible for different national systems of regulation to compete alongside each other throughout the Community. Let me illustrate this with an example from the banking sector.

Under the principle of mutual recognition, a bank authorised in one member state is able to operate throughout the European Community without further authorisation and under the supervision of its home country's banking authority. So branches of banks supervised by the Bank of England are able to operate in Germany in competition with banks supervised from France.

This not only makes life simpler for the banks, it also gives an extra dimension of choice to banking customers. Customers are able to choose not only between different banks but, in effect, between different banking supervisory regimes. Their choice will depend partly on whether a bank operates under a regulatory regime which is inexpensive and flexible, but also on whether the regulator can be relied upon to insist on high standards of integrity and prudence. Each government has an incentive to get the balance right.

The same concept of choice applies in the general field of taxation. If businesses and individual citizens are free to choose the jurisdiction in which to pay tax and to enjoy government services, this will give governments a strong incentive:

1. to increase the efficiency of their service provision, and
2. to achieve an attractive balance between taxation and service provision.

Some people will prefer to locate their business in a country with higher tax, but a better infrastructure and education system, health services and social security provision. Others would be prepared to put up with less extensive services in return for paying lower taxes.

This is the sort of choice that people should be free to make. The government that will clearly lose out where this freedom exists is the government which imposes high taxes without giving appropriate high quality services.

In short, our vision of choice and diversity does lead to an alternative vision of Europe, a Europe in which governments give their citizens rights to choose between competing jurisdictions, where, as a result, citizens have power over governments.

Historically, Europe's strengths as a continent were drawn from the diversity and independence of the states and governments which it comprised. The challenge for the future is to maintain that diversity and independence while, at the same time, replacing conflict and enmity by cooperation and friendship.

21 Growing Up with Europe – A Memoir

Patrick Robertson

When we were children my brother and I used to visit England in September and go to Kew Gardens, buy our school uniform at Selfridges and watch the Last Night of the Proms on television, enraptured by the atmosphere of an alien Britishness.

Kew Gardens was a far cry from the dusty parks of Rome. We did not understand why, at a scruffy international school in Italy, we had to wear a 'school uniform'. Neither did our Italian, Dutch, German and French pals. In Italy there is nothing that vaguely resembles the Proms. And the various shades of purple on our school jackets, each from a different shop in a different country, emphasised the rich variety of people who went to the Junior English School of Rome.

Looking back, it is incredible that British schoolmasters bothered with a school so distant from academic aspirations, hidden on the outskirts of a Rome which, in 1975, was exotic though provincial and dirty. But they did bother. The school was on the beautiful Appia Antica. We played football on the ruins of an ancient Roman temple, and our ghastly purple jackets were rapidly consigned to satchels the moment Assembly was over in the morning. Yet a Britishness prevailed. The Headmaster behaved just as dictatorially as the functionaries of The British Public School, constrained only, perhaps, by the equally autocratic demands of the Italian Mamma whose progeny was, she never doubted, much more valuable than the eccentricities of a British school teacher.

For those British children whose parents worked in Rome, Britain was where we went for medical checkups, when we had 'Home Leave' every two years. Marmite, All-Bran and Cadbury's chocolate came from there, and the memories faded as soon as supplies ran out.

To be sent to a real Public School in London therefore came as a great cultural shock. Friends in Italy, who regularly visit Britain, point out that the two countries have very little in common. Italians do not understand English reserve, confusing it for arrogance and coldness, and the English just think the Italians are chaotic.

The Public School and I did not always get on, but all the same it bred an ambition I had never felt on the Appia Antica. London was a fantastic city, full of rude and independent people, particularly south of the river. We had to prove ourselves in a way which Rome had never demanded. In Rome, we did not know what a 'short-back-and-sides' was, nor were we thrashed by the local comprehensive boys for having one, or for wearing a 'school uniform' whose jackets were not just identical but actually emblazoned with the college crest. Rome never asked us to hand over our pocket-money to a bully outside Brixton tube station, nor did it demand that we become aware of a class system whose roots were, to us, incomprehensible.

But we came to understand. And we became aware – perhaps too aware – of the nuances of British life. At that age, it meant how to deal with bullies, to sleep in a dormitory full of strangers, or to finish homework quickly so as to watch television in the evening.

The most striking aspect of coming to Britain was the fact that the people were remarkably proud of their country. Whereas in Italy the joke of the day was about who was sharpest at avoiding taxes, or who had ignored the greatest number of laws, in London the accent was on who had progressed the furthest up the ladder of established authority, who had got to Oxford, Sandhurst or whatever. This attitude is ingrained in so many British people, and I naturally became affected by it.

For those who aspire to politics, the question of where to practise rarely comes up. But for those brought up abroad most of their life, as I was, the choice is real. There is no doubt that each European country has a political culture, and different cultures are not easily reconciled. For example, a shrewd Italian friend told me that Italy would benefit the most from European integration: by ignoring the laws it did not like and twisting those it did. Italian politicians are careful not to attach themselves to any particular initiative, so that if it fails they remain in power. How else could Giulio Andreotti have remained a minister since the end of the Second World War?

But the satisfaction of holding your own, of fighting the good fight – all this is admirable, particularly if you are of a romantic frame of mind. There is something honourable about a political culture which bestows few privileges on its political class, which forces it to justify itself before Parliament, and which elects a government to *govern*, not escape responsibility on a waterbed of consensus.

It is in this spirit that I became captivated by the European debate. This was going to become the greatest battle of them all. From being a politician's speech against the centralisation of European politics, the Bruges crusade has become a small part of our national conscience which should never disappear. The European debate is about every country's right to govern itself, to be master of its own destiny, to judge its mistakes in the light of its past, not the wishful promises of the future. The battle is between those who would risk merging and submerging Europe's cultural diversity and those who would preserve it.

But the issues are obscured by the mischief of those who would cheerfully pass national sovereignty to an unproven entity in Brussels on the grounds that 'Europe' represents all that is progressive and wise. It is true that anyone who travels Europe regularly is bound to recognise a genuine idealism, a desire to bury a horrible past in a federal arrangement which will consummate our common future. But the reality is that European politics is as hard-nosed as ever.

Apart from proposals to do with the creation of a single European market, there are very few coming from Brussels in the name of Europe which suggests that there is such an entity as 'Europe'. From the CAP to the Social Charter to Monetary and Political Union, the evidence supports the European tradition of competing nation-states. A political union which suits France's ambition to constrain Germany, a monetary union which makes Germany the 'good European', and a foreign policy which satisfies the domestic political exigencies of whichever country is holding the EC presidency – these do not culminate in genuine European endeavour. They are, rather, the ephemeral confabulations of a continent obsessed with its own self-importance, its visions of grandeur, its over-hasty refurbishment of a recent past littered with disaster. To many, therefore, 'Europe' has become a convenient mask with which to disguise even more ambitious national aspirations.

Much of The Bruges Group's work must therefore be dedicated to debunking myths. There are questions which must be asked. Are nation-states truly outdated, or are they simply too small for socialists to control, given the internationalisation of capital and industry? Do the similarities between European nations preclude their right to be also different, according to the wishes of the populations which inhabit them? Most fundamental of all, are economic calculations really more important than political judgments, given the intractible problems which require a keen respect for politics and self-government if they are to be resolved satisfactorily?

For it is a belief in the primacy of economics which is the Trojan Horse of European socialists and economic liberals alike. Starting from completely opposite positions, social democracy argues that the Europeanisation of economics requires a similar expansion of political faculties, an argument refined by Professor David Marquand, while economic liberals, such as the German Professor Peter Bernholz, view the internationalisation of economics as an ideal opportunity to emasculate the nation-state – which admittedly in the past has been exploited by statists and corporatists to suppress individual liberty and pursue beggar-my-neighbour mercantilism. But both positions ignore the new recognition by nation-states that their true national interest lies in open and free trade with all comers, whereby economic forces are channelled into peaceful, mutually beneficial competition. The most successful parts of the world today are, as ever, nation-states, whether Japan, Switzerland, Germany, or even Singapore, Korea and Taiwan.

One thing which is emerging more clearly every day, is that we Europeans have created a monster. In the supposed cause of promoting free trade and economic integration between nations, we have constructed a centralising Community with a dynamic of its own. What started as the European Economic Community is now decked out with an easily-packaged vision, European Union. Those who dare to question the direction of events are dismissed as outdated troglodytes. They come face to face with a barrage of pitying abuse by intellectual pickets who chant accusations of being 'bad Europeans'. Apart from being unhealthy for debate, this loaded vocabulary suggests that faith in bureaucratic institutions is more powerful than the wishes of the Europeans whom those institutions are supposed to serve.

An example of this sort of treatment comes to mind. A colleague in The Bruges Group was invited by a student at the

College of Europe in Bruges to take part in a debate on Europe. The rector, a certain Professor Lukaszewski, vetoed the event on the grounds that we were spreading propaganda against the European Commission. This was, of course, untrue, but Sir John Hoskyns had just delivered the first of his broadsides against EC fraud and the federalists were still smarting. The point of Hoskyns' speech had eluded the good rector.

It seems never to have occurred to Lukaszewski to question the nature of European institutions. For him, and, sadly, too many others, fraud, dishonesty and bureaucracy are a minor price to pay for so good a cause as the realisation of European Union.

And there is worse. A Conservative Euro-MP, Michael Welsh, recently spent the best part of a conference telling delegates that The Bruges Group wanted Britain to leave the EC. His excuse for these distracting remarks was quite extraordinary. We had published a paper by Dr Alan Sked proposing radical changes to European institutions, which, amongst many other things, would have removed direct elections from the European Parliament whilst reinforcing cooperation procedures through the creation of a powerful European cabinet.[1] This was our positive contribution to the institutional debate. When I wrote to Mr Welsh, he justified his remarks by saying that since our proposals would never be accepted by anyone (least of all well-padded MEPs) our ideas amounted to a call for withdrawal!

Sir Leon Brittan treated our proposals in a similar fashion when he came to address the group in London. His speechwriters had included a lengthy rejection of Dr Sked's ideas in his address. But Sir Leon cut every bit, on the grounds that (as we later discovered) he did not want to make him feel too important.

There are many examples of mischief in the present European debate. It is important that Europeans should know that the President of the Commission, M. Jacques Delors, having supported the repayment of subsidy to Rover on privatisation, abstained on a vote recommending that Renault return state-aids to the French government, amounting to many hundred million pounds. Or how another Commissioner asked a prominent member of the British Cabinet whether the UK was going to vote down some proposal for a European withholding-tax, so that he would not have to vote against – on instructions from his own government. How the Irish Commissioner uses his influence to take care of his Irish constituents, usually powerful businessmen and farmers. So much for European Commissioners abiding by the 'European interest'.

Ordinary Europeans are therefore rudely discouraged from setting their own agenda for the development of the Community. If they question the efficiency or usefulness of an EC policy, they can be all too easily ignored as being chauvinists or nationalists. The people who are allowed to dictate the agenda are the professional Europeans. An example comes to mind. At a meeting of the Kensington Conservatives Association[2] a semi-professional European, Nicholas Colchester of *The Economist*, told his audience that economic liberalism was incompatible with having a national, as opposed to a European, identity. But he did not think he was expressing an opinion, for to him this was fact, 'and if you don't understand that you don't understand Europe'. Given the bureaucratic complexity of many European policies it is all too easy for these professionals to say that the rest of us 'do not understand . . . ' But that is precisely the point: whilst we are asked to trust this outfit to govern a large chunk of our lives, we are treated as ignorant outsiders if we dare question policy.

One of the most common federalist techniques is to say that European politics requires everyone to commit themselves to a goal before the details of how to get there are worked out. Britain's view on monetary and political union will not even be 'taken seriously' unless we accept this rule, according to Sir Leon Brittan. This is certainly not the case in domestic British politics, nor in Germany and France, for that matter. Nevertheless, for *Europe* we all have to enter into a new word-game, and the guardians of the rules are Eurocrats. This means that whoever sets the agenda is able to protect any particular initiative with the armour of Europeanness. When we too try to play the game – by, for example, proclaiming our support for 'monetary union' whilst putting an alternative route forward – the Eurocrats step in and suddenly change the rules. That is what happened when Jacques Delors recently rubbished Britain's 'hard ECU' plan.

I have often asked why this debate is conducted so dishonestly. At heart lies the question of government: who is going to rule? For the time being, Europe is a community of sovereign nations, with no constitutional authority vested in the centre. But the issue is already becoming more blurred, and the very existence of this grey area permits centralisers constantly to expand it. To understand this we must look at the question of sovereignty. Ultimately, sovereignty is a legal concept: what institution has the final say to act on behalf of a state? In Britain it is Parliament, as is the case in every other member state of the Community. The fact that other countries may have greater division of powers in the everyday conduct of domestic government – whether constitutional courts or federal assemblies – should not be allowed to obscure the issue.

Without doubt, therefore, Parliaments are sovereign. Relations between modern, civil societies are sufficiently harmonious for each to require very little military or economic power to enforce any number of quite independent decisions, as the eccentricities of a little country like Switzerland illustrate. But today states increasingly exercise their sovereignty by freely submitting certain issues to international cooperation, whether NATO, the IMF, GATT or even the European Community. Only in the Community, however, is the issue confused by majority voting. Since majority voting fundamentally conflicts with the notion of a confederation of sovereign states, it can only work if the contracting parties are clearly aware in advance what issues are subjected to this procedure. The problem in the EC arises because the contractual agreement – the Treaty of Rome – is not sufficiently clear to define the limits of central authority. Not only is this the case (mostly, but not always, on relatively minor matters) but the institution with the authority to *interpret* the Treaty – the Court of Justice – increasingly rules in a manner which conflicts with the original intentions of its authors. And example is the manner in which the EC is seeking to pass social legislation by majority vote, on the grounds that a legally worthless political declaration in favour of the Social Charter indicates its importance to the Single Market.

This means that there is plenty of scope for centralisers and Eurocrats to abuse the constitutional contract. They argue, erroneously but effectively, that sovereignty is 'shared' or 'pooled' because of the existence of majority voting. They conveniently forget that Parliaments had to approve those areas covered by majority voting beforehand. They also argue that, given the extent of EC competence, the Community should be made more 'democratic' (which they usually take to mean more powers for the European Parliament). They are aware, but do not tell us, that this would eventually lead to the demise of the democratic *national* parliaments. Finally, they argue that, since the contractual agreement between nations seems to work, there is no reason why the centre can't take over its management. But by doing this the centre would take on a life of its own, and therefore become *sovereign*. It is revealing that many of those who argue that sovereignty means nothing are the very people who support the creation of a new sovereignty based in a city in Belgium. It is this chain of thought which is so perverse and consequently so infuriating.

The urgency, panic and even hysteria behind the drive to European Union stems from the fragility of Europe's contractual arrangement. Relationships between nations and EC institutions are changing. The ways and means to alter the status quo surreptitiously are multiplying. The community is now sitting on top of a fence: it can either become a fully-fledged federation or a clearly-defined confederation. In, both cases, however, the powers will have to be apportioned, and honesty will eventually have to enter the debate. For as long as we live in a grey area there will be ambiguity about the real nature of the EC. It will be crippled by the ever increasing frustration of the confederates on the one hand the the underhand technique of the federalists on the other. It is a formula for tension, discord and division, only recently illustrated by Europe's response during the Gulf War.

All government rests upon the citizen's willingness to be persuaded and, if necessary, coerced. It is no different if we are talking about transferring government from one institution to another. European government is as yet a dream. There are promises for the naive and traps for the unwary. Without the formal consent and the understanding of the citizens of every European country, the political institutions of Europe will founder at the first unforseen test. Personally, I hope and believe that Europe will prove as tolerant of its differences as my old headmaster was of the various shades of our purple school jackets. For if it does not, its fruit must prove bitter, if not poisonous.

NOTES

1. Alan Sked, *A Proposal for European Union* (The Bruges Group, 1990), reproduced in this book in Chapter 1.
2. 12 November 1990.

Index